Comfort Food

Every dish you love, every recipe you want

By Ken Haedrich and the Almanac editors

Photography by Becky Luigart-Stayner

254

120

78

The Old Farmer's Almanac Books
PUBLISHER: Sherin Pierce
EDITOR: Janice Stillman
ART DIRECTOR: Colleen Quinnell
RECIPE DEVELOPER AND TESTER: Ken Haedrich
COPY EDITOR: Jack Burnett
EDITORIAL STAFF: Mare-Anne Jarvela, Sarah Perreault, Heidi Stonehill, Tim Clark
INDEXER: Samantha A. Miller

V.P., NEW MEDIA AND PRODUCTION: Paul Belliveau
PRODUCTION DIRECTORS: Susan Gross, David Ziarnowski
PRODUCTION ARTISTS: Lucille Rines, Rachel Kipka, Janet Grant

NEW MEDIA EDITOR: Catherine Boeckmann
WEB DESIGNERS: Lou Eastman, Amy O'Brien
E-COMMERCE MANAGER: Alan Henning
PROGRAMMING: Reinvented, Inc.

CONSUMER MARKETING MANAGER: Kate McPherson

COVER AND FULL-PAGE FOOD PHOTOGRAPHY: Becky Luigart-Stayner
FOOD STYLIST: Ana Kelly
PROP STYLIST: Jan Gautro

For additional information about this and other publications from The Old Farmer's Almanac, visit ALMANAC.COM or call 1-800-ALMANAC.

Distributed in the book trade by Houghton Mifflin Harcourt.

YANKEE PUBLISHING INC., P.O. BOX 520, 1121 MAIN STREET, DUBLIN, NEW HAMPSHIRE 03444

Thank you for buying this cookbook! We hope you enjoy every dish that it inspires. Thanks, too, to everyone who had a hand in it, including printers, distributors, and sales and delivery people.

ISBN/EAN: 978-1-57198-648-1
First Edition

Printed in the United States of America

COOK UP SOME COMFORT!

Everybody has a favorite "comfort food." Melt-in-your-mouth mac 'n' cheese is at the top of many lists. Other faves are chicken noodle soup, bacon baked beans, chocolate pudding, and home-baked cinnamon raisin bread. And let's not forget lasagna. *Comfort food* is so many things: It's familiar, it makes you feel good, it's not fancy, it's classic, and it's perfect for any situation or occasion, like when . . .

• You're hungry, you don't know what you want—melt-y, gooey, chewy, hearty, crispy, crunchy, soupy, saucy?—but you want it to be satisfyingly filling, yummy, and easy.

• The gang is coming over. You want to serve them a dish that won't take too long to fix and will make them dig right in.

• There's a potluck supper coming up. You want to make and bring a dish that's so good, it will all be gone.

• It's tailgate time! You need something that's finger-lickin' fun, will travel well, and "that'll eat," as some Southern cooks say.

• You're cooking for the family reunion, club meeting, or Sunday supper. You want to make the meal an event, and you want friends and family to feel the love.

Every recipe in this collection fills that bill—and more. Here you have more than 200 mouthwatering, heartwarming, craving-killing recipes, including the favorites named above. We're sure that you'll love them; we've tried them all. So cook, eat, and enjoy—and go to **Almanac.com/Feedback** to give us a taste of what you think.

Ken Haedrich and the Almanac editors

40

238

108

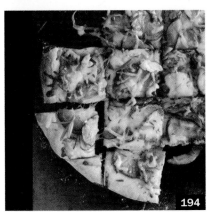
194

CONTENTS

156

134

64

30

Crab Cakes With Special Seafood Sauce
recipe on page 30

appetizers

Buffalo Wing Sauce

Buffalo wing sauce, which is sold under a variety of brand names, is a spicy blend of hot-pepper sauce, butter (or other fat), seasonings, and vinegar used most often in the preparation of Buffalo chicken wings. (Did you know that the wings originated in the New York city of the same name?) The heat intensity varies between brands, so apply a little and taste (then add more, if desired) whenever you try a new one.

Hot Buffalo Chicken and Cheese Dip

Spicy, chunky, and oh, so cheesy!

2 tablespoons (¼ stick) unsalted butter
½ cup finely chopped onion
2 cloves garlic, minced
1 cup frozen corn kernels, slightly thawed
2½ cups finely chopped rotisserie chicken meat
⅔ cup prepared Buffalo wing sauce (see box)
12 ounces cream cheese, softened
⅔ cup mayonnaise
1 packet (1 ounce) ranch dressing mix
½ cup crumbled blue cheese
1 ripe tomato, halved, seeded, and finely diced
3 cups shredded sharp cheddar cheese

■ Preheat the oven to 350°F. Butter three or four shallow gratin dishes or one or two deep ones.

■ Melt the butter in a skillet over medium heat. Add the onion and cook for 4 minutes, stirring often. Add the garlic and corn and cook for 3 to 4 minutes. Add the chicken and Buffalo wing sauce. Simmer for 3 minutes, stirring often. Remove from the heat and set aside.

■ Combine the cream cheese, mayonnaise, and ranch dressing mix in a large bowl. Beat with an electric mixer for about 1 minute, or until soft and fluffy. Add the blue cheese and chicken mixture. Blend evenly with a wooden spoon.

■ Divide the mixture among the prepared dishes. Sprinkle diced tomato and cheddar cheese evenly over the portions. Bake on the center oven rack for 25 to 30 minutes, or until bubbly and golden.

Makes 8 to 10 servings.

Note: This dip can be prepared up to 24 hours before baking. Fill the gratins with dip, cover with plastic wrap, and refrigerate.

Preheat the oven, then remove the plastic wrap and bake as directed. Starting cold, the dip may need a few more minutes in the oven.

Barbecue Chicken Empanadas

The filling can be made up to 24 hours ahead of time. The dough is tender and flaky but durable and makes an excellent wrapper for other savory or sweet turnovers.

Dough:

2¼ cups all-purpose flour

1¼ teaspoons salt

6 tablespoons (¾ stick) cold unsalted butter, cut into ¼-inch pieces

2 tablespoons cold vegetable shortening, in several small pieces

⅓ cup cold water

1 large egg

1 tablespoon white vinegar

Filling:

2½ tablespoons vegetable oil

½ cup finely chopped onion

½ green or red bell pepper, finely chopped

2 cloves garlic, minced

1½ teaspoons chili powder

½ teaspoon smoked paprika

½ teaspoon ground cumin

3 cups diced cooked chicken

1 cup fresh or frozen corn kernels

1 cup chicken stock

¼ cup barbecue sauce

¼ cup salsa

salt and freshly ground black pepper, to taste

¼ cup chopped green olives with pimientos

1 cup finely diced sharp cheddar or pepper jack cheese

1 egg beaten with 1 tablespoon milk, for glaze

For dough:

■ Line a small baking sheet with plastic wrap.

■ Combine the flour and salt in a food processor. Cover and pulse several times to mix. Remove the processor lid and scatter the butter and shortening over the dry ingredients, re-cover, then pulse six or seven times, breaking the fat into pea-size bits.

■ In a small bowl, whisk together the water, egg, and vinegar. Add the egg mixture to the flour mixture. Cover and pulse briefly and repeatedly, just until the dough starts to clump together.

■ Turn the dough out onto your work surface. Divide the dough into 12 or 16 equal-size pieces (the number depends on how large you want the empanadas to be) and roll each piece into a ball. Flatten each ball into a fat disk and place on the prepared baking sheet. Cover loosely with plastic wrap and refrigerate for at least 1 hour.

Makes dough for 12 to 16 empanadas.

How to Make Empanada Dough by Hand

You don't need to buy a processor—or even turn on an existing one:

■ Mix the flour and salt in a large bowl. Using two forks, two knives, or a pastry blender, cut in the butter and shortening until it is broken into fine bits.

■ In a small bowl, whisk together the water, egg, and vinegar. Add the liquid to the flour mixture all at once and stir until the dough pulls together. Turn the dough out onto your work surface.

■ Continue as directed above.

For filling:

■ Heat the oil over medium heat in a large skillet. Add the onion and bell pepper and cook for 6 to 7 minutes. Add the garlic, chili powder, smoked paprika, and cumin and cook for 30 seconds. Add the chicken and corn, and stir to coat with the spices. Add the stock, barbecue sauce, and salsa and stir. Bring to a boil, then reduce the heat and simmer for several minutes, stirring often, until much of the liquid evaporates but the mixture is still saucy. Sprinkle with salt and pepper. Remove from the heat and set aside to cool completely. Add the olives and stir to blend.
(**Note:** The filling can be made to this point up to 24 hours ahead.)

■ Transfer to a bowl, then cover and refrigerate.

■ Put the cooled filling into a food processor and pulse to chop, four or five times quickly. (Do not overchop; the meat should maintain some texture.)

■ Preheat the oven to 375°F. Lightly grease or line a large baking sheet with parchment paper.

To assemble:

■ Working with one piece of dough at a time on a floured surface, roll it into a 6-inch-long oval about 4½ inches wide. Place about 3 tablespoons of filling on one half of a dough oval. Top with a tablespoon of cheese. Moisten the edge of the oval with a wet fingertip, then fold the uncovered half over the filling, lining up the edges. Press the edges together and place the empanada on the prepared baking sheet. Repeat for the remaining empanadas. Poke the top of each empanada with a fork, to vent, then brush lightly with the egg-milk glaze. Bake on the center oven rack for 25 minutes, or until golden brown. Cool on a rack for at least 10 minutes before serving.

Makes 12 to 16 servings.

SAME DIFFERENCE

Yellow and red bell peppers are actually just green bell peppers that were left on the plant to mature.

Roasting Peppers

A good time to roast bell peppers is summer, when they're big and sweet. Do it outside on the grill: Keep turning them until they're charred all over, then place them in a glass bowl and cover the bowl with plastic wrap. Let them sit for 10 to 15 minutes to loosen the skins and allow the peppers to cool.

Make a slit in each pepper and drain off any liquid. Remove the core and seeds, then peel and scrape off the charred skin with the edge of a paring knife. Add the peppers to a dish or pack them in a jar with olive oil and refrigerate to use during the week.

White Bean and Roasted Red Pepper Dip

Serve with pita chips or crackers.

2 cans (19 ounces each) cannellini beans, drained and rinsed
⅔ cup roasted red bell pepper strips, blotted dry
⅓ cup olive oil
2 cloves garlic, chopped
2 tablespoons freshly squeezed lemon juice
1 tablespoon tomato paste
3 tablespoons coarsely chopped fresh Italian parsley
1 teaspoon dried oregano
several pinches chopped fresh or dried rosemary
¾ teaspoon salt, plus more to taste
1 or 2 pinches cayenne pepper, or to taste
¼ cup finely grated Parmesan cheese (optional)

■ In a food processor, combine all of the ingredients, including Parmesan cheese, if using. Pulse until well blended but not puréed (it should still have some texture), stopping to scrape down the sides of the bowl, if necessary.

■ Taste and add additional seasonings, if desired, and pulse to blend. Transfer to a serving dish. Cover and refrigerate for several hours or overnight. Add 2 or 3 tablespoons more of Parmesan cheese, if desired, and stir, before serving.

Makes 8 or more servings.

Garlicky Eggplant Dip

Similar to the popular Middle Eastern dip called baba ganoush, this should be served with crisp pita chips or sesame crackers. Smoked paprika adds an exotic flavor.

3 medium, ripe eggplants, about 2 pounds total
¼ cup tahini, or sesame paste
¼ cup olive oil
¼ cup loosely packed fresh Italian parsley
1½ tablespoons freshly squeezed lemon juice
2 or 3 cloves garlic, coarsely chopped
½ teaspoon salt, plus more to taste
¼ teaspoon smoked paprika
freshly ground black pepper, to taste

■ Preheat the oven to 425°F. Line a large rimmed baking sheet with foil.

■ Pierce each eggplant three or four times with a paring knife and place them on the sheet. Bake for 60 to 70 minutes, or until the eggplants can be easily pierced with a knife. Transfer to a cooling rack. Cut a slit in each eggplant to release steam. Set aside for 30 minutes to cool.

■ Scrape all of the eggplant flesh out of the skin and put the flesh into a colander set inside a large bowl. Allow the flesh to drain for at least 1 hour, until cool.

■ Discard the liquid. Spread the eggplant flesh on a chopping board and use a paring knife to scrape out as many of the seeds as possible. Discard the seeds. (See box.) Pat the eggplant flesh with paper towels, then transfer to a food processor. Add the remaining ingredients. Pulse repeatedly to purée. Taste and add more seasonings, if desired, and pulse to blend. Transfer the mixture to a bowl, cover, and refrigerate for at least 2 hours before serving.

Makes 6 or more servings.

The Bitter Truth About Eggplant

Always buy ripe, fresh eggplant. Unripe or less-than-fresh specimens often have a bitter taste that can adversely affect the flavor of your dish. Draining and then removing the seeds from the eggplant, as we do here, also helps to rid it of any bitterness.

If, when you finish making it, your dip tastes a little bitter, stir in up to 4 tablespoons of mayonnaise, 1 tablespoon at a time, to balance the flavor.

Baking Soda & Baking Power

Baking soda, which contains sodium hydroxide and carbonic acid, requires an acidic ingredient, such as buttermilk or yogurt, in a batter to help a baked good rise.

Baking powder, which contains cream of tartar and sodium bicarbonate, does not require an acidic ingredient in a batter to help a baked good rise.

Whereas baking soda has an unlimited shelf life as long as it stays dry, the acid ingredient(s) in baking powder can cause it to lose its strength in about a year.

Silver Dollar Cheese Biscuits

Small in size but big in flavor, these are best right out of the oven and "refreshed" when reheated.

2 cups all-purpose flour
1 tablespoon sugar
2 teaspoons baking powder
½ teaspoon baking soda
½ teaspoon salt
5 tablespoons cold, unsalted butter, cut into ¼-inch pieces
1½ cups shredded sharp cheddar cheese, divided
¾ cup buttermilk

■ Combine the flour, sugar, baking powder, baking soda, and salt in a large bowl and whisk to blend. Add the butter and cut it into the dry ingredients with a pastry blender or rub it with your fingers, until the mixture resembles a coarse meal. Refrigerate for 10 minutes.

■ Preheat the oven to 400°F. Lightly butter a large baking sheet or line it with parchment paper.

■ Add 1 cup of the cheese to the flour mixture and toss lightly, to combine. Make a well and add the buttermilk. Using a large fork or wooden spoon, stir until the mixture forms dough that sticks together and pulls away from the side of the bowl. Let it rest for 1 minute.

■ Turn the dough out onto a lightly floured surface. Using floured hands, knead the dough two or three times. Pat or roll to be about ⅔ of an inch thick. Press a 1¼-inch (or similar) biscuit cutter into the dough. Place the rounds on the baking sheet, evenly spaced and close together. Gather, shape, and cut the scraps. Sprinkle with the remaining ½ cup of cheese. Bake for 15 minutes, or until golden brown and crusty. Serve. To reheat, wrap in aluminum foil and place in a warm oven for 10 minutes.

Makes 18 to 20 biscuits.

French Onion Toasts

This handheld fare will remind you of the soup that inspired it.

4 tablespoons (½ stick) unsalted butter, plus more for the bread
2 or 3 very large onions, halved and sliced (8 cups)
salt and freshly ground black pepper, to taste
¾ cup beef stock
1 tablespoon dry sherry or cognac
2 cloves garlic, thinly sliced
1 loaf (13 to 14 inches long) French bread, or baguette,
    halved lengthwise
2 cups shredded Jarlsberg or Swiss cheese
2 tablespoons crumbled, crisp-cooked bacon or bacon bits

■ Preheat the oven to 400°F.

■ Melt the butter in a large skillet or Dutch oven over medium-high heat. Add the onions and salt and pepper and cook for about 10 minutes, or until the onions wilt. Add the beef stock, ¼ cup at a time, as the liquid evaporates. This should take about 15 minutes.

■ Add the sherry and garlic and cook for a few minutes more, or until the liquid cooks off. Remove the skillet from the heat and season with additional salt and pepper, if desired.

■ Butter the cut sides of the French bread and place them butter side up on a baking sheet. Warm the bread on the center oven rack for 7 to 8 minutes. Remove it from the oven and spread half of the onion mixture on each piece of bread. Sprinkle with the cheese and bacon. Return the bread to the oven for a few minutes, or until the cheese melts. Transfer the bread to a cutting board and slice into 1½-inch-wide pieces.

Makes 8 servings.

The appetite is sharpened by the first bites.

–José Rizal, Philippine writer (1861–96)

Creamy Pimiento Cheese

*Every cook has his or her favorite version of this Southern staple
and you can, too.*

½ **pound extra sharp white cheddar cheese, shredded**
½ **pound medium orange cheddar cheese, shredded**
⅔ **cup mayonnaise**
3 **ounces cream cheese, softened**
1 **teaspoon Worcestershire sauce**
¼ **teaspoon salt**
⅛ **teaspoon cayenne pepper**
⅛ **teaspoon freshly ground black pepper**
1 **jar (4 ounces) drained and chopped pimientos**

■ Combine all of the ingredients, except the pimientos, in a food
processor. Pulse the mixture briefly and repeatedly until well blended
but not puréed.

■ Add the pimientos and pulse until the mixture is well blended but
not puréed. It should have some texture, with flecks of pimientos.
Transfer to jars or crocks with lids, seal, and refrigerate. If possible,
allow the cheese to sit for at least a few hours before serving.

Makes 3 cups.

Variations:

■ If you want to fancy up your pimiento cheese even more, add
2 to 3 tablespoons of any combination of fine bacon bits, minced red
onion, diced jalapeños, bourbon (1 tablespoon recommended),
and/or Dijon-style mustard (1 teaspoon recommended).

**Please Pass the
Pimiento Cheese**

*Pimiento cheese is
often served as a dip
with crackers or on tea
sandwiches or celery.
However, inventive
Southern cooks
put pimiento cheese on
burgers, use it as filling for
grilled cheese sandwiches,
add it to the stuffing
for butterflied chicken
breasts, and mix it into
deviled egg filling.*

A Deviled Egg Trio

Dare to devil eggs differently. You won't be disappointed!

12 large eggs

■ Place the eggs in a large saucepan or pot and add enough water to cover by 1 inch. Put the pan over high heat and bring to a boil. When the boil starts, reduce the heat to a simmer and cook for 10 minutes. Transfer the eggs to a bowl of ice water and set them aside to cool completely.

■ Peel, rinse, and blot each egg dry. Refrigerate the whole eggs until you're ready to "devil" them. Choose one of the following variations when you're ready to proceed.

Note: Hard-boiled eggs, refrigerated, will last up to a week if they're not peeled. However, they're easier to peel if it's done shortly after they've cooled.

Tuna Deviled Eggs

12 hard-boiled eggs
1 can (5 ounces) tuna (in water is preferable), drained and broken into small pieces
½ cup mayonnaise
2 tablespoons minced dill pickle
1 tablespoon minced Italian parsley
¼ to ½ teaspoon seafood seasoning
salt and freshly ground black pepper, to taste

■ Slice the eggs in half lengthwise. Remove the yolks and place them in a large bowl. Set aside the egg white halves. Using a fork or pastry blender, break the yolks into small pieces. Add the tuna and stir. Add the mayonnaise, dill pickle, parsley, seafood seasoning, and salt and pepper, to taste, and mix. Spoon the filling into the egg white halves, creating a small mound in each. Refrigerate until serving.

Makes 24 deviled eggs.

EGGS-CELLENT IDEA

The night before
you make hard-boiled
eggs, tape the egg
carton closed and turn
it on its side. This will
"center" the yolks.

Guacamole Deviled Eggs

12 hard-boiled eggs
1 ripe avocado
1½ tablespoons freshly squeezed lemon juice
2 tablespoons minced pickled jalapeño slices
1 tablespoon minced roasted red pepper or green olives with pimientos
2 tablespoons mayonnaise
1 tablespoon minced fresh Italian parsley
1 to 2 teaspoons minced onion
¼ teaspoon salt
freshly ground black pepper, to taste

■ Slice the eggs in half lengthwise. Remove the yolks and place them in a large bowl. Set aside the egg white halves. Using a fork or pastry blender, break the yolks into small pieces. Add the avocado flesh and the lemon juice and mix. Add the jalapeño slices, roasted red pepper, mayonnaise, parsley, onion, and salt and pepper, to taste. Stir to blend. Spoon the filling into the egg white halves, creating a small mound in each. Refrigerate until serving.

Makes 24 deviled eggs.

Bacon Ranch Deviled Eggs

12 hard-boiled eggs
¼ cup mayonnaise
¼ cup ranch dressing
2 tablespoons sour cream
2 tablespoons finely chopped bacon bits
1 tablespoon chopped green olives with pimientos
½ teaspoon Dijon-style mustard
1 or 2 dashes hot-pepper sauce
salt and freshly ground black pepper, to taste

■ Slice the eggs in half lengthwise. Remove the yolks and place them in a large bowl. Set aside the egg white halves. Using a fork or pastry blender, break the yolks into small pieces. Add the mayonnaise, ranch dressing, sour cream, bacon bits, green olives, mustard, and hot-pepper sauce and stir to blend. Add salt and pepper, to taste, and mix. Spoon the filling into the egg-white halves, creating a small mound in each. Refrigerate until serving.

Makes 24 deviled eggs.

Baked Stuffed Creamer Potatoes

Here's a hearty finger food that even kids will love.

TUBER TIPS

When preparing
potatoes, remove any
eyes, sprouts, and
green parts.
(Sprouts emerge
from the eyes.)

If the tuber has a
few sprouts but
is still firm,
cut off the sprouts
and use the potato.

If it has sprouts
and has become soft,
discard it.

Discard green
potatoes; they are
bitter and mildly toxic.
Green skin indicates
that the potato
has been exposed
to sunlight.

1½ pounds white-skinned creamer potatoes, about 1¼ to 1½ inches
    across (see box, opposite)
2 tablespoons (¼ stick) unsalted butter
½ cup minced onion
2 cloves garlic, minced
3 tablespoons sour cream, divided
½ teaspoon Dijon-style mustard
2 tablespoons finely grated Parmesan cheese
4 tablespoons finely crumbled, crisp-cooked bacon or bacon bits, divided
¼ teaspoon salt
¼ teaspoon freshly ground black pepper
1 cup shredded cheddar cheese
paprika (optional)

■ Preheat the oven to 400°F.

■ Rinse the potatoes, then spread them on a large baking sheet. Using the tip of a paring knife, pierce each potato about ¼ inch deep. Bake for 25 to 30 minutes, or until the potatoes can be pierced easily with a toothpick. When done, transfer the baking sheet to a cooling rack.

■ Melt the butter in a skillet over medium heat. Add the onion and cook for 5 to 7 minutes, or until light golden. Add the garlic and cook for 1 minute more. Remove from the heat and set aside.

■ When the potatoes are cool enough to handle, slice each one in half. Using a melon baller or small spoon, scoop out the potato flesh, leaving a wall approximately ⅛-inch thick. Put the flesh into a large bowl. Set aside the potato skins.

■ Reduce the oven to 375°F. Oil a large baking dish.

■ Add the cooked onion mixture to the potato flesh and mix to combine.

■ In a small bowl, combine the 3 tablespoons of the sour cream with the mustard. Add this plus the Parmesan cheese, 2 tablespoons of bacon, salt, and pepper to the potato flesh. Mash the mixture well with a hand masher. (A slightly dry mixture will help the potatoes to hold their shape. If you think that it's too dry, mash in another tablespoon of sour cream.)

■ Pack the potato shells with the filling, forming a dome shape on the top. Arrange the stuffed potatoes closely in the baking dish. Sprinkle with the cheddar cheese and the remaining bacon bits. Dust with paprika, if desired. Bake for about 20 minutes, or until heated through.

Makes 8 servings.

> **What I say is that if a man really likes potatoes, he must be a pretty decent sort of fellow.**
>
> *–A. A. Milne, English writer (1882–1956)*

The Creamers of the Crop

Creamer potatoes, also known as new, mini, petite, or baby potatoes, are red- or white-skinned spuds that are harvested before they fully mature.

HOT STUFF

The heat of a pepper is measured in Scoville units. A mild pepper such as a Mexican bell registers between 100 and 500 Scoville units. The habanero 'Red Savina' is a scorching 577,000 Scoville units!

Sweet and Tangy Meatballs and Sausage

The meatballs can be cooked up to a day in advance and refrigerated.

1 bottle (12 ounces) tomato-based chili sauce
½ cup ketchup
⅓ cup barbecue sauce
1 cup grape jelly
½ cup hot-pepper jelly
1 tablespoon Dijon-style mustard
1 batch small-size Old-Fashioned Meatballs (page 24)
¾ to 1 pound mini smoked sausages

■ Combine the chili sauce, ketchup, barbecue sauce, grape jelly, hot-pepper jelly, and mustard in a saucepan. Gradually raise the heat to a simmer, whisking occasionally.

■ Pour the chili mixture into a slow cooker or large, heavy-bottomed pan and add the meatballs and sausages. If using a slow cooker, heat for 2 to 4 hours on high, stirring from time to time. On the stovetop, simmer gently, stirring often, until heated through. Serve warm.

Makes 10 or more servings.

Old-Fashioned Meatballs

Now, this is meatballs!

1 pound ground chuck
½ pound ground veal
½ pound hot or mild Italian sausage
   meat, removed from casings
¾ cup fine Italian-style bread crumbs or
   plain cracker crumbs
½ cup finely grated Parmesan cheese
2 cloves garlic, minced

1¼ teaspoons anise seed,
   preferably crushed (optional)
1½ teaspoons dried basil
1½ teaspoons dried oregano
1¼ teaspoons salt
½ teaspoon freshly ground black pepper
2 large eggs, lightly beaten
⅓ cup milk
olive oil, if panfrying

■ Combine the meats in a large bowl and break them up with your hands. Add the bread crumbs, Parmesan cheese, garlic, anise seed (if using), basil, oregano, and salt and pepper and, with your hands, work until well blended. Add the eggs and milk and continue to mix by hand until evenly combined. Do not overwork the mixture, or the meatballs will not be tender.

■ Measure and shape the meatballs: For small meatballs, use about 2 tablespoons. For golf ball–size meatballs, use about ¼ cup.

Choose a cooking method:

To bake:

■ Preheat the oven to 400°F. Lightly grease a large, rimmed baking sheet or coat it with cooking spray.

■ Place the meatballs on the sheet. Bake for 22 to 30 minutes, or until, when you cut one open, you see that the center is no longer pink. (Larger meatballs need to cook longer.) Transfer the meatballs to a large platter and set them aside to cool.

To panfry:

■ Coat the bottom of a large skillet with olive oil and warm it over medium-low heat. Add the meatballs, leaving enough space between them to be able to turn them to brown all surfaces evenly. (Do this in batches, if necessary.) Cook, turning the meatballs frequently, until, when you cut one open, you see that the center is no longer pink.

Makes 24 to 48 meatballs.

Hunger is the best seasoning for meat.

–Cicero,
Roman philosopher
(106–43 B.C.)

Sausage and Spinach–Stuffed Mushrooms

Use any leftovers as omelet filling.

16 to 20 medium to large white mushrooms (not jumbo)
1 tablespoon olive oil
¼ pound hot or mild Italian sausage meat, removed from casings
¼ cup finely chopped onion
2 to 3 cups packed baby spinach, coarsely chopped
⅓ cup chopped walnuts
10 Ritz or saltine crackers, broken up
small handful fresh Italian parsley
½ teaspoon dried basil
¼ cup finely grated Parmesan cheese, plus more for topping
¼ cup cream cheese, softened
2 or 3 oil-packed sun-dried tomato halves, drained and chopped (optional)
salt and freshly ground black pepper, to taste

■ Preheat the oven to 375°F. Line a plate with paper towel.

■ Remove the stems from the mushrooms and discard or set aside for another use. Wipe the caps with paper towels to clean off dirt and debris. Using a paring knife or small melon baller, enlarge the cavity to make room for a generous portion of stuffing. Set the mushrooms aside.

■ Heat the olive oil in a skillet over medium heat. Add the sausage and onion and cook for 3 to 4 minutes, stirring and breaking up the meat. Add the spinach, stir, cover, and cook for 2 minutes. Uncover and cook for 2 minutes more. Remove the skillet from the heat, transfer the mixture to a plate, and set aside to cool.

■ Put the walnuts, crackers, parsley, and basil into a food processor. Pulse to chop. Add the sausage mixture, Parmesan cheese, cream cheese, sun-dried tomatoes (if using), and salt and pepper, to taste. Pulse repeatedly, until the mixture just starts to clump together. Do not overprocess.

■ Spoon the filling into the mushroom caps, mounding it on top. Dust each mushroom with Parmesan cheese. Place on a large baking sheet. Bake for 22 to 25 minutes, or until light golden and heated through. Don't worry if the mushrooms weep.

■ Transfer to the plate and set aside to rest. Transfer to a platter and serve.

Makes 8 servings.

Cleaning Mushrooms

Wiping is a generally accepted way to clean off mushrooms. Rinsing them usually just traps water in the gills and can make them sodden. Never rinse them unless they're really dirty.

Baked Stuffed Clams

24 small or medium clams (such as littlenecks)
3 slices bacon
⅓ cup minced green or red bell pepper
⅓ cup minced onion
¼ cup minced celery
2 cloves garlic, minced
¼ cup dry white wine
1 cup panko bread crumbs
3 tablespoons finely grated Parmesan cheese
3 tablespoons finely chopped Italian parsley
salt and freshly ground black pepper, to taste
¼ to ½ cup reserved clam-cooking water
3 tablespoons unsalted butter (half soft, half cold)

■ Preheat the oven to 375°F.

■ Scrub the clams well under running water. Bring 1 inch of water in a large saucepan or pot to a boil. Add the clams, cover, and boil-steam them, covered, for 7 to 8 minutes, or until they open. (Discard any clams that look damaged or have not opened after 8 minutes.) Using a slotted spoon, transfer the clams to a colander placed over a plate. Reserve the cooking water.

■ When the clams are cool enough to handle, remove the meats from the shells (reserve the shells) and chop the meats coarsely. Transfer to a bowl and set aside.

■ In a large skillet, cook the bacon until crisp. Transfer it to paper towels (do not drain the skillet). Add the bell pepper, onion, and celery to the skillet and cook over medium heat for 5 minutes, stirring often. Add the garlic and cook for 1 minute more. Add the wine and cook for 1 minute, stirring, until the liquid is reduced by half. Set aside.

■ Crumble the bacon.

■ Add the bread crumbs, Parmesan cheese, parsley, bacon, chopped clams, and salt and pepper, to taste, to the skillet and stir. Sprinkle with 1 to 2 tablespoons of reserved clam-cooking water to dampen (not soak) the filling. It should hold together.

■ Rinse and dry the largest clamshells. Break each one apart at the hinge. Lightly spread soft butter on the inside of each half. Pack each half generously with filling and place on a large baking sheet. Put a small slice of cold butter on each mound of filling. Bake for 20 minutes, or until heated through.

Makes 4 to 6 servings.

CLEANING CLAMS

Before cooking fresh clams, soak them in a bowl of cool, salted water for an hour or so; during this time, the clams will spit out sand. Then, lift out each clam from the sandy water and scrub its shells with a stiff brush under cold running water. Softshell types (such as steamers) tend to have more grit than hardshells (such as littlenecks).

Bacon-Wrapped Scallops With Creamy Chili Sauce

A spin on a classic: surf and turf with heat.

Scallops:

½ **pound bacon**

chili powder and freshly ground black pepper, to taste

1 pound large scallops

3 tablespoons unsalted butter, melted

Sauce:

½ **cup mayonnaise**

2 tablespoons sour cream

2 tablespoons red chili paste

1 teaspoon Dijon-style mustard

2 to 3 teaspoons lime juice

1 tablespoon chopped Italian parsley

salt and cayenne pepper, to taste

For scallops:

■ Preheat the broiler. Get out a large, rimmed baking sheet.

■ Lay the bacon slices on a large piece of wax paper. Dust each slice with chili powder and pepper. Put a scallop at one end and roll it up in the bacon. If desired, trim the bacon to just overlap around the scallop. Stick a toothpick into the bacon to hold it in place. Repeat for all of the scallops. Place them in a large bowl.

■ Drizzle with butter, turning to coat.

■ Place the scallops, uncrowded, on the baking sheet. Broil for 15 to 20 minutes, or until the scallops are cooked through and appear opaque. Remove the sheet from the oven—be careful of the hot juices—and serve with the sauce.

For sauce:

Combine all of the ingredients in a small bowl and stir to blend. Cover and refrigerate until needed.

Makes 4 to 5 servings.

FOOD FOR THOUGHT

In ancient Rome, parsley was thought to preserve sobriety.

Salmon Pâté

Elegant and easy! Serve with crackers or toast points, or indulge and use as sandwich spread.

8 to 9 ounces smoked salmon or 4 to 5.5 ounces smoked salmon
   with 1 can (5 ounces) salmon, flaked
8 ounces cream cheese, softened
2 tablespoons capers or finely chopped dill pickle
2 tablespoons chopped fresh dill
2 teaspoons freshly squeezed lemon juice
1½ teaspoons Dijon-style mustard
1 teaspoon Worcestershire sauce
½ teaspoon prepared horseradish
¼ teaspoon smoked paprika
¼ teaspoon salt
¼ teaspoon freshly ground black pepper
1 cup toasted walnuts, chopped fine

■ Put all of the ingredients except the nuts into a large bowl. Using an electric mixer on medium speed, beat until the ingredients are thoroughly combined but still have some texture. Taste, adding more seasonings, if desired. Cover with plastic wrap and refrigerate for about 1 hour.

■ Transfer the mixture to a 12-inch-long sheet of plastic wrap and shape into a 2-inch-thick log. Wrap the log in the plastic and roll to give it uniform shape. Refrigerate until shortly before serving.

■ Remove the plastic wrap. On a fresh sheet of plastic wrap, sprinkle the nuts close together and roll the log over them, to coat. Transfer the log to a serving tray.

Makes 8 to 10 servings.

In the hands of an able cook, fish can become an inexhaustible source of perpetual delight.

–Anthelme Brillat-Savarin, French writer (1755–1826)

Hot Crab Dip

Dig—or dip—in, with whole grain crackers, baguette toasts, or celery sticks.

2 tablespoons (¼ stick) unsalted butter
1 cup finely chopped onion
2 cloves garlic, minced
2 teaspoons seafood seasoning (such as Old Bay)
4 ounces cream cheese, softened
⅓ cup sour cream
⅓ cup mayonnaise
2 teaspoons lemon juice
1½ teaspoons Worcestershire sauce
1½ teaspoons Dijon-style mustard
salt and freshly ground black pepper, to taste
8 ounces crabmeat, fresh or canned (drained)
2 cups shredded sharp cheddar cheese, divided
paprika, for dusting

■ Preheat the oven to 375°F. Butter a shallow 1½-quart casserole.

■ In a skillet over medium heat, melt the butter. Add the onion, stir, and cook for 5 minutes, or until soft. Add the garlic and seafood seasoning, stir to blend, and cook for 1 minute more. Set aside.

■ Combine the cream cheese, sour cream, and mayonnaise in a bowl and, using an electric mixer on medium-low speed, mix until just blended. Add the lemon juice, Worcestershire sauce, and mustard and mix until smooth and creamy. Add salt and pepper, to taste. Fold in the crabmeat and 1 cup of the cheese.

■ Spread the mixture in the prepared casserole. Sprinkle with the remaining 1 cup of cheese and dust with paprika. Bake for 25 minutes, or until bubbly. Serve warm.

Makes 8 or more servings.

GARLIC TIP

If you have a lot of garlic cloves to peel, place them in a small bowl. Pour hot water onto them and let stand for a minute. Discard the water, and the papery skins will come off easily by hand.

Crab Cakes With Special Seafood Sauce

Everyone has a different expectation of a crab cake. This one beats them all.

Crab cakes:

1 pound lump crabmeat

2 scallions, white parts only, minced

2 tablespoons minced red bell pepper

2 tablespoons minced fresh Italian parsley

1½ tablespoons minced fresh dill

¾ cup fine, plain cracker crumbs,
  plus extra for rolling, divided

1 large egg, lightly beaten

3 tablespoons mayonnaise

2 teaspoons seafood seasoning (such as Old Bay)

1½ teaspoons Dijon-style mustard

½ teaspoon Worcestershire sauce

olive oil and unsalted butter, for frying

Sauce:

¾ cup mayonnaise

3 tablespoons sour cream

¼ cup dill pickle relish

2 tablespoons tomato-based chili sauce

1 tablespoon minced red onion

1 tablespoon minced fresh Italian parsley

¾ teaspoon seafood seasoning (such as Old Bay)

½ teaspoon Dijon-style mustard

¼ teaspoon sugar

For crab cakes:

■ Preheat the oven to 300°F. Line a baking sheet with wax paper.

■ Combine the crabmeat, scallions, bell pepper, parsley, dill, and ¾ cup cracker crumbs in a large bowl and mix to blend. Put the remaining crumbs in a shallow bowl and set aside.

■ In a third bowl, combine the egg, mayonnaise, seafood seasoning, mustard, and Worcestershire sauce and whisk to blend. Add the egg mixture to the crab mixture and stir until the ingredients cohere.

■ Shape the crabmeat mixture: For "silver dollar"–size cakes, use 1 heaping tablespoon of the mixture; for larger cakes, use about ⅓ cup. Form crab balls. Roll each ball in the cracker crumbs. Flatten each ball into a ¾-inch-thick disk and place on the prepared baking sheet.

■ Heat 1 tablespoon of olive oil and 1 tablespoon of butter in a large, nonstick skillet over medium heat; don't let the butter smoke. In batches, cook the crab cakes for about 3 minutes on each side, turning once. Between batches, wipe the skillet with paper towels to remove burned crumbs and add fresh olive oil and butter.

■ Transfer the crab cakes to an unlined baking sheet and hold in the oven until all are cooked.

For sauce:

■ Put the mayonnaise and sour cream into a bowl and whisk to combine. Add the dill pickle relish, chili sauce, onion, parsley, seafood seasoning, mustard, and sugar. Stir to blend thoroughly. Cover and refrigerate until serving. Serve crab cakes with the sauce on the side.

Makes 12 to 30 crab cakes.

Party Tarts

What's a party without mini quiches? Use your favorite dough or the one for empanadas.

FARM FRESH

To keep eggs fresh, store them in your refrigerator in their original carton. It protects them from drying out and absorbing odors.

Dough:

Empanada Dough (page 10), handled as directed here

Custard:

2 large eggs
⅔ cup light cream
¼ teaspoon Dijon-style mustard
¼ teaspoon salt
freshly ground black pepper, to taste
¼ teaspoon dried basil

For dough:

■ Lightly butter the cups of a 12-cup muffin pan.

■ Prepare the dough as directed and divide it into equal halves. (You will need only one half; save the other for another use.) Refrigerate for at least 1 hour. (If longer, let it sit at room temperature for 5 to 10 minutes before rolling.)

■ On a floured surface, roll the dough to slightly less than ⅛-inch thick. Using a 3- or 3¼-inch round cutter, cut 12 circles into the dough and place one in each muffin cup, pressing it in evenly and flat against the bottom and about ½ inch up the side of the cup. Reroll to cut the dough scraps, if necessary. Refrigerate for 30 minutes.

For custard:

■ In a bowl, combine the eggs, light cream, mustard, salt, pepper, and basil and whisk until blended. Pour into a spouted measuring cup.

■ Prepare one of the fillings and add the custard as directed.

To bake:

■ Preheat the oven to 350°F.

■ Bake for 25 minutes, or until the pastry has browned and the filling is set. Transfer to a cooling rack for 10 minutes. Slide a knife around each tart's edge, to loosen, then transfer to a rack to cool. Serve warm or at room temperature. To serve later, refrigerate and reheat later on a baking sheet at 325°F for 10 minutes.

Makes 12 servings.

Filling Variations

Olive and Feta Tarts

¼ cup chopped, pitted olives
¼ cup finely crumbled feta cheese
paprika, for dusting

■ Evenly divide the chopped olives and feta cheese among the cups. Pour enough custard into each cup to almost reach the top of the dough. Lightly dust each tart with paprika. Bake as directed.

Sun-Dried Tomato Tarts

24 oil-packed sun-dried tomato halves
½ cup finely crumbled feta cheese or
    ½ cup slivers of mozzarella

■ Lay two pieces of sun-dried tomato in each dough cup. Evenly divide crumbled feta cheese or slivers of mozzarella among the cups. Pour in enough custard to almost reach the top of the dough. Bake as directed.

> **I feel a recipe is only a theme, which an intelligent cook can play each time with variation.**
>
> *—Madame Jehane Benoît, Canadian writer (1904–87)*

Broccoli Cheddar Tarts

1¼ to 1½ cups small broccoli florets,
    steamed to al dente
½ to ¾ cup finely diced sharp cheddar cheese

■ Place one or two broccoli florets in the bottom of each dough cup. Evenly divide the cheddar cheese among the cups. Pour in enough custard to almost reach the top of the dough. Bake as directed.

Onion and Bacon Tarts

2 tablespoons (¼ stick) butter
1 medium onion, roughly chopped
¼ to ⅓ cup crumbled, crisp-cooked bacon
½ to ¾ cup finely shredded cheddar cheese

■ Melt the butter in a skillet over medium heat. Add the onions and cook until wilted. Transfer to a plate and set aside to cool.

■ Put a spoonful of onions into each dough cup. Evenly divide the bacon and cheddar cheese among the cups. Pour in enough custard to almost reach the top of the dough. Bake as directed.

Beef and Mushroom Stew
recipe on page 54

soups, stews, & chilis

How to Make a Bread Soup Bowl

The best loaves for this are firm, crusty, and about 5 inches across.

• *Preheat the oven to 350°F.*

• *Slice off the top third of the loaf with a serrated knife. (Save these ends for another use, or warm them separately, wrapped in foil, and serve with the soup.)*

• *Carefully, so that you don't puncture the sides, carve or pull out the bready interior, leaving relatively thick walls.*

• *Wrap the hollowed loaf in aluminum foil and put it into the oven for 10 minutes, or until warm. Remove the foil. Ladle in the soup and serve on a plate.*

Broccoli Cheddar Soup

For a special treat, serve this in a bread bowl.

1 large head broccoli
1 medium baking potato, peeled and diced
5 cups chicken stock
4 tablespoons (½ stick) unsalted butter
1 medium onion, finely chopped
1 cup sliced mushroom caps
1 clove garlic, minced
⅓ cup all-purpose flour
⅔ cup half-and-half or milk
½ teaspoon salt, plus more to taste
freshly ground black pepper, to taste
1 tablespoon Dijon-style mustard
2 cups shredded sharp cheddar cheese

■ Cut the broccoli tops into 1-inch florets (about 3 cups). Peel and dice the broccoli stalks to make 1 cup. Put all of the broccoli and potato into a large saucepan, add the chicken stock, and bring to a boil. As soon as the boil starts, use a slotted spoon to transfer about half of the broccoli florets to a bowl and set aside. Reduce the heat, cover, and simmer the remaining broccoli and potato for about 10 minutes, or until tender. Remove the pan from the heat.

■ In a large soup pot over medium heat, melt the butter. Add the onion and cook for 5 minutes, or until soft. Add the mushrooms and garlic, and cook for 5 minutes more. Add the flour and cook, stirring, for 2 minutes. Ladle all but a cupful of broccoli broth into the soup pot. Stir, until the mixture thickens.

■ Transfer the broccoli pieces (except the reserved florets) and remaining broth to a food processor. Pulse to purée. Add the purée to the soup pot, then add the half-and-half, salt, and pepper. Bring to a simmer, stirring. Add the mustard and the cheese, ½ cup at a time, stirring until it melts. Add the reserved broccoli florets. Taste and add more salt and pepper, if desired.

Makes 6 servings.

Cheesy Cream of Cauliflower Soup

*For white soup, use only Jarlsberg cheese. For a tint of color,
use half yellow sharp cheddar and half Jarlsberg.*

6 tablespoons (¾ stick) unsalted butter, divided
1 large onion, chopped
5 cups chicken stock
2 cups peeled and diced baking potatoes
3½ cups small cauliflower florets, cut into 1-inch pieces, divided
½ teaspoon salt, plus more to taste
3 tablespoons all-purpose flour
1½ cups half-and-half or milk
1 pound Jarlsberg cheese, shredded, or ½ pound each yellow sharp
   cheddar and Jarlsberg, shredded
2 teaspoons Dijon-style mustard
freshly ground black pepper or cayenne pepper, to taste
chopped fresh Italian parsley or thyme, for garnish

■ In a large soup pot over medium heat, melt 3 tablespoons of butter.
Add the onion and cook until soft, about 10 minutes. Add the chicken
stock, potato, 2½ cups of cauliflower, and salt. Bring to a boil, then
reduce to a simmer and cook for 10 to 12 minutes, or until the
vegetables are tender.

■ Working in batches, use a slotted spoon to transfer the solids to a
ricer or food mill and purée. (You may also purée the vegetables in a
food processor, with ¼ cup of the broth.) Return the vegetables to the
pot along with the remaining 1 cup of cauliflower florets. Simmer for
7 to 8 minutes more, or until the florets are tender.

■ Melt the remaining 3 tablespoons of butter in a saucepan over
medium heat. Add the flour and whisk for 1 minute; do not brown.
Add the half-and-half and cook for 2 to 3 minutes, whisking
constantly, until thickened. Add the mixture to the soup and heat for
several minutes, stirring often.

■ Just prior to serving, add the cheese, ½ cup at a time, and stir until
it melts. Add the mustard. Taste and add salt and pepper, if desired.
Serve hot, garnished with parsley or thyme.

Makes 8 or more servings.

> It is on a good stock,
> or first good broth and
> sauce, that excellence
> in cookery depends.
>
> *—Mrs. Isabella Beeton,
> English writer (1836–65)*

BOILING POINTS
What is the difference
between a "low boil"
and a "rapid boil"?

While both might
occur at the same
temperature, 212°F,
the difference is what
you see happening on
the surface. With a
"low boil," you would
see some bubbling
on the surface, but it
would seem in control.
With a "rapid boil,"
you would see a good
deal more surface
action. The variations
are more apparent
when there's food
in the vessel.

Cabbage Paprikash Soup

Use vegetable stock in place of chicken stock, if desired.

4 tablespoons (½ stick) unsalted butter
1 large onion, finely chopped
1 green bell pepper, chopped
4 cups thinly sliced green cabbage
1 clove garlic, minced
¼ cup paprika
5 cups chicken stock
1 large baking potato, peeled and diced
1 large carrot, grated
1 bay leaf
¾ teaspoon salt, plus more to taste
freshly ground black pepper, to taste
1½ tablespoons tomato paste
⅓ cup all-purpose flour
1 cup sour cream

■ In a large soup pot or Dutch oven over medium heat, melt the butter. Add the onion and bell pepper and cook for 5 minutes. Add the cabbage and cook for 7 to 8 minutes more, or until the cabbage is wilted. Add the garlic and paprika. Cook for 1 minute more, stirring. Add 1 cup of water plus the stock, potato, carrot, bay leaf, salt, and black pepper. Bring to a low boil, then reduce the heat and simmer gently for 10 minutes, stirring occasionally.

■ Ladle 1 cup of broth into a small bowl and set aside to cool for 1 to 2 minutes. Add the tomato paste and stir. Add the flour and whisk until smooth. Add this mixture to the soup pot and simmer, stirring, for 5 minutes more, or until thick.

■ Combine the sour cream and a ladle of hot soup in a bowl and stir to blend. (This step, "tempering" the sour cream, will help to prevent it from separating when you add it to the pot.) Add to the soup and heat for 3 to 4 minutes, but do not boil. Taste and add seasonings, if desired. Remove the bay leaf before serving.

Makes 6 or more servings.

French Onion Soup

Red or white wine, with either beef or chicken stock, is suitable.

8 tablespoons (1 stick) unsalted butter, divided
4 large onions, halved and sliced (8 to 10 cups)
salt, to taste
2 cloves garlic, minced
1 bay leaf
several large pinches fresh or dried thyme leaves
1 cup dry white wine, divided
1 tablespoon all-purpose flour
5 cups beef stock
freshly ground black pepper, to taste
1 to 2 teaspoons Worcestershire sauce, or to taste
1 French bread, or baguette
2 to 2½ cups shredded Swiss or Gruyère cheese

**Warm food,
warm friendships.**
—Czech proverb

■ In a large soup pot over medium heat, melt 6 tablespoons of butter. Add the onions and salt lightly. Add the garlic, bay leaf, and thyme. Cover for 10 minutes, then uncover, cooking for a total of 35 to 45 minutes, or until the onions are soft and golden caramel in color, stirring frequently and scraping the bottom of the pan.

■ Add the wine, ½ cup at a time, and cook, stirring, until the wine evaporates. Add the flour and cook for 2 minutes while continuing to stir. Add the stock and bring to a simmer. Taste and add salt and pepper, if desired. Add a teaspoon of Worcestershire sauce. Taste and add more, if desired.

■ Preheat the oven to 350°F.

■ Slice the French bread, cutting eight to ten ¾-inch-thick slices on the diagonal. With the remaining butter, coat one side of each slice and place the pieces, buttered side up, on a large baking sheet. Toast in the oven for 12 to 15 minutes, or until light golden and crusty. Remove the bread from the oven and set aside.

■ Turn off the oven and turn on the broiler.

■ Remove the bay leaf. Ladle the soup into heatproof serving bowls, to within about 1 inch of the rim. Float two slices of bread in each bowl. Cover thickly with shredded cheese. Place the bowls on a baking sheet and broil for 3 to 4 minutes, or until bubbly. Avoid scorching the cheese or bread.

Makes up to 6 servings.

Cream of Green Pea Soup

Even when made with frozen peas, this soup has fresh-from-the-garden flavor. Of course, fresh peas will also work nicely, if you're lucky enough to have some.

3 tablespoons unsalted butter
1 medium sweet onion, finely chopped
5 cups chicken stock
4 cups frozen green peas
1 medium baking potato, peeled and diced
½ teaspoon salt, plus more to taste
¼ cup heavy or whipping cream
freshly ground black pepper, to taste
finely grated Parmesan cheese, for garnish

■ In a large pot over medium heat, melt the butter. Add the onion and cook, partially covered, for 10 minutes, or until the onion is soft. Add the chicken stock, peas, potato, and salt. Bring to a boil. Reduce the heat, cover, and simmer for 7 to 8 minutes, or until the peas are soft. Remove from the heat.

■ Process the mixture in batches: Using a slotted spoon, transfer some of the peas to a blender. (The blender should be no more than one-third full.) Add enough of the liquid to cover. Process until smooth, then transfer to a large bowl. Repeat for the remaining mixture. Save a few peas for garnish. (You'll have more broth than you need, which is fine: Just leave it in the pot.)

■ Return the pea mixture to the pot, add the heavy cream, and stir. Gently reheat the soup. Taste and add pepper and more salt, if desired. Serve hot, passing the cheese and peas at the table.

Makes 4 to 5 servings.

**Beautiful Soup,
so rich and green,
Waiting in a hot tureen!**

*–Lewis Carroll,
English writer (1832–98)*

WHAT'S THE DIFFERENCE?

Summer squash is harvested before it is ripe; the skin is tender and the seeds are immature. Winter squash is picked when it is ripe; the skin has toughened and the seeds are mature.

Curried Butternut Squash Soup

Substitute another cooked winter squash, if desired.

1 large butternut squash
3 tablespoons unsalted butter
4 cups halved and thinly sliced onion
2½ cups chicken stock, divided
1 cup half-and-half or light cream
2 tablespoons brown sugar
1½ teaspoons curry powder
salt and freshly ground black pepper, to taste
½ cup apple butter, for garnish

■ Preheat the oven to 375°F.

■ Halve the squash lengthwise, scoop out the seeds, and place it on an oiled, rimmed baking sheet, cut sides down. Bake for 45 to 60 minutes, or until the squash can be pierced easily with a paring knife. Transfer the sheet to a rack and turn the squash over to cool.

■ Melt the butter in a large skillet over medium heat. Add the onions and cook, stirring often, for 15 to 18 minutes, or until golden and caramelized. If the onions become dry, add water, 1 tablespoon at a time, as needed.

■ Transfer the onions to a food processor. Scoop the squash out of the skins and add to the processor with 1 cup of the chicken stock. Process until smooth.

■ Transfer the onion–squash mixture to a large saucepan. Add the remaining 1½ cups of stock, half-and-half, and brown sugar. Bring to a simmer, stirring often (do not boil).

■ Ladle ½ cup of soup into a small bowl and add the curry powder. Stir to blend, then return it to the soup. Stir and simmer for 5 minutes more, adding salt and pepper, to taste. Serve hot, passing the apple butter at the table.

Makes 6 servings.

Really Good Gazpacho

Three rules ensure that this lives up to its name: ripe tomatoes in season; not overprocessing the ingredients; chilling, as directed.

4 or 5 large, ripe tomatoes
1 large cucumber, peeled, halved lengthwise, and seeded
1 medium zucchini, coarsely chopped
1 large green or red bell pepper, coarsely chopped
1 cup coarsely chopped red onion
3 cloves garlic, chopped
¼ cup olive oil
¼ cup red-wine vinegar, plus more to taste
½ teaspoon salt, plus more to taste
freshly ground black pepper, to taste
2 to 3 cups tomato juice
¼ cup finely chopped Italian parsley
1 cup avocado chunks, for garnish
½ cup sour cream, for garnish

■ Halve the tomatoes crosswise and gently squeeze out and discard the seeds. Coarsely dice the tomatoes to make 3 cups and transfer to a food processor. Process until finely chopped. Transfer to a large bowl.

■ Put the cucumber and zucchini into the processor, finely chop, and add to the tomatoes. Process the bell pepper, onion, and garlic and add to the tomatoes.

■ Add the olive oil, vinegar, salt, and pepper, to taste, and stir. Add the tomato juice; the amount depends on the desired thickness of the soup. Cover and refrigerate for at least 2 hours, or overnight.

■ Shortly before serving, taste and adjust the salt, pepper, and vinegar, if desired. Add the parsley and stir. Pass the avocado chunks and a ramekin of sour cream at the table for topping each bowl.

Makes 6 servings.

BEST BUY

When buying bell peppers, choose firm, richly colored ones that are the heaviest for their size.

KEEP THE CRUNCH

If celery stalks
become wilted,
separate them and
place in a bowl
of ice water for
10 to 15 minutes
before use.

Chicken Noodle Soup

There is simply nothing like chicken noodle soup made from scratch.

3 tablespoons unsalted butter
1 medium onion, finely chopped
2 stalks celery, finely chopped
2 carrots, peeled and finely chopped
8 cups chicken stock (or combination of stock and water, to taste)
1 bay leaf
½ teaspoon dried oregano
½ teaspoon dried thyme
½ teaspoon dried basil
2 cups shredded cooked chicken
2 cups wide egg noodles, uncooked
2 tablespoons chopped fresh Italian parsley
salt and freshly ground black pepper, to taste

■ Melt the butter in a large soup pot over medium-low heat. Add the onion, celery, and carrots, cover, and cook for 10 minutes, stirring occasionally. Add the stock, bay leaf, oregano, thyme, and basil and bring to a boil. Add the chicken, noodles, parsley, and salt and pepper, to taste. Reduce the heat and simmer, partially covered, until the noodles are tender. Taste and adjust the seasonings, if desired. Remove the bay leaf before serving.

Makes 6 to 8 servings.

Chicken Tortilla Soup With All the Fixin's

Don't skimp on the fixin's; they're half the fun.

Soup:

3 tablespoons olive oil

1 large onion, chopped

1 medium green bell pepper, chopped

3 to 4 cloves garlic, minced

1 jalapeño, finely chopped

2 teaspoons chili powder

1 teaspoon cumin

1 teaspoon smoked paprika

4 cups chicken stock

1 cup frozen or fresh corn kernels

2 cans (15 ounces) diced tomatoes (chili-style, if possible), with juice

1¼ to 1½ pounds boneless skinless chicken breasts or skinless thighs

¾ teaspoon salt, plus more to taste

1 can (15 ounces) black beans, drained and rinsed

freshly ground black pepper, to taste

3 tablespoons fine yellow cornmeal

3 corn tortillas, cut in half, then into thin strips

Fixin's:

diced ripe avocado

finely chopped red onion

chopped fresh Italian parsley

shredded Monterey Jack or sharp cheddar cheese

broken tortilla chips

pickled jalapeño slices

For soup:

■ Heat the olive oil in a large soup pot over medium heat. Add the onion and bell pepper and cook for 8 minutes, or until the onion is soft. Add the garlic, jalapeño, chili powder, cumin, and smoked paprika. Cook for 1 minute more, then add 2 cups of water plus the stock, corn, tomatoes with their juice, chicken, and salt. Bring to a boil, then reduce the heat and simmer, partially covered, for 25 minutes.

■ Using a slotted spoon, transfer the chicken to a plate. Add the black beans and black pepper to the soup pot.

■ Cut the chicken into thin, bite-size pieces and return to the soup.

■ Put the cornmeal into a small bowl and add 2 to 3 tablespoons of water (more, if necessary), stirring to make a thick slurry. Add this to the soup and simmer, stirring often, for 20 to 30 minutes, or until the soup thickens slightly. Taste and adjust the seasonings, if desired. Just prior to serving, add the tortillas to the soup and stir. Serve, passing the fixin's at the table.

Makes 8 servings.

> **Food is the most primitive form of comfort.**
>
> *–Sheilah Graham, English-born American writer (1904–88)*

Spiced Turkey Soup

Day-after-Thanksgiving leftovers never tasted so good!

3 tablespoons vegetable oil
1 large onion, chopped
1 stalk celery, chopped
½ green bell pepper, chopped
1 carrot, peeled, halved lengthwise, and diced
2 cloves garlic, minced
1 teaspoon cumin
1 teaspoon chili powder
1 teaspoon paprika
1 teaspoon dried oregano
½ teaspoon dried coriander
6 cups chicken or turkey stock
2 to 2½ cups chopped cooked turkey
1 cup frozen or fresh corn kernels
1 cup frozen or fresh green beans
1 tablespoon tomato paste
salt and freshly ground black pepper, to taste
2 to 3 tablespoons chopped Italian parsley

Soup is liquid comfort.

—Author unknown

■ Heat the oil in a large, heavy soup pot over medium heat. Add the onion and cook for 5 minutes, or until soft. Add the celery, bell pepper, and carrot and cook for 5 minutes more, partially covered, stirring often. Add the garlic, cumin, chili powder, paprika, oregano, and coriander and cook for 1 minute, stirring. Add the stock, turkey, corn, green beans, and tomato paste. Bring the soup to a simmer, stirring often. Taste and add salt and pepper, if desired. Simmer for 10 to 15 minutes. Add the parsley just before serving.

Makes 6 servings.

Chorizo and Black Bean Soup With Avocado Cream

Chorizo, a spicy Spanish sausage, lends a rich, meaty flavor.

Soup:

1½ cups dried black beans, picked
 over, well rinsed, and drained

3 tablespoons vegetable or olive oil

1 medium onion, chopped

1 medium green bell pepper, chopped

2 stalks celery, thinly sliced

½ cup chopped carrot

salt, to taste

1 tablespoon chili powder

2 teaspoons cumin

1 teaspoon smoked or regular paprika

2 cloves garlic, minced

6 cups chicken stock

½ pound raw chorizo sausage,
 removed from casings and broken up

2 tablespoons tomato paste

freshly ground black pepper, to taste

Avocado cream:

1 ripe avocado

⅓ cup sour cream

handful fresh Italian parsley, chopped

1 to 2 teaspoons lime juice

pinch of salt

Heavy Bottoms vs. Light Weights

Generally speaking, the thickness of the bottom of your pan can make a difference in your cooking. The more metal you put between your food and heat source, the better, especially for long-simmering dishes. This is because more metal results in more even cooking. Also, when you're browning a cut of meat—before, say, braising something such as pot roast—the even heat from a heavy-bottom pan will result in more even browning because of fewer hot spots.

For soup:

■ Put the beans into a soup pot and add enough water to cover by several inches. Bring to a boil and cook for 1 minute, then remove from the heat. Cover and set aside for 3 hours.

■ Heat the oil in a separate pot over medium-high heat. Add the onion, bell pepper, celery, carrot, and salt. Cook for 8 minutes, stirring often. Add the chili powder, cumin, paprika, and garlic and cook for 1 minute more. Add the chicken stock and stir.

■ Drain the beans, discarding the liquid, and add the beans to the soup. Bring the soup to a boil, then reduce to a simmer. Add the chorizo. Simmer, partially covered, stirring occasionally, for 2 hours, or until the beans are tender.

■ In batches and using a slotted spoon, transfer the solids and a cup or two of the broth to a food processor. Process to a rough purée and pour into a large bowl. Return the purée to the soup pot and add the tomato paste. Simmer for 10 minutes more, stirring. Taste and add salt and pepper, if desired.

For avocado cream:

■ Cut the avocado in half and spoon out the flesh in each half, putting it into a food processor. Add the sour cream, parsley, lime juice, and salt and process to a smooth purée, scraping down the sides once or twice. Transfer to a small serving bowl. Serve the soup hot and pass the avocado cream at the table.

Makes 6 or more servings.

Kale, Sausage, and White Bean Soup

To add color and sweetness, substitute diced winter squash for the potato. Whether you use potato or squash, add cooked pasta at the end and you've got minestrone.

BE KIND TO RINDS

Save the hard, thin rind remnants of fresh Parmesan cheese that are too difficult to grate and toss them into simmering Italian-style soups like this one, where they'll add subtle flavor. Remove the cheese rinds before serving the soup.

½ pound fresh kale
3 to 4 links (about 1 pound) hot or mild Italian sausage
3 tablespoons olive oil
1 large onion, chopped
1 stalk celery, chopped
1 carrot, chopped
2 cloves garlic, minced
3 cups chicken stock
1 medium baking potato, peeled and diced
1 can (14 ounces) diced tomatoes, with juice
2 tablespoons tomato paste
1 teaspoon salt, plus more to taste
1 teaspoon dried basil
½ teaspoon dried thyme
freshly ground black pepper, to taste
1 can (15 or 19 ounces) cannellini beans, drained and rinsed
finely grated Parmesan cheese, for garnish

■ Strip the kale leaves from their stems and tear the leaves into large pieces. Discard the stems. Rinse the leaves in a large bowl of cool water. Transfer to a colander and set aside.

■ Bring a large pan of water to a boil. Pierce each sausage link several times with a paring knife, place the links in the boiling water, and cook for 10 minutes. Transfer to a plate. When the sausages are cool enough to handle, remove the casings and cut the links into ¼-inch-thick slices.

■ Heat the olive oil in a large soup pot over medium heat. Add the onion, celery, and carrot and cook for 10 minutes, or until the onion is soft. Add the garlic and cook for 1 minute more. Add 3 cups of water plus the stock, kale, and sausage. Bring to a simmer, stirring occasionally. Add the potato, tomatoes with juice, tomato paste, salt, basil, thyme, and pepper. Simmer for 20 to 25 minutes, or until the kale is tender. Add the beans and simmer for 5 to 10 minutes more. Taste and adjust the seasonings, if desired. Serve hot and pass the Parmesan at the table.

Makes 8 or more servings.

ONION ADVICE

If a recipe calls
for half an onion,
use the top half.
The root will help to
preserve the lower
half for use later.

Lentil and Turkey Sausage Soup

Turkey sausage makes a good alternative to red meat.

1½ cups dry green lentils, picked over
¼ cup olive oil
1 large onion, chopped
1 cup chopped celery
1 cup chopped green or red bell pepper
3 cloves garlic, minced
1½ teaspoons ground cumin
1½ teaspoons smoked paprika
4 cups chicken stock
1½ cups chopped carrot
1¼ teaspoons salt, plus more to taste
1 teaspoon dried thyme
1 teaspoon dried oregano
⅓ cup tomato paste
1 pound smoked turkey sausage, cut into ¼-inch slices
1 bay leaf
freshly ground black pepper, to taste

■ Put the lentils into a large bowl. Cover with boiling water and set aside for 10 to 15 minutes. Drain the lentils and set aside.

■ Heat the olive oil in a large soup pot over medium heat. Add the onion, celery, and bell pepper and cook for 10 minutes. Add the garlic, cumin, and smoked paprika and cook for 1 minute more. Add 4 cups of water plus the lentils, stock, carrot, salt, thyme, and oregano. Bring the mixture to a boil, then reduce the heat and simmer for 20 to 30 minutes, or until the lentils are soft.

■ Using a slotted spoon, transfer about two-thirds of the solids to a food processor. Process to a smooth purée, then return the purée to the soup pot.

■ Add the tomato paste, sausage, bay leaf, and pepper, to taste. Simmer, uncovered, for about 30 minutes, stirring often. Taste, adding more salt and pepper, if desired. Remove the bay leaf before serving.

Makes about 8 servings.

Beer Cheese Soup

Great for a gang, especially in cool weather.

1 cup peeled and diced carrot
1 cup peeled and diced potato
2 cups chicken stock
3 tablespoons unsalted butter
1 large onion, chopped
1 cup diced smoked beef or turkey sausage
2 cloves garlic, minced
¼ cup all-purpose flour
1 bottle (12 ounces) beer, ale, or stout
1½ cups half-and-half or light cream
2 to 3 teaspoons Dijon-style mustard
2 teaspoons Worcestershire sauce
1 teaspoon salt, plus more to taste
3 to 4 cups shredded extra sharp cheddar cheese
freshly ground black pepper, to taste
sugar, to taste (optional)

■ Combine the carrot, potato, and stock in a saucepan and bring to a boil. Reduce the heat, cover, and simmer for 10 minutes, or until the vegetables are tender. Set aside, uncover, and cool briefly.

■ Transfer to a food processor and purée. Set aside.

■ Melt the butter in a large soup pot over medium heat. Add the onion and cook for 8 minutes, or until soft. Add the sausage and garlic and cook for 1 minute. Add the flour and cook for 1 minute more, stirring. Add the beer and half-and-half and cook for 3 to 4 minutes, stirring. Add the puréed vegetable mixture, mustard, Worcestershire sauce, and salt. Add the cheese in three stages, stirring between additions and adding more as it melts. Add black pepper, to taste. Simmer (do not boil) for 5 minutes more, adding more salt and cheese, if desired. If slightly bitter, add sugar, to taste, a pinch at a time.

Makes 6 servings.

Spud Check

To determine what kind of potatoes you have, drop one in a pot containing 11 parts water to one part salt. Waxy potatoes, best for boiling, will float. Mealy potatoes, best for baking or mashing, will sink.

Creamy Mussels Chowder

Serve with crusty French or Italian bread and a large green salad.

4 pounds fresh mussels, scrubbed and picked over (see box, opposite)
1 cup dry white wine
2 cups peeled and diced waxy potatoes
½ cup halved and thinly sliced carrot
1 teaspoon salt, divided, plus more to taste
2 leeks, white part only
4 tablespoons (½ stick) unsalted butter
2 stalks celery, thinly sliced
1 clove garlic, minced
2½ tablespoons all-purpose flour
½ teaspoon seafood seasoning (such as Old Bay)
1 bottle (8 ounces) clam juice
1 teaspoon dried thyme
1½ cups light cream or half-and-half
freshly ground black pepper, to taste

■ Put the mussels into a large pot and add the wine and ½ cup of water. Cover and steam over medium to high heat for 5 to 7 minutes. Using a slotted spoon, transfer the mussels to a large bowl and set aside to cool.

■ Line a colander with cheesecloth and place it inside another bowl. Pour the mussel broth through it to strain, then set the liquid aside. Set aside 12 mussels in the shell for garnish. Remove the meats from the remaining shells. Coarsely chop half of the meats.

■ Put the potatoes and carrots into a small saucepan; add 1 cup of water, or enough to barely cover; and ½ teaspoon of salt. Bring to a boil and cook gently for 6 to 7 minutes, uncovered, or until the potatoes are almost tender. Remove from the heat.

COMING CLEAN

A leek's layers can trap dirt. To clean, submerge slices in a bowl filled with cold water. Swirl them in the water and then let sit for several minutes. Remove from the water, rinse, and pat dry with paper towels.

■ Leaving the root end intact, cut the leeks lengthwise, into quarters. Fan the leeks and thoroughly rinse them. Roughly chop the leeks and set aside.

■ In a large soup pot over medium heat, melt the butter. Add the leeks and celery and cook for 8 to 9 minutes, or until soft. Add the garlic, flour, and seafood seasoning and cook for 1 minute more. Add the clam juice, thyme, reserved mussel broth, and contents of the potato saucepan and simmer. When the soup starts to thicken, add the cream and a scant ½ teaspoon salt. Add the chopped and whole mussel meats, stir, and simmer for about 5 more minutes. Taste and add salt and pepper, if desired. Serve hot, with two mussels in the shell on each portion as garnish.

Makes 6 servings.

**Chowder breathes reassurance.
It steams consolation.**

*–Clementine Paddleford,
American food writer
(1898–1967)*

How to Prepare Mussels

Under running tap water, scrub the mussels with a bristle brush to remove grit and dirt. Tap the smooth surface of any open shells with a fingertip; if the shell doesn't close, discard it. Use scissors to trim off or your hands to pull off the little "beards" that may be attached. After steaming, discard any mussels that have not opened.

Beef and Mushroom Stew

Watch this pot so that it never boils, or the meat will become tough.

1½ pounds stew beef, cut into
    bite-size pieces
¼ cup plus 2 tablespoons all-purpose
    flour, divided
4 tablespoons vegetable oil, divided
1 large onion, chopped
2 stalks celery, thinly sliced
½ pound mushrooms, sliced
2 cloves garlic, minced
2½ cups beef broth
1 cup tomato juice
½ cup dry red wine
¾ teaspoon salt, plus more to taste

2 bay leaves
2 large baking potatoes,
    peeled and cut into chunks
2 carrots, peeled and cut into
    thin rounds
2 cups fresh green beans,
    cut into bite-size pieces
1 teaspoon dried thyme
1 teaspoon dried oregano
freshly ground black pepper, to taste
1 tablespoon brown sugar
1 tablespoon Worcestershire sauce
1 tablespoon ketchup

■ Combine the stew beef and ¼ cup of flour in a large plastic bag and shake well to coat the meat.

■ Heat 2 tablespoons of oil in a large soup pot over medium heat. Working in two batches, shake the excess flour off half of the meat, put that meat into the pot, and cook for 3 minutes, or until browned, stirring occasionally. Transfer the meat to a heatproof dish. Add the remaining 2 tablespoons of oil to the pan and brown the remaining meat.

■ Add the onion, celery, mushrooms, garlic, and first batch of browned beef to the pot. Cook for 3 minutes, stirring often, or until the onion is soft. Add the beef broth, tomato juice, wine, salt, and bay leaves. Bring to a simmer. Reduce the heat, cover, and cook for 1 hour, stirring occasionally.

■ Ladle ¾ cup of the broth into a medium bowl and set aside.

■ To the large pot, add the potatoes, carrots, green beans, thyme, oregano, pepper, brown sugar, Worcestershire sauce, and ketchup. Cover and continue to simmer for 1 hour more, or until the vegetables are tender.

■ About 10 minutes before serving, add the remaining 2 tablespoons of flour to the reserved broth. Whisk until smooth, then add to the stew. Simmer for 10 minutes more, stirring often, until thickened. Remove the bay leaves before serving.

Makes 6 to 8 servings.

GOING GREEN

Green beans will keep for up to 1 week in a plastic bag in the crisper of your refrigerator.

Chicken Stew With Dumplings

In some parts of the country, nothing says "comfort food" quite like dumplings.

Stew:

2 cups all-purpose flour

3½ to 4 pounds split chicken breasts, thighs, or other chicken parts

salt, to taste, plus 1 teaspoon

freshly ground black pepper, to taste

paprika, to taste

3 tablespoons olive oil

2 tablespoons unsalted butter

1 large onion, chopped

2 stalks celery, thinly sliced

2 cups sliced mushroom caps

1 cup thinly sliced carrot

3 cups chicken stock

½ teaspoon dried thyme

½ cup light cream

⅓ cup all-purpose flour

Dumplings:

¾ cup all-purpose flour

¼ cup yellow cornmeal

1½ teaspoons baking powder

scant ½ teaspoon salt

½ teaspoon crumbled sage

1 tablespoon cold butter, in pieces

1 large egg

⅓ cup milk

For stew:

■ Put the flour into a pie plate or shallow bowl. Rinse the chicken pieces and pat dry with paper towels. Remove and discard the skin. Lightly salt and pepper the chicken, dust with paprika, and dredge the pieces in the flour.

■ Heat the olive oil and butter in a large pot over medium heat. Add the chicken, leaving space between the pieces. Cook for 3 to 4 minutes per side, or until browned. Transfer to a platter. Add the onion, celery, mushrooms, and carrot to the pot. Cook for 5 to 6 minutes, stirring often. Return the chicken pieces to the pot, add 2 cups of water plus the stock, thyme, salt, and pepper, to taste, and bring to a boil. Lower the heat, cover, and simmer for 30 minutes.

■ Remove the pot from the heat. Using a slotted spoon, transfer the chicken pieces to a platter. Set the broth aside to cool for 1 hour. With a large spoon, skim off and discard as much fat as possible.

■ When the chicken is cooled to the touch, pick off the meat, cut it into bite-size pieces, and return to the pot.

■ In a small bowl, whisk the light cream and flour until smooth. Add to the broth and simmer, until thickened, stirring occasionally.

For dumplings:

■ About 20 minutes before serving, combine the flour, cornmeal, baking powder, salt, and sage in a bowl. Add the butter and rub it in with your fingers until it resembles a coarse meal. Make a well in the center of the mixture. Drop the egg into the center, then add the milk. Whisk to combine the liquids, then stir the mixture to make a batter.

■ Carefully drop the batter, one rounded tablespoon at a time, into the barely simmering stew. Cover the pot and cook the dumplings for 15 minutes. (If you hear the liquid boiling, lower the heat.) Remove the cover, remove the pan from the heat, and allow the stew to rest briefly for 5 minutes before serving.

Makes 6 servings.

White Bean Chicken Chili

White chili contains chicken or turkey, instead of beef or pork, and no tomato products.

3 tablespoons unsalted butter
2 stalks celery, thinly sliced
1 large onion, chopped
1 large yellow, orange, or green
   bell pepper
2 cups thinly sliced mushrooms
3 cloves garlic, minced
1 jalapeño, finely chopped
2½ tablespoons all-purpose flour
4 teaspoons chili powder
2½ teaspoons cumin
2 teaspoons dried oregano
1½ teaspoons ground coriander

4½ cups chicken stock
2 to 3 cups cooked chicken,
   cut into bite-size pieces
1 can (19 ounces) cannellini
   beans, drained and rinsed
1 cup frozen or fresh corn
1 can (4 ounces) chopped
   green chiles
1 medium carrot, grated
scant ½ teaspoon salt
sour cream, for garnish
shredded cheddar cheese,
   for garnish

■ In a large soup pot or Dutch oven over medium heat, melt the butter. Add the celery, onion, and bell pepper and cook for 5 minutes, or until soft. Add the mushrooms, garlic, and jalapeño, stir, and cook for 4 to 5 minutes more, or until the mushrooms are soft and release a good deal of moisture. Add the flour, chili powder, cumin, oregano, and coriander and cook for 1 minute, stirring. Add the chicken stock, chicken, beans, corn, chiles, carrot, and salt. Gradually bring the mixture to a boil, then reduce the heat and simmer, covered, for about 30 minutes, stirring often. Taste and adjust the seasonings, if desired. Serve hot, passing the sour cream and cheese at the table.

Makes 6 or more servings.

> One can not think well,
> love well, sleep well,
> if one has not dined well.
> –*Virginia Woolf,*
> *English writer (1882–1941)*

Cincinnati Chili

Instead of browning, this method boils the beef, resulting in a fine-textured chili.

2 pounds ground beef (chuck)
1 medium onion, finely chopped
2 cloves garlic, minced
1 can (15 ounces) tomato sauce
½ cup thick barbecue sauce
3 tablespoons chili powder
2 tablespoons unsweetened cocoa powder
1½ tablespoons tomato paste
1 tablespoon light-brown sugar
1 tablespoon apple cider vinegar
1 tablespoon Worcestershire sauce
1½ teaspoons salt, plus more to taste
1 teaspoon cumin
½ teaspoon cinnamon
¼ teaspoon ground coriander
¼ teaspoon ground cloves
freshly ground black pepper, to taste
½ pound spaghetti, cooked according to package directions
2 cups shredded sharp cheddar cheese, for garnish
1 cup finely chopped red onion, for garnish
1 can (15 ounces) red kidney beans, drained and rinsed, for garnish

■ Combine 5 cups of water with the ground beef in a large, enameled pot or Dutch oven. Bring to a boil, then reduce the heat and simmer for 30 to 40 minutes, skimming off the scum and fat that floats to the top.

■ Add the remaining ingredients, except the spaghetti and garnishes, and continue to simmer for 45 minutes to 1 hour, stirring often, until the liquid is full-bodied and saucy. Taste and adjust the seasonings, if desired. Serve over spaghetti, passing the garnishes at the table.

Makes 6 to 8 servings.

Life is a combination of magic and pasta.

–Federico Fellini, Italian film director (1920–93)

*Crunchy Asian Salad
With Chicken
recipe on page 78*

salads

dressings and condiments

Mustardy Beet Salad

A kaleidoscope of color that's creamy, too.

4 or 5 medium beets, scrubbed, or 1 jar (16 ounces) pickled beets,
   drained and diced
salt, to taste
2½ cups diced red-skinned potatoes, peeled, if desired
2 tablespoons red-wine vinegar
1 cup chopped dill pickles
2 stalks celery, finely chopped
½ cup finely chopped red onion
¼ cup sour cream
¼ cup mayonnaise
1½ tablespoons Dijon-style mustard
1 tablespoon chopped fresh dill
freshly ground black pepper, to taste

■ Put the beets into a large pot, add water to cover, and salt, to taste.
Bring to a boil, then reduce the heat and boil gently for 20 to 30
minutes, or until the beets can be pierced easily with a fork.
Drain and set aside to cool. Slip off the skins, dice the beets, and
put into a bowl.

■ Put the potatoes into a saucepan, add water to cover, and salt, to
taste. Bring to a boil, then reduce the heat slightly and cook for 8 to 10
minutes, or until the potatoes are barely tender.

■ Drain and spread the potatoes in a shallow casserole. Sprinkle
with the vinegar and toss lightly. Add the pickles, celery, red onion,
and beets.

■ In a small bowl, combine the sour cream, mayonnaise, mustard,
and dill and whisk to blend. Pour over the beet–potato mixture
and add salt and pepper, to taste. Cover and refrigerate for at least
1 hour before serving.

Makes 6 or more servings.

Save 'n' Store

To store beets, trim the leaves, leaving about 2 inches of stem. Keep the unwashed beets in a plastic bag in the crisper of the refrigerator for up to 4 weeks. Store beet greens, or leaves, in a plastic bag in the crisper for up to 3 to 4 days.

Creamy Broccoli Carrot Salad

A palate- and eye-pleaser! Shredded cheese could clump together in a cold salad such as this, so diced is preferable.

1½ heads broccoli
salt, to taste, plus ¼ teaspoon
1 cup finely diced cheddar cheese
½ cup finely chopped carrot
½ cup toasted chopped walnuts
2 to 3 tablespoons crisp-cooked bacon, crumbled,
    or 1 to 1½ cups diced ham
2 tablespoons finely chopped red onion
½ cup mayonnaise
⅓ cup sour cream
2 tablespoons sugar
1½ tablespoons champagne or apple cider vinegar
freshly ground black pepper, to taste

■ Rinse the broccoli and cut the florets into bite-size pieces. Reserve the stems for another use. Put 1 inch of water into a large pot and bring to a boil. Working in two batches, put the florets into a basket steamer and place it in the pan, cover, and steam for 2 minutes. Immediately drain and spread the florets on paper towels; salt, to taste; and cool completely. (Do not transfer to an ice bath; the florets would soak up water and then dilute the salad.)

■ Transfer the florets to a large bowl. Add the cheese, carrot, walnuts, bacon, and onion. Toss to mix, then refrigerate.

■ One to 2 hours before serving, combine the mayonnaise, sour cream, sugar, vinegar, salt, and pepper in a small bowl and whisk to blend. Pour the dressing over the broccoli mixture and toss well. Taste, adding more seasonings, if desired. Cover and refrigerate.

Makes 6 to 8 servings.

CREATIVE CARROTS

Purée leftover cooked carrots and use to thicken soups.

Chop leftover cooked carrots and add to hamburger meat or use to extend meat loaves or meatballs.

Asparagus Vinaigrette Salad

Asparagus is a sure sign of spring, and this is a taste of it!

2 pounds fresh asparagus, rinsed and trimmed
3 or 4 large handfuls fresh baby spinach
handful fresh Italian parsley
salt and freshly ground black pepper, to taste
1 cup Mustard Vinaigrette (page 81), divided
1 hard-boiled egg, finely chopped
1 cup herb-flavored croutons (whole, if small,
   otherwise partially crushed)
shavings of fresh Parmesan cheese (optional)

■ Put two dinner plates into the freezer.

■ Lay the asparagus in a steamer basket. Put ½ inch of water into a large pot and bring to a boil. Carefully put the steamer basket into the boiling water, cover, and steam for 3 minutes, or until the spears are bright green in color. (Pencil-thin spears cook quickly; thumb-thick ones require 1 to 2 minutes more. Avoid wilting the spears.)

■ Remove the plates from the freezer and immediately transfer the asparagus onto them, spreading the spears so that they do not overlap. Set aside to cool. (Do not plunge the asparagus into cold water; this often leaves it waterlogged.) Or cover and refrigerate for 1 to 2 hours before serving.

■ Mix the spinach and parsley and arrange in a bed on a large platter. Season with salt and pepper. Lay the asparagus spears over the greens. Drizzle with ¼ cup of the vinaigrette and top with the egg, croutons, and Parmesan cheese, if using. Pass the remaining vinaigrette at the table.

Makes 6 servings.

Asparagus Tips

Look for firm spears—between pinky- and forefinger-diameter—with tight, unblemished tips and fresh (not dry or woody) white to light green bottoms. Use as soon as possible after purchasing. Asparagus grows in sandy soil, so always rinse it well. Snap off and discard the pale, woody, lower third or quarter of each spear.

The word "cabbage" comes from the Old French word *caboche,* meaning head and referring to the vegetable's round form.

The botanical name for cabbage is *Brassica oleracea,* Capitata group.

Sweet Chopped Coleslaw

This is creamy sweet, with just the right amount of tang.

1 small head green cabbage, quartered and cored
½ cup shredded carrot
⅓ cup mayonnaise
¼ cup sugar
2 tablespoons sour cream
1½ tablespoons white vinegar
1 tablespoon finely minced onion
2 teaspoons freshly squeezed lemon juice
scant ½ teaspoon salt
freshly ground black pepper, to taste

■ Cut one quarter of the cabbage into several large chunks. Fit the food processor with the regular cutting blade and put the chunks into it. Using 1-second pulses, chop the cabbage well. (Do not overchop the cabbage, or it will turn into a watery mess.) Transfer to a large mixing bowl. Continue with each quarter to make 6 cups. Save the remainder for another use. Add the carrot and toss lightly.

■ In a separate bowl, combine the remaining ingredients and whisk to blend. Pour the mixture onto the cabbage and mix well. Cover with plastic wrap and refrigerate for at least a few hours or overnight, stirring occasionally.

Makes 8 servings.

Cucumber, Onion, and Cherry Tomato Salad

A great way to use garden-fresh cukes.

½ large red onion, sliced
2 large or 3 medium cucumbers, peeled, halved lengthwise,
 seeded, and thickly sliced
1½ to 2 cups halved cherry or grape tomatoes
⅓ cup Herb Vinaigrette (page 81)
salt and freshly ground black pepper, to taste
½ cup crumbled feta cheese, for garnish

■ Put the onion into a large bowl. Add boiling water to cover. Let stand for 20 minutes, then drain. Transfer to a paper towel-lined plate and blot dry.

■ Return the onion to the bowl. Add the cucumbers, tomatoes, vinaigrette, and salt and pepper, to taste, and mix well. Cover and refrigerate for at least an hour, stirring occasionally. Transfer to a serving plate and crumble the cheese on top.

Makes 6 servings.

Take the Bite Out of Onions

To tame the flavor of sliced or chopped (not whole) raw onion without eliminating its pleasant crunch, place in a bowl and cover with boiling water. Let it sit for 15 to 20 minutes. Then drain and blot up the excess liquid with paper towels.

Tomato, Watermelon, and Feta Salad

Nothing says "Summer!" quite like this dish.

1 pint grape or cherry tomatoes
salt and freshly ground black pepper, to taste
juice of ½ lime
2 tablespoons olive oil
2 tablespoons chopped fresh mint
2 tablespoons chopped fresh Italian parsley
2 tablespoons minced red onion
4 cups cold, bite-size watermelon chunks (preferably seedless)
sherry vinegar, white-wine vinegar, or balsamic vinegar,
    to taste (optional)
1 cup feta cheese, in bite-size chunks (not crumbled)

■ Cut the tomatoes into halves or quarters and place in a bowl. Sprinkle with salt and pepper, to taste. Add the lime juice, olive oil, mint, parsley, and onion and toss to coat. Set aside for 10 to 15 minutes.

■ Immediately before serving, add the watermelon and toss gently. Sprinkle with vinegar, to taste, if desired. Transfer to a serving dish and sprinkle with feta cheese.

Makes 6 servings.

KEEP OUT

Store fresh tomatoes at a cool room temperature in a dry spot away from direct sunlight. A tomato's flavor and texture deteriorates when it is kept in the refrigerator.

Quinoa Tabbouleh

A new twist on a dish traditionally made with cracked wheat.

1 cup quinoa
salt, to taste
½ pint cherry or grape tomatoes, halved lengthwise
1 medium cucumber, peeled, halved lengthwise, seeded, and sliced
1 can (15 to 16 ounces) garbanzo beans, drained and rinsed
1 cup crumbled feta cheese
4 scallions, white and pale green parts only, chopped
3 to 4 tablespoons chopped fresh Italian parsley
2 tablespoons chopped fresh mint (optional)
2 to 3 tablespoons lemon juice
2 to 3 tablespoons olive oil
freshly ground black pepper, to taste

■ Rinse the quinoa in a fine mesh sieve and transfer to a saucepan. Add 2 cups of water and salt, to taste. Bring to a boil, reduce the heat, and simmer, covered, for 15 to 20 minutes, or until all of the water is absorbed. Remove from the heat, covered, and set aside for 10 minutes.

■ Gently "fluff" the quinoa with a fork and transfer to a large bowl. Cool thoroughly.

■ Add the tomatoes, cucumber, garbanzo beans, feta cheese, scallions, parsley, and mint, if using, to the quinoa and mix lightly.

■ In a small jar with a lid, combine 2 tablespoons each of the lemon juice and olive oil. Cover, shake, and pour on the quinoa mixture. Toss to coat and add salt and pepper, to taste. Add more lemon juice and olive oil, if desired. Cover and refrigerate for at least 1 hour before serving, stirring occasionally.

Makes 6 servings.

Variation:
■ Instead of mint, add 2 to 3 tablespoons of pesto. Reduce or eliminate the olive oil, as desired.

Quinoa
This staple crop of rural Peruvians is pronounced KEEN-wah and means "mother grain" in the language of the Incas. Although it's in the same botanical family as beets and spinach, quinoa is the highly nutritious seed of the goosefoot plant. Its preparation is similar to that for rice or other grains.

Olives' Origin

An olive is a fruit from the tree Olea europaea. *It is harvested either when it is immature and green or after it ripens and turns black. Freshly picked olives are bitter and inedible. To be edible, they must be cured in brine, water, or oil.*

Panzanella With Tuna and Olives

Panzanella is a bread salad. For best results, toss the ingredients shortly before serving so that the bread retains some crunch.

1 large loaf crusty sourdough bread
2 tablespoons olive oil
salt, to taste
3 medium to large ripe tomatoes, cored, halved, and seeded
1 large cucumber, halved and seeded
1 medium yellow or red bell pepper, finely chopped
½ red onion, thinly sliced
2 tablespoons drained capers
freshly ground black pepper, to taste
small handful torn fresh basil leaves
⅓ cup Mustard Vinaigrette (page 81), made with champagne
    or red-wine vinegar, to taste
1 to 2 cans (5 ounces) olive oil–packed tuna, undrained, flaked
1 cup pitted green or black olives, halved
crumbled feta cheese, for garnish

■ Preheat the oven to 375°F.

■ Cut several ¾-inch-thick slices of bread. Cut the slices into ¾-inch cubes to make 6 cups and put them into a large bowl. Drizzle the olive oil on the bread cubes, salt to taste, and toss well. Spread the bread cubes on a large baking sheet and bake for 15 to 20 minutes, or until light golden brown. Set aside on a cooling rack.

■ Cut the tomatoes into coarse chunks and place in a large bowl. Cut the cucumber into ¼-inch-thick slices and add to the tomatoes. Add the bell pepper, onion, capers, and salt and pepper, to taste. Toss to mix.

■ Moments before serving, add the bread cubes and basil to the bowl. Toss well to combine. Add about ⅓ cup of vinaigrette. Toss again, adding more vinaigrette, if desired. Set aside for 5 minutes. Serve, passing chunks of tuna, olives, and feta cheese.

Makes 5 to 6 servings.

**To Peel or
Not to Peel?**

*Red-skinned or waxy
potatoes are a good
choice for potato salads
because they hold their
shape with cooking.
Recipes often advise
peeling them, but the
skins are paper-thin
and tasteless. So you
can leave the skin on,
if you prefer.*

Country-Style Potato Salad

The one you grew up on—or wish you had.

2 to 2½ pounds red-skinned potatoes
1 tablespoon, plus ¾ teaspoon salt
¼ cup dill pickle juice
2½ tablespoons apple cider vinegar
1 teaspoon sugar
4 hard-boiled eggs, peeled and chopped
¾ cup finely chopped celery
½ cup chopped dill pickles
2 tablespoons minced red onion
2 tablespoons chopped fresh Italian parsley
⅔ cup mayonnaise
2 teaspoons yellow mustard
freshly ground black pepper, to taste

■ Put the potatoes into a large pot and add water to cover by at least 1 inch. Add 1 tablespoon of salt. Bring the water to a boil, then reduce the heat slightly and cook for 20 to 25 minutes, or until the potatoes can be easily pierced with a fork. Transfer to a plate. Set aside to cool thoroughly.

■ Peel the potatoes, cut them into bite-size pieces, and put them into a large, shallow bowl.

■ In a small bowl, combine the pickle juice, apple cider vinegar, and sugar and whisk to blend. Drizzle the liquid over the potatoes and toss them gently, by hand, to coat. Sprinkle ¾ teaspoon of salt over the potatoes and toss again to mix. Set aside for 30 minutes. Add the hard-boiled eggs, celery, pickles, onion, and parsley and mix gently.

■ In a small bowl, combine the mayonnaise and mustard and stir to blend. Add the mixture to the potatoes, sprinkle with pepper, and mix gently. Cover with plastic wrap and refrigerate until serving.

Makes 10 or more servings.

Pesto and Tomato Potato Salad

Pesto's not just for pasta!

2 to 2½ pounds red-skinned potatoes

1 tablespoon salt, plus more to taste

⅓ cup plus 2 tablespoons Mustard Vinaigrette (page 81),
    made with champagne or red-wine vinegar, divided

freshly ground black pepper, to taste

3 tablespoons prepared pesto

1 cup halved or quartered cherry tomatoes

½ cup thinly sliced red onion

¼ cup finely chopped red or green bell pepper

2 tablespoons capers

2 tablespoons chopped fresh Italian parsley

■ Put the potatoes into a large pot and add water to cover by at least 1 inch. Add 1 tablespoon of salt. Bring the water to a boil, then reduce the heat slightly and cook for 20 to 25 minutes, or until the potatoes can be easily pierced with a fork. Transfer to a plate. Set aside to cool thoroughly.

■ Pour ⅓ cup of the Mustard Vinaigrette into a large, shallow casserole or bowl, tilting the dish to spread the vinaigrette and cover the bottom.

■ Peel the potatoes, cut them into bite-size pieces, and put them into the casserole. Salt and pepper lightly, then gently stir to coat with the vinaigrette. Set aside for 30 minutes.

■ In a small bowl, combine the pesto with the 2 tablespoons of remaining vinaigrette and whisk to blend. Pour the pesto mixture over the potatoes. Add the tomatoes, onion, bell pepper, capers, and parsley. Stir lightly, and serve.

Makes 8 servings.

A world without tomatoes is like a string quartet without violins.

–*Laurie Colwin,
American writer (1944–92)*

Tex-Mex Cobb Salad

Nearly all of the measurements are purposely imprecise; use more or less, as desired, arranged in rows.

½ head iceberg lettuce, coarsely chopped
3 to 4 cups bite-size pieces cooked chicken
4 or 5 hard-boiled eggs, sliced or quartered lengthwise
3 medium tomatoes, cut into 6 or 8 wedges each
1 or 2 ripe avocados, peeled, pitted, and diced
2 cups corn kernels, cooked, drained, and blotted dry
1 can (16 ounces) black beans, drained and rinsed
1 to 2 cups finely diced pepper jack or Monterey Jack cheese
½ cup halved black olives
several slices crisp-cooked bacon, crumbled (optional)
2 cups Barbecue Ranch Dressing (page 80)

■ On a large platter, arrange the lettuce in a single row down the center. Arrange the chicken, eggs, tomatoes, avocados, corn, and black beans in rows on each side. (If using a round platter, pile lettuce in the center and arrange the other ingredients in concentric circles around it.) Top with the cheese, olives, and bacon, if using. Serve the dressing on the side.

Makes 4 to 5 servings.

FUN FOOD FACT

Hass avocados are named for Rudolph Hass, a postman who planted avocado seeds at his small grove in the mid-1920s and later patented the variety. That first tree survived until 2002, when root rot killed it.

Three-Bean Pasta Salad

Whether you add in the optional ingredients or serve them on the side, this can be a complete meal in one bowl.

½ teaspoon salt
1½ to 2 cups fresh green beans, cut into 1-inch pieces
1 can (16 ounces) red kidney beans, drained and rinsed
1 can (16 ounces) chickpeas, drained and rinsed
¼ cup finely chopped red onion
1 cup Tomato Vinaigrette (page 81), divided
½ pound rotini
2 stalks celery, thinly sliced
1 cup halved or quartered cherry tomatoes
½ cup chopped green olives with pimientos
¼ cup chopped fresh Italian parsley
2 tablespoons chopped fresh basil or 2 teaspoons dried basil
freshly ground black pepper, to taste
2 tablespoons capers (optional)
diced ham (optional)
1 or 2 cans (5 ounces) olive oil–packed tuna, undrained, flaked (optional)
vinegar, to taste
olive oil, to taste
crumbled feta cheese, for garnish

> The secret of staying young is to live honestly, eat slowly, and lie about your age.
>
> –Lucille Ball, American actress (1911–89)

■ Fill a saucepan half full of water. Add salt and bring to a boil. Add the green beans and boil for 5 to 6 minutes, or until tender. Drain and transfer to a large bowl.

■ Add the kidney beans, chickpeas, onion, and about ⅓ cup of the vinaigrette to the beans. Stir to coat. Cover and refrigerate for at least 1 hour or overnight.

■ Prepare the rotini according to the package directions. Drain, cool briefly, then add to the beans. Mix, add ⅓ cup more of vinaigrette and mix again.

■ Stir in the celery, tomatoes, olives, parsley, basil, and pepper, to taste. If using, add the capers, ham, or tuna. Toss, adding more dressing, if desired. Cover and refrigerate until serving.

■ If possible, bring to room temperature before serving. If the salad seems dry, add 1 tablespoon of hot water and stir. Then, if desired, add a few splashes of vinegar and/or olive oil and mix. Top with feta cheese before serving.

Makes 6 to 8 servings.

Great American Chicken Salad

A classic combination that always hits the spot.

4 cups bite-size cooked chicken pieces
2 stalks celery, chopped
¼ cup finely chopped dill pickles
2 tablespoons minced pickled jalapeño slices
2 tablespoons minced red onion
2 tablespoons chopped fresh Italian parsley
⅔ cup mayonnaise
⅓ cup sour cream
1 tablespoon apple cider vinegar
2 teaspoons Dijon-style mustard
1 teaspoon sugar
splash or two hot-pepper sauce
1 or 2 hard-boiled eggs, chopped (optional)
¼ teaspoon salt
freshly ground black pepper, to taste
pickle juice (optional)

■ In a large bowl, combine the chicken, celery, pickles, jalapeño, onion, and parsley.

■ In a separate bowl, combine the mayonnaise, sour cream, vinegar, mustard, sugar, hot-pepper sauce, eggs (if using), salt, and pepper, to taste. Stir to blend.

■ Add the dressing to the chicken and mix well. Taste, adding more seasonings and vinegar or pickle juice, if desired. Serve immediately or refrigerate for 1 to 3 hours.

Makes 4 to 6 servings.

Chicken Salad as Stuffing

This chicken salad is delicious stuffed in cherry tomatoes or other small tomatoes. First, chop the chicken salad in the food processor using a series of short pulses. The smaller the tomatoes, the finer the stuffing should be. Remove the seeds from the tomatoes with a serrated paring knife, then spoon the salad into each hollow.

EDA-WHO?

Edamame
(ed-a-MAH-may;
"beans on branches"
in Japanese) are soy
beans picked before
they harden. Half a cup
of shelled edamame
has as much fiber as
4 slices of whole-wheat
bread, 11 grams of
protein, all the iron
in 4 ounces of roasted
chicken, and plenty
of vitamins A and C.

Crunchy Asian Salad With Chicken

Asian Ginger-Garlic Dressing (page 80), at room temperature, divided
2 to 3 cups bite-size cooked chicken pieces
2 cups frozen shelled edamame
2 cups thinly sliced green cabbage
2 cups grated carrot
5 scallions (white part only), thinly sliced
½ cup thinly sliced almonds
¼ cup chopped fresh Italian parsley or 2 tablespoons
   chopped fresh cilantro
1 tablespoon sugar
2 tablespoons apple cider vinegar
¼ teaspoon salt
2 cups chow mein noodles

■ Pour about ⅓ cup of dressing into a bowl. Add the chicken, stir to coat, then set refrigerate.

■ Prepare the edamame according to the package directions. Drain, then transfer to a paper towel–lined plate to dry.

■ In a large bowl, combine the cabbage, carrot, scallions, almonds, parsley, and edamame. Add the sugar, vinegar, and salt and mix well. Cover and refrigerate for 30 minutes, stirring once or twice.

■ Just before serving, add the chicken and noodles and toss well to combine. Mix in only as many noodles as will be eaten at each service. Noodles that sit in the salad will get soggy. Pass the remaining dressing.

Makes 6 or more servings.

Barbecue Ranch Dressing

DRESSINGS AND CONDIMENTS

Asian Ginger-Garlic Dressing

½ cup smooth peanut butter
¼ cup vegetable oil
¼ cup water
3 tablespoons apple cider vinegar
2 tablespoons sugar
1½ tablespoons soy sauce
1½ tablespoons hoisin sauce
1 tablespoon coarsely chopped fresh ginger
½ teaspoon salt
2 cloves garlic, chopped
dash or two cayenne pepper

■ Put all of the ingredients into a blender and pulse to a purée that is smooth and full-bodied, not thin. Taste and adjust the seasonings, if desired. Transfer to a container. Cover and refrigerate. Bring to room temperature and shake before using.

Makes about 1¼ cups.

Barbecue Ranch Dressing

1¼ cups thick ranch dressing
1½ tablespoons mild barbecue sauce
¼ cup finely chopped dill pickle
3 tablespoons minced pickled jalapeño slices
2 tablespoons chopped fresh Italian parsley
sour cream, as needed

■ Combine all of the ingredients in a small bowl and stir to blend. To thin, add pickle juice or water, ½ teaspoon at a time. Stir. To thicken, add 1 to 2 tablespoons of sour cream. Stir. Cover and refrigerate.

Makes about 3 cups.

Mustard Vinaigrette

Creamy Dijon-style mustard emulsifies better than the grainy, whole seed type, so use creamy if you can.

¼ cup balsamic, champagne, or red-wine vinegar
2 to 3 teaspoons Dijon-style mustard
1 clove garlic, finely minced
2 to 3 teaspoons light-brown sugar
¾ cup olive oil
½ teaspoon salt, or to taste
freshly ground black pepper, to taste

■ Combine the vinegar, mustard, garlic, and brown sugar in a bowl and whisk well. Add the olive oil in a slow, steady stream, while whisking. Add the salt and pepper, to taste, continuing to whisk.

Note: Alternatively, combine all of the ingredients in a small jar with a tight lid and shake it vigorously. Taste and adjust the seasonings, if desired.
Makes about 1 cup.

Variations

Tomato Vinaigrette

■ Whisk 1 tablespoon of tomato paste into Mustard Vinaigrette after adding the olive oil. Taste and adjust the seasonings with a pinch of brown or regular sugar, if desired.

Herb Vinaigrette

■ Add up to 1 tablespoon of chopped fresh or ¾ teaspoon of dried basil, oregano, or thyme to Mustard Vinaigrette when you add the salt and pepper.

Herb Vinaigrette

Chunky Blue Cheese Dressing

Makes a great veggie dip, too!

¾ cup mayonnaise
¾ cup sour cream
1 tablespoon red-wine vinegar
1 teaspoon Worcestershire sauce
½ teaspoon prepared yellow mustard

1 clove garlic, minced
1 cup crumbled blue cheese
salt and freshly ground black pepper,
 to taste

■ In a bowl, combine the mayonnaise, sour cream, vinegar, Worcestershire sauce, mustard, and garlic and whisk until blended. Add the blue cheese, stir, and add salt and pepper, to taste. To thin, add 1 to 2 teaspoons of water and stir. Refrigerate until serving. Store any remaining dressing in a sealed jar.

Makes about 2½ cups.

JUST PEACHY

Peeling a peach
is similar to
peeling a tomato.
Completely submerge
it in boiling water
for 30 seconds,
then plunge it
immediately into
ice water for 10
seconds. Score the
skin with a paring
knife and peel it off.

Peach, Red Onion, and Tomato Salsa

Serve with chips or on grilled fish or burgers.

1½ cups peeled and finely diced fresh,
 ripe peaches
1½ cups cored, seeded, and finely
 diced tomatoes
½ cup finely chopped red onion
½ cup finely chopped bell pepper
1 to 2 tablespoons fresh lime juice

¼ cup chopped pickled jalapeños,
 plus 1 teaspoon juice
1 tablespoon chopped fresh basil
1 tablespoon chopped fresh
 Italian parsley
2 to 3 teaspoons sugar
salt, to taste

■ Combine all of the ingredients in a bowl. Refrigerate for several hours. Stir and taste occasionally, adjusting the seasoning as needed.

■ Transfer to one or more jars with a lid, cover, and refrigerate for up to a week.

Makes about 4 cups.

Quick Dill Pickle Slices

Pucker up! These crisp, chunky chips go with grilled foods, barbecue, sloppy Joes, and sandwiches.

1¼ cups distilled white vinegar
3 tablespoons sugar
2 tablespoons kosher salt
1 tablespoon coriander seeds
1 teaspoon yellow mustard seeds
1½ cups cold water
¼ cup chopped fresh dill
2 cloves garlic, thickly sliced
2 pounds Kirby cucumbers, rinsed and
 sliced ¼-inch thick

■ Combine the vinegar, sugar, and salt in a small, nonreactive saucepan. Bring to a boil and cook, stirring, until the sugar and salt dissolve. Remove from the heat and add the coriander and mustard seeds.

■ Pour the mixture into a bowl, add the water, and stir. Set aside to cool.

■ Divide the dill and garlic among three clean pint jars or the equivalent. Divide the cucumber slices evenly among the jars, packing them tightly. Ladle liquid into each jar to cover the cucumbers, cover with lids, and refrigerate overnight. These pickles will keep at least a week in the refrigerator.

Makes 3 pints.

Refrigerator Bread and Butter Pickles

2 pounds Kirby cucumbers, sliced about ⅛-inch thick
3 teaspoons salt, divided
½ red onion, thinly sliced
1½ cups sugar
1 cup distilled white vinegar
1 tablespoon mustard seed
1 tablespoon celery seed
3 cloves garlic, halved and bruised

■ Put 1 cup of sliced cucumbers into a large bowl and sprinkle with ⅛ teaspoon of salt. Repeat with the remaining cucumbers, 1 cup at a time. (Use 1 teaspoon of salt, total.) Add the onion and toss gently. Cover with plastic wrap and set aside for 1 hour. Drain and set aside.

■ Combine ½ cup of water plus the sugar, vinegar, mustard seed, celery seed, garlic, and remaining 2 teaspoons of salt in a saucepan. Gradually bring to a boil, stir, and cook for 2 minutes, or until the sugar is dissolved.

■ Pour the vinegar mixture over the cucumbers and set aside for 10 minutes, stirring occasionally.

■ Divide the cucumber slices among three clean pint jars or the equivalent, making sure that each jar has some garlic in it. Pour enough liquid into each to cover the cucumbers, cover with lids, then set aside to cool. Refrigerate for 24 hours before serving.

Makes 3 pints.

Roasted Autumn Vegetables
recipe on page 98

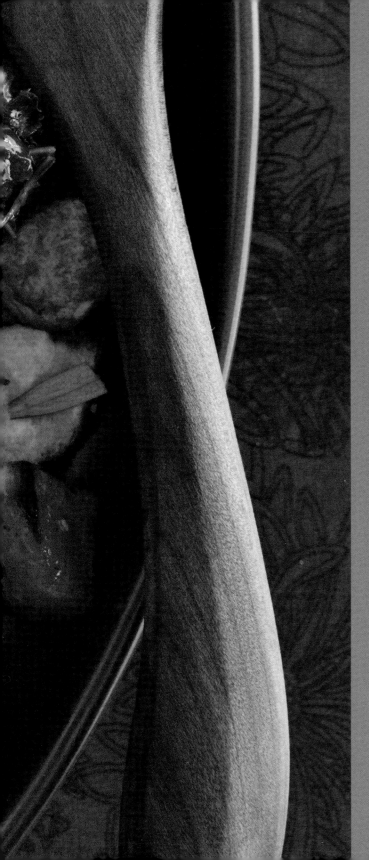

vegetables

Potato and Artichoke au Gratin

If Yukon Golds are not available, use russets.

2 tablespoons (½ stick) unsalted butter, plus extra for the pan
1 large onion, quartered and thinly sliced
2 cloves garlic, thinly sliced
1 can (14 ounces) artichoke hearts, drained
5 medium to large Yukon Gold potatoes, peeled and thinly sliced
1 scant teaspoon salt
freshly ground black pepper, to taste
1½ cups shredded Gouda cheese
⅓ cup finely grated Parmesan cheese
1½ cups heavy cream
1¼ cups half-and-half

■ Preheat the oven to 375°F. Butter a 13x9-inch shallow casserole or gratin dish.

■ Melt 2 tablespoons of butter in a skillet over medium heat. Add the onion and cook for 10 to 12 minutes, or until soft. Add the garlic, cook for 1 minute more, then remove from the heat.

■ Starting at the stem end, slice the artichoke hearts into three or four pieces each. Lay the slices out on paper towels and blot away excess moisture.

■ Arrange half of the potato slices in the casserole. Sprinkle with salt and pepper. Arrange half of the sliced artichoke hearts on top. Sprinkle with half of each cheese, then spoon on half of the onions. Repeat the layers.

■ Combine the heavy cream and half-and-half in a saucepan and cook over medium heat until the mixture shimmers. Slowly pour the liquid over the layers of vegetables and cheese. Cover with aluminum foil and bake for 30 minutes. Remove the foil and bake for 25 to 30 minutes more, or until golden and bubbly and the potatoes are tender.

Makes 8 servings.

Test for Freshness

When buying artichokes, look for plump, compact globes, heavy for their size, with tightly closed, green bracts (the "leaves" of the bud) that squeak if gently squeezed. Avoid those that have blemishes, mold, an "off" color, or wilted bracts.

Cheesy, Creamy Potatoes au Gratin

As the ingredients melt into one another, they will form a sort of baked potato pancake.

2 cups half-and-half or light cream
2 cups heavy or whipping cream
4 large baking potatoes, peeled and thinly sliced
1¼ teaspoons salt
2 cloves garlic, minced
freshly ground black pepper, to taste
1½ cups shredded Swiss cheese, divided
⅓ cup finely grated Parmesan cheese

■ Preheat the oven to 375°F. Generously butter a 13x9-inch shallow casserole or gratin dish.

■ Pour the half-and-half and heavy cream into a large, heavy-bottom pot. Add the sliced potatoes, salt, and garlic. Gently heat the mixture, stirring often, until it shimmers.

■ With a slotted spoon, transfer about half of the potatoes into the prepared casserole. Pour half of the hot cream over the potatoes. Sprinkle with pepper, to taste, and half of the Swiss cheese. Cover with the remaining potatoes and cream. Sprinkle with pepper and the remaining Swiss cheese. Top with Parmesan cheese. Bake for 45 to 55 minutes, or until the potatoes are tender and the cheese is golden brown. Cool for 10 minutes before serving.

Makes 8 servings.

> The discovery of a new dish does more for human happiness than the discovery of a new star.
>
> *–Jean Anthelme Brillat-Savarin, French writer (1755–1826)*

QUICK GARLIC

When you don't have time to roast garlic heads, mince a couple of cloves and cook them very gently in butter for 1 minute. Add the garlic and butter to the potatoes and mix to combine.

Roasted Garlic Mashed Potatoes

Roasting garlic deepens its flavor and reduces its pungency.

2 large heads garlic
1 tablespoon olive oil
4 large baking potatoes, peeled and cut into coarse chunks
2½ teaspoons salt, divided
½ to ⅔ cup warm half-and-half or milk
6 tablespoons unsalted butter, in pieces, softened
¼ cup sour cream, at room temperature
freshly ground black pepper, to taste
2 to 3 tablespoons finely grated Parmesan cheese (optional)

■ Preheat the oven to 400°F.

■ Rub off the papery outer skin of the garlic. Slice off the upper third of each head, exposing the cloves. Stand the heads on a square piece of aluminum foil and drizzle with olive oil. Wrap the foil around the garlic and bake for 50 to 60 minutes.

■ Remove the garlic from the foil and cool for 15 minutes. Squeeze out the soft garlic in the cloves into a small bowl and mash well with a fork.

■ Put the potatoes into a large pot and add enough water to cover by about 2 inches. Bring to a boil, add 2 teaspoons of salt, and cook, uncovered, for 15 to 20 minutes, or until tender but not falling apart. Drain and return the potatoes to the pan. Shake the pan several times, letting the heat of the pan dry up any moisture clinging to the potatoes. Add the half-and-half, butter, mashed garlic, and ½ teaspoon of salt. Using a hand masher or fork, mash the potatoes, leaving them a little lumpy.

■ Add the sour cream, pepper, to taste, and Parmesan cheese, if desired, and mash to blend.

Makes 6 or more servings.

Firehouse Potatoes

With leftover baked potatoes, this dish comes together in a jiffy.

3 tablespoons olive or vegetable oil
1 medium onion, halved and thinly sliced
1 medium green or red bell pepper, seeded and chopped
4 small to medium baked potatoes, skins on, quartered lengthwise and
   cut into chunks
2 cloves garlic, minced
1½ teaspoons chili powder
¾ cup prepared salsa
½ teaspoon salt
freshly ground black pepper, to taste
⅓ cup sour cream or ranch dressing
½ cup pickled jalapeño slices, chopped
½ cup chopped olives with pimientos
1 cup shredded pepper jack cheese

■ Preheat the oven to 375°F.

■ In a large, ovenproof skillet over medium heat, warm the oil.
Add the onion and green pepper and cook for 8 minutes, or until the
onion is soft. Add the potatoes, garlic, and chili powder and cook
for 1 minute more. Add the salsa and salt and cook for 2 to 3 minutes,
stirring often. Remove from the heat and add the pepper, to taste.
Drop dollops of sour cream onto the potatoes. Spread the jalapeños
and olives on top. Sprinkle with the cheese. Bake for 20 to 25 minutes,
or until bubbly and heated through.

Makes 4 to 6 servings.

Cheese Bits

*When a recipe calls for
shredded, crumbled,
or grated cheese, use
these guidelines for
purchasing cheese by
weight:*

*4 ounces regular
cheese = 1 cup shredded*

*4 ounces blue or feta
cheese = 1 cup crumbled*

*3 ounces hard-grating
cheese = 1 cup grated*

Pecan-Crusted Sweet Potato Casserole

Anyone who likes to have dessert first will love this dish.

Filling:

4 large sweet potatoes, scrubbed
4 tablespoons (½ stick) unsalted butter, in pieces, softened
½ cup sugar
⅓ cup light cream or milk
2 large eggs, at room temperature
1 teaspoon vanilla extract
½ teaspoon salt
¼ teaspoon allspice

Topping:

⅔ cup packed light-brown sugar
⅔ cup pecan halves
¼ cup all-purpose flour
¼ teaspoon cinnamon
¼ teaspoon salt
4 tablespoons (½ stick) unsalted butter, melted

**Life is uncertain.
Eat dessert first.**

*—Ernestine Ulmer,
American writer
(1892–1987)*

For filling:

■ Preheat the oven to 350°F. Butter a 2-quart casserole. Line a baking sheet with aluminum foil.

■ Pierce each sweet potato several times with a paring knife or fork and place on the baking sheet. Bake for 60 to 70 minutes, or until soft and tender when pierced with a paring knife. Transfer the baking sheet to a cooling rack. Cut a slit in the potatoes lengthwise and cool for 15 to 20 minutes.

■ Scoop the sweet potato flesh into a large bowl and mash it with a potato masher or fork. Add the butter, sugar, and cream and, using an electric mixer on medium-high speed, beat to blend. Add the eggs, one at a time, and beat to combine. Add the vanilla, salt, and allspice and beat until evenly mixed. Spread the mixture in the casserole.

For topping:

■ Combine the brown sugar, pecans, flour, cinnamon, and salt in a food processor. Pulse briefly until the pecans are chopped. Add the butter and pulse until the nuts are finely chopped.

■ Spread the topping evenly over the sweet potato mixture. Bake for 45 minutes, or until the ingredients are puffed slightly and the topping is rich light brown. Transfer to a cooling rack for 15 to 20 minutes before serving.

Makes 8 or more servings.

Variation for topping:

■ Combine all of the ingredients, except the pecans, in a food processor and pulse briefly. Spread the topping and pecans over the sweet potato mixture. Bake for 45 minutes.

Bee Wise

*Before you measure
honey for cooking,
oil the measuring
cup so that the
honey will pour out
easily. Or, if the
recipe calls for oil,
measure it first.*

Sweet Potato Oven Fries
With Honey Mustard Dipping Sauce

These are finger-lickin' good!

Fries:

3 large sweet potatoes, peeled
3 tablespoons olive oil
2 cloves garlic, minced
½ teaspoon paprika
½ teaspoon salt
freshly ground black pepper,
   to taste

Sauce:

½ cup mayonnaise
2 tablespoons sour cream
1 tablespoon honey
2 teaspoons Dijon-style mustard
2 teaspoons prepared yellow
   mustard
cayenne pepper, to taste

For fries:

■ Preheat the oven to 400°F. Coat a large baking sheet with nonstick cooking spray.

■ Cut the sweet potatoes in half, lengthwise, then slice each half into long sticks roughly ⅓ of an inch think. Transfer to a large bowl; sprinkle with the oil, garlic, paprika, salt, and pepper, to taste; and toss with your hands, taking care to make the seasonings "stick" as well as possible.

■ Spread the sweet potatoes in a single layer on the baking sheet, keeping them from touching. Bake for 15 minutes. Remove the sheet from the oven and turn the sweet potatoes with a spatula. Reduce the heat to 375°F and bake for 15 minutes more.

For sauce:

■ Combine all of the ingredients in a small bowl and whisk to blend. Refrigerate until serving.

Makes 4 to 5 servings.

Variation:

■ For thicker "steak" fries, quarter the potatoes lengthwise, then cut each quarter into two or three long wedges. Proceed as above, but bake at 400°F for 30 to 35 minutes, turning them after 15 minutes.

Bacon Baked Beans

Long, slow baking and the right seasonings make the best beans.

1 pound dried navy beans, picked over to remove any debris
3 tablespoons vegetable oil
1 cup chopped onion
1 cup chopped green bell pepper
2 cloves garlic, minced
½ cup packed light-brown sugar
½ cup tomato-based chili sauce
¼ cup barbecue sauce
2 tablespoons apple cider vinegar
2 tablespoons Dijon-style mustard
1½ teaspoons salt
½ teaspoon ground black pepper
6 to 8 slices bacon

BROWN SUGAR STORAGE

Place a few marshmallows in your bag or box of brown sugar to prevent it from turning rock-hard.

■ Rinse the beans and place in a large bowl with water to cover. Set aside to soak for 2 hours or overnight.

■ Drain the beans and transfer them to a large pot. Add 1 gallon of water, bring to a boil, reduce the heat, and simmer, partially covered, for 1½ to 2 hours, or until tender. Drain, reserving the cooking water.

■ Heat the oil in a large skillet over medium heat. Add the onion and bell pepper and cook for 5 minutes, or until soft. Add the garlic and cook for 1 minute more.

■ Preheat the oven to 325°F. Oil a large, shallow casserole.

■ Combine the brown sugar, chili sauce, barbecue sauce, vinegar, mustard, salt, and pepper in a large bowl. Add 1½ cups of the bean cooking water and whisk to blend.

■ Put the drained beans and sautéed vegetables into the casserole, pour the sauce over, then stir to coat. (If you make the sauce in a suitably large bowl, you can add the beans to it, stir to coat, and then transfer to the casserole.) Lay the bacon over the beans. Bake, uncovered, stirring occasionally without disturbing the bacon, for 2 hours, or until the beans are covered in thick sauce.

Makes 8 or more servings.

Asian-Style Green Beans

*Plain green beans are transformed into a spicy Asian side dish—
a natural accompaniment to pork or roast chicken.*

2 tablespoons vegetable oil or 5 teaspoons vegetable oil and 1 teaspoon
    sesame oil
1 tablespoon chopped fresh ginger
3 cloves garlic, minced
¼ teaspoon red pepper flakes
1 pound green beans, trimmed and cut into 1-inch pieces
salt, to taste
3 tablespoons hoisin sauce
½ to 1 teaspoon soy sauce

■ Heat a large, heavy skillet with a tight-fitting lid. When the pan
is hot, add the oil and heat it for 30 seconds. Add the ginger, garlic,
pepper flakes, and green beans and cook over high heat for 1 minute,
stirring constantly. Add ½ cup of water and a generous pinch or two
of salt. Cover the pan and steam for 6 minutes, or until almost fully
tender. Check on the water once or twice; if more is needed, add
¼ cup. Add the hoisin and soy sauces and stir. Cook, uncovered, until
the water evaporates and the sauce coats the beans thickly. Serve hot.

Makes 4 to 6 servings.

What's a "Hill of Beans"?

*Beans are commonly
used in everyday
expressions to indicate
something of little
value. Consequently,
someone who isn't
worth a hill of beans is
seen as being worth
very little.*

Creamed Brussels Sprouts

The stock reduction reduces the need to add salt. Taste for yourself!

3 tablespoons unsalted butter

1 pound brussels sprouts, halved lengthwise

1 medium onion, thinly sliced

2 cloves garlic, minced

1 cup chicken stock

¼ cup heavy cream

1 tablespoon Dijon-style mustard

salt and freshly ground black pepper, to taste

■ Melt the butter in a large skillet over medium heat. Add the brussels sprouts, onion, and garlic and cook for 2 minutes, stirring frequently. Add the chicken stock, stir, and bring to a simmer. Cover and cook for 3 minutes, or until not quite tender. Uncover and cook until the liquid is reduced by half. Add the cream and mustard and cook, stirring often, until the liquid is reduced to a thick sauce that coats the sprouts. Season with salt and pepper, to taste.

Makes 4 to 6 servings.

STORING SPROUTS

Do not wash brussels sprouts before storing them; do it only right before use.

WHAT'S THAT SMELL?

A small bowl with
baking soda or white
vinegar placed next
to the stove while
cooking cabbage will
absorb the smell.

Bacon-Braised Cabbage

The vinegar enhances the flavor. Serve with roast meats.

1 tablespoon vegetable or olive oil
2 strips bacon, cut into 1-inch pieces
1 medium onion, halved and thinly sliced
1 small to medium head green cabbage, quartered, cored,
    and thinly sliced
salt and freshly ground black pepper, to taste
¾ cup chicken stock
cider vinegar or champagne vinegar (optional)

■ Heat the oil in a large, heavy-bottom pot over medium heat. Add
the bacon and cook for 2 to 3 minutes. Add the onion and cook
for 5 minutes. Add the cabbage, about a third at a time, cooking each
batch for 1 to 2 minutes before adding the next. Sprinkle with salt
and pepper, to taste.

■ When the cabbage starts to wilt, add the chicken stock and bring to
a boil. Cover tightly, reduce the heat, and cook (or braise) the cabbage
for about 30 minutes, or until tender, stirring occasionally. Serve hot,
passing the vinegar at the table, if desired.

Makes 6 to 8 servings.

**May the leaves
of your cabbage be
free of worms.**
—Irish blessing

Herb-Roasted Cauliflower

It's quick, easy, and tasty!

1 head cauliflower
½ medium onion, halved and sliced
1 or 2 cloves garlic, minced
3 tablespoons olive oil
½ teaspoon chopped fresh rosemary or thyme
½ teaspoon salt
paprika, to taste

■ Preheat the oven to 425°F. Lightly oil a large, rimmed baking sheet (not nonstick).

■ Cut the cauliflower into florets, rinse well, and drain. Put the florets into a large bowl, add the remaining ingredients, and toss thoroughly.

■ Spread the mixture evenly on the baking sheet. Bake for 22 to 25 minutes, or until tender. Serve immediately.

Makes 5 to 6 servings.

Mild vs. Smoked Paprika

Mild, or regular, paprika is not as strong as the smoked variety and will add a lovely tinge of color to the cauliflower without masking its subtle flavor in the way that the smoked variety would.

Roasted Autumn Vegetables

This dish features kale as its secret ingredient.

1 pound small red-skinned potatoes, quartered,
    or whole creamer potatoes
2 cups peeled butternut squash, cut into ½-inch dice
2 large carrots, peeled and cut into ½-inch-thick diagonal slices
2 parsnips, peeled and cut into ½-inch-thick diagonal slices
2 to 3 cups packed kale, rinsed and chopped
3 tablespoons olive oil
1 tablespoon chopped fresh rosemary or 1 teaspoon dried rosemary
2 cloves garlic, minced
salt and freshly ground black pepper, to taste

■ Preheat the oven to 450°F. Lightly oil two large, rimmed baking sheets.

■ Combine the vegetables, olive oil, rosemary, garlic, salt, and pepper, to taste, in a large bowl and toss by hand to coat. Spread the mixture evenly onto the baking sheets and bake for 15 minutes on separate oven racks. After 15 minutes, stir the vegetables with a spatula and return to the oven, switching the rack position of the sheets. Bake for 15 minutes more, or until the vegetables are tender and browned.

Makes 6 servings.

SEASONING WITH BAY LEAVES

Bay leaves impart a delicate, eucalyptus-like flavor and help to meld the flavors of other seasonings. Use the dried leaves whole in condiments, soups, and stews. Remove the leaves just before serving; with their sharp edges, they can lodge in the digestive system. (Bay leaves do not dissolve in the stomach.)

Marinated Vegetables

For best taste, prepare this dish at least 12 hours before serving. Try substituting small, halved white mushrooms or green beans in season.

⅔ cup dry white wine
½ cup olive oil
1 tablespoon lemon juice
1 teaspoon salt
1 clove garlic, crushed
2 bay leaves
½ teaspoon fennel seed, crushed
½ teaspoon dried thyme or 3 sprigs fresh thyme
3 large carrots, peeled and cut into 1½-inch matchsticks
½ to ¾ head cauliflower, cut into bite-size florets
1 large green pepper, cut into thin strips
1 red onion, halved and thinly sliced
freshly ground black pepper, to taste

■ Combine the wine, olive oil, lemon juice, salt, crushed garlic, and 1 cup of water in a large, nonreactive pot. Add the bay leaves, fennel seed, and thyme. Add the carrots, cauliflower, green pepper, and red onion and bring to a gentle boil. Cover and simmer for 6 to 7 minutes, or until the vegetables are cooked but still have some crunch. Using a slotted spoon, transfer the vegetables to a large bowl and set the liquid aside to cool.

■ Pour the cool liquid over the vegetables. Sprinkle generously with pepper, cover, and refrigerate.

■ Transfer the vegetables to a serving dish with a slotted spoon. Remove the bay leaves before serving.

Makes 6 servings.

Slow-Cooked, Smoky Southern Collards

Collards take patience and a sure hand with the seasonings, but the results keep you coming back for more.

3 tablespoons vegetable or light olive oil
4 strips bacon, cut into 1-inch pieces
1 large onion, halved and thinly sliced
1 clove garlic, crushed
2 to 2½ pounds fresh collard greens, rinsed and chopped
1 ham hock
1 teaspoon salt, plus more to taste
2 beef bouillon cubes
3 tablespoons light-brown sugar
1 tablespoon barbecue sauce
1 teaspoon Worcestershire sauce
several dashes hot-pepper sauce
½ teaspoon red-wine or balsamic vinegar, plus more to taste

■ Heat the oil in a large, heavy-bottom soup pot over medium heat. Add the bacon and cook for 3 to 4 minutes, stirring often, until the bacon has rendered a good deal of fat. Add the onion and garlic and cook for 7 minutes.

■ Add the collards and just enough water to cover. Add the ham hock and salt, bring to a boil, then reduce the heat to a simmer.

■ With a ladle, remove 1 cup of the simmering water to a small bowl, add the bouillon cubes, and stir until dissolved. Add the bouillon to the pot, with the brown sugar, barbecue sauce, Worcestershire sauce, and hot-pepper sauce, and stir. Simmer the mixture, uncovered, for 2 to 3 hours, stirring occasionally, until the leaves are tender but not mushy and the mixture resembles a stew. Add water, ½ cup at a time, if necessary to keep the greens stewing but not drowning. Taste and adjust the seasonings, if desired.

■ During the last 30 minutes of cooking, add ½ teaspoon of vinegar at a time and taste. You want to perk up the flavor with the vinegar, not disguise it. Serve the collards separate from the broth, in cups or bowls. Pass vinegar for sprinkling.

Makes 6 servings.

How to Prepare Collards

You can cook collards with the stems; however, even after extended cooking, the stems still can be chewy. It's better to remove the stems before cooking. Tear the leaves from the stems or use a paring knife to cut them out. Then rinse the leaves and chop them coarsely into large pieces.

All Ears

The best way to enjoy the flavor of sweet corn is to cook it as soon as it is picked. If that is not possible, place the ears, unshucked, in a paper bag and store in the refrigerator. If they are left on the kitchen counter, the sugars in them will turn more quickly to starch.

Grilled Corn on the Cob

Grilling corn in the husks (instead of foil) maximizes flavor.

6 ears corn on the cob
3 tablespoons unsalted butter, softened
salt and freshly ground black pepper, to taste

■ Peel off and discard most of the husks on all of the ears of corn; leave the last couple of layers in place. Peel those last layers back, but do not remove them. Pull off as much silk as possible. Return the last layers of husks to cover the corn.

■ Submerge the corn in a tub of fresh, cold water for 15 minutes.

■ Preheat the grill.

■ Peel the husks back and smear ½ tablespoon of soft butter over the kernels of each ear. Salt and pepper, to taste. Return the husks to cover the corn.

■ Place the ears over medium, direct heat for about 5 minutes, turning often to prevent charring any exposed corn. Move the ears to the side of the grill and cover the grill. Cook over indirect heat for 10 to 12 minutes more. Remove to a platter, then let cool for 5 minutes in the husks.

Makes 6 servings.

Variations

Grilled Corn on the Cob
With Chili Lime Butter

■ Mix 1 teaspoon of chili powder and ¼ teaspoon of finely grated lime zest into the soft butter. Proceed as directed.

Grilled Corn on the Cob
With Pesto and Parmesan Cheese

■ Omit the butter. Brush each ear with ½ tablespoon of pesto. Proceed as directed. When the husks are removed after grilling, dust the ears with freshly grated Parmesan cheese.

Grilled Corn on the Cob With Bacon

■ Remove the husks completely. Soak the corn as directed, including 18 10-inch lengths of cotton kitchen string in the soaking water. Pepper the ears (omit the butter and salt), to taste, and wrap two pieces of bacon around each ear. Secure the bacon with the string. Grill as directed.

ADD SOME ZEST!

To gather zest from the rind of citrus fruit, use a zester, grater, or even a vegetable peeler. Longer strips make great garnishes, while tiny flakes evenly distribute citrus flavor in cooking.

SCALLION STORAGE

Store green onions,
including scallions, in a
plastic bag in the
refrigerator for 3 to 5 days.

Spiced Corn Fritters

Chunky and pancake-like, these are best hot off the skillet with a dab of sour cream.

2 cups fresh or frozen corn
⅔ cup all-purpose flour
1½ teaspoons sugar
1 teaspoon baking powder
½ teaspoon salt
½ teaspoon cumin
½ teaspoon chili powder
1 large egg
½ cup milk
2 tablespoons (¼ stick) unsalted butter, melted
2 tablespoons minced scallions (white part only) or onions
1 tablespoon vegetable oil, for the pan

■ If using fresh-cut corn kernels, put them into a saucepan with lightly salted water to cover. Bring to a boil and cook for 5 minutes. Drain and cool. If using frozen corn kernels, thaw and drain.

■ In a large bowl, combine the flour, sugar, baking powder, salt, cumin, and chili powder. Mix and make a well in the center.

■ In a separate bowl, beat the egg lightly, add the milk, butter, and scallions, and whisk to blend.

■ Pour the liquid into the well of the dry ingredients and stir to blend. Set aside for 5 minutes. Add the corn and mix to combine.

■ Heat the oil in a large, nonstick skillet over medium heat. Add generous spoonfuls of batter and cook for 2 minutes per side, or until there is no sign of raw batter when you cut into it.

Makes 4 to 6 servings.

Variation:
■ Substitute ½ cup of canned black beans, drained and rinsed, for an equal amount of the corn.

Cheddar and Corn Pudding With Green Chiles

Enjoy with lightly dressed tomatoes in summer and as a side at holiday dinners.

2 cups milk

¼ cup fine yellow cornmeal

4 tablespoons (½ stick) unsalted butter, divided

1 tablespoon sugar

1¼ teaspoons salt

¼ teaspoon freshly ground black pepper

1 cup finely chopped onion

4 cups fresh or frozen and thawed corn

1 can (4 or 5 ounces) green chiles, drained

¾ cup fine-curd cottage cheese

5 large eggs, lightly beaten

2 cups shredded sharp white cheddar cheese, divided

■ Preheat the oven to 325°F. Butter a 13x9-inch baking dish or other large, shallow casserole.

■ Combine the milk and cornmeal in a small saucepan over medium heat. Gradually bring to a simmer, whisking constantly, until the mixture thickens to a creamlike consistency. Pour the mixture into a large bowl. Add 2 tablespoons of butter in pieces, sugar, salt, and pepper and whisk to combine.

■ Melt the remaining 2 tablespoons of butter in a skillet over medium heat. Add the onion and corn and cook for 5 minutes, or until soft. Remove from the heat. Transfer the corn mixture to a food processor and pulse to make a rough-textured purée.

■ Combine the corn and onion with the milk-cornmeal mixture. Add the chiles, cottage cheese, eggs, and 1 cup of the cheddar cheese and stir until combined. Pour the mixture into the buttered baking dish. Sprinkle with the remaining 1 cup of cheese. Bake for 35 to 40 minutes, or until the mixture is set (not liquid) and lightly browned. (If the top isn't browning, move the dish to a higher rack during the last 10 minutes.) Transfer to a cooling rack for at least 10 minutes before serving.

Makes 10 or more servings.

A-Maize-ing!

Cornmeal is a flour made from ground maize (corn). It comes in yellow, white, blue, and red varieties.

HOW TO CLEAN KALE

Kale's curly leaves trap
dirt and grit, so wash
them well. Submerge the
leaves in a large basin
of cool water, then
agitate the leaves to
loosen the dirt. Drain
in a colander or if
your recipe requires
completely dry kale,
use a salad spinner.

Tomato-Stewed Kale

This dish marries well with pasta, polenta, or rice.

1½ pounds fresh kale, washed
3 tablespoons olive oil
1 large onion, chopped
2 cloves garlic, minced
1 cup chicken stock
1 can (14 ounces) diced tomatoes with juice
1 teaspoon dried basil or 1 tablespoon chopped fresh basil,
    added at the end
salt and freshly ground black pepper, to taste
1 to 2 teaspoons balsamic or red-wine vinegar
1 to 3 teaspoons tomato paste (optional)
finely grated Parmesan cheese (optional)

■ Strip or cut the kale leaves from the stems and rip the leaves into large pieces. Discard the stems.

■ Warm the oil in a large, heavy-bottom pot or Dutch oven over medium heat. Add the onion and cook for 8 to 9 minutes, or until soft. Add the garlic and cook for 1 minute more. Add all of the kale and chicken stock to the pot. Bring the mixture to a boil, reduce the heat, then cover and simmer for 15 minutes, stirring occasionally.

■ Add the tomatoes and their juice, dried basil, and salt and pepper, to taste. Cover and simmer for 15 to 25 minutes more, or until the kale is tender. Taste, adding more salt and pepper, if desired.

■ Just before serving, stir in 1 to 2 teaspoons of vinegar, tasting between each, and the fresh basil, if using. If the broth is thin and/or you are serving this over pasta, add 1 to 3 teaspoons of tomato paste. Pass the Parmesan cheese at the table, if using.

Makes 6 servings.

Spaghetti Squash Alfredo

Eating this vegetable "pasta" right out of its shell is fun for even finicky eaters.

2 spaghetti squashes (about 4 to 5 pounds each)
4 to 8 teaspoons olive oil
salt and freshly ground black pepper, to taste
4 tablespoons (½ stick) unsalted butter, softened
½ cup heavy cream or ranch salad dressing
½ cup finely grated Parmesan cheese, plus extra for topping
¼ cup crisp-crumbled bacon or bacon bits (optional)
red pepper flakes (optional)

■ Preheat the oven to 375°F. Line a baking sheet with aluminum foil.

■ Carefully cut the squashes in half lengthwise. Scoop out and discard the seeds. Pour 1 to 2 teaspoons of olive oil into each squash half and brush it on the flesh. Sprinkle with salt and pepper, to taste, then place the halves on the prepared baking sheet, cut side up. Bake for 1 hour, or until tender and the spaghetti "strands" flake easily when raked with a fork. Transfer the sheet to a cooling rack for 5 to 10 minutes.

■ Preheat the oven to 425°F.

■ Using a fork, scrape the spaghetti strands away from, but not out of, the outer shell. Leave some of the squash flesh intact to help support the sides. Add to each half 1 tablespoon of butter, 2 tablespoons of heavy cream, and 2 tablespoons of Parmesan cheese. Using two forks, toss the ingredients with the strands. Taste, and adjust the seasonings, if desired. Spread the squash mixture evenly in each shell. Sprinkle with bacon bits (if using), pepper flakes (if using), and Parmesan cheese. Return the squashes to the oven and bake for 15 minutes more. Cut in half and serve hot, in the shells.

Makes 8 servings.

Spaghetti or Squash?

Cup for cup, spaghetti squash has fewer than 25 percent of the calories and carbohydrates of regular spaghetti— and beats pasta in most nutrient categories.

Pondering Parsley

Most markets carry both curly leaf and Italian, or flat leaf, parsley. These usually can be used interchangeably, although to some people's taste the curly herb makes a more attractive garnish, while Italian parsley seems slightly sweeter.

Fresh Tomato and Zucchini au Gratin

This dish is perfect for harvesttime. Draining the tomatoes keeps the dish from getting watery.

4 medium tomatoes, cored
salt, to taste, plus ¼ teaspoon
3 zucchini (each 6 to 7 inches long)
⅓ cup heavy cream (optional)
1 large slice dense white or whole wheat bread, cut into cubes
½ cup finely grated Parmesan cheese
small handful fresh Italian parsley
2 teaspoons dried basil or 6 to 7 leaves fresh basil, finely chopped
¼ teaspoon freshly ground black pepper
3 tablespoons olive oil

■ Cut the tomatoes into ¼-inch-thick slices. Place the slices in a colander over a large bowl. Salt, to taste, and toss to coat. Set aside to drain for 30 minutes.

■ Rinse and dry the zucchini. Slice each one into ¼-inch-thick slices, cutting slightly on the diagonal. Put the slices into a large bowl, salt, to taste, and toss lightly. Set aside for 15 to 20 minutes.

■ Preheat the oven to 400°F. Butter a shallow, 13x9-inch baking dish or large gratin dish. (For a slightly richer version, if using the heavy cream, pour it into the dish and tilt to coat.)

■ Combine the bread, Parmesan cheese, and parsley in a food processor. Pulse to reduce the bread to fine crumbs. Transfer to a bowl and add the basil, salt, and pepper. Mix to blend.

■ Lay the zucchini slices on paper towels and pat dry.

■ Lay tomato slices in the bottom of the prepared baking dish. Place the zucchini slices on top. Spread the bread crumbs over the zucchini and evenly drizzle the olive oil on top. Bake for about 30 minutes, or until bubbly.

Makes 6 servings.

How to Use Roasted Tomatoes

Almost anything goes well with roasted tomatoes— and that's a good reason to have a batch on hand:

• Coarsely chop a batch and mix to coat cooked pasta. Garnish with chopped olives and feta cheese.

• Spread on toasted bagels or English muffins, with cream cheese.

• Use atop bruschetta or on burgers.

• Chop and add to tuna and other sandwich salads.

• Use as omelet filling, with cheddar cheese.

Slow-Roasted Plum Tomatoes

Roasting meaty plum tomatoes concentrates their flavor and brings out the sweetness that you seldom get from fresh tomatoes.

10 plump or large plum tomatoes, cored, halved, and seeded
salt and freshly ground black pepper, to taste
⅓ to ½ cup Mustard Vinaigrette (page 81) or olive oil
and balsamic vinegar
½ medium onion, finely chopped
2 cloves garlic, finely chopped

■ Preheat the oven to 350°F. Oil a large, rimmed, preferably nonstick baking sheet or line it with parchment paper.

■ Place the tomato halves on the baking sheet, cut side up. Salt and pepper, to taste. Drizzle with vinaigrette. Sprinkle a little bit of onion and garlic over each tomato. Bake for 1¼ to 1½ hours, or until the tomatoes have collapsed.

■ Transfer the baking sheet to a cooling rack for 10 minutes. Using a spatula, transfer the roasted tomatoes to a covered glass or ceramic container. Refrigerate.

Makes 6 or more servings.

Crispy Fried Green Tomatoes

A Southern classic as American as apple pie.

½ cup panko bread crumbs
½ cup fine yellow cornmeal
1 teaspoon paprika
1 cup all-purpose flour
½ cup buttermilk
3 large green tomatoes
salt and freshly ground black pepper, to taste
3 to 4 tablespoons vegetable oil, for the pan

■ Combine the bread crumbs, cornmeal, and paprika in a shallow bowl. Put the flour into another shallow bowl. Pour the buttermilk into a third bowl and put all of the bowls near the stove.

■ Cut the tomatoes into ¼-inch-thick slices. Lay them on a large sheet of wax paper and sprinkle both sides with salt and pepper, to taste. Heat a large, nonstick or cast iron skillet. When it is hot, add the oil, using just enough to coat the pan. Working quickly and with one tomato slice at a time (but cooking four to six slices at once), dredge both sides in flour, dunk the slice in buttermilk, generously coat with the cornmeal mixture, and place in the skillet. Cook each slice for 2 minutes on each side, or until golden brown, turning once. If the slices get dark too quickly, reduce the heat. Serve immediately or transfer to a baking sheet and hold in a 300°F oven until ready to serve.

Makes 6 servings.

It's difficult to think anything but pleasant thoughts while eating a homegrown tomato.
–Lewis McDonald Grizzard Jr., American writer (1946–94)

Cheese-Stuffed Baked Tomatoes

*Because plum tomatoes are less likely to fall apart than other types,
they are preferable for this dish.*

6 to 8 large plum tomatoes
salt, to taste
1 tablespoon unsalted butter, plus more for the tops
¼ cup minced onion
1 clove garlic, minced
2 cups tightly packed baby spinach, rinsed
¾ cup ricotta cheese
½ cup finely shredded provolone cheese
⅓ cup finely grated Parmesan cheese
1 tablespoon pesto or chopped fresh basil
freshly ground black pepper, to taste
1 cup fine cracker crumbs

■ Preheat the oven to 350°F. Line a rimmed baking sheet with foil. Line a platter with paper towels.

■ Cut the tomatoes in half lengthwise. (Do not remove the cores.) Using a paring knife and spoon, carve out the seeds and sections of each tomato half, leaving the walls intact. Discard the seeds and sections or save for another use. Salt the tomato interiors lightly, then place them cut side up on the baking sheet. Bake for 8 minutes.

■ Transfer the tomato halves to the prepared platter, inverting the halves to allow them to drain.

■ Preheat the oven to 375°F.

■ Melt 1 tablespoon of butter in a skillet over medium heat, add the onion, and cook for 3 minutes. Add the garlic and spinach, cover, and cook for 4 to 5 minutes, stirring often. Remove from the heat and cool briefly.

■ In a bowl, combine the cheeses, pesto, and salt and pepper, to taste. Add the spinach mixture and stir. Spoon this filling into the tomato halves, mounding it slightly. Put the crumbs into a small bowl and press the top of each tomato into them or sprinkle a heavy coating of crumbs on top of each, pressing lightly. Return the tomato halves to the baking sheet and top with a thin pat of butter. Bake for 30 minutes, or until puffed and golden brown. Cool briefly before serving.

Makes 6 or more servings.

> **A nickel will get you on the subway, but garlic will get you a seat.**
> —*Yiddish proverb*

Breaded Fried Zucchini Rounds

Never say "No!" to a gift of zucchini from the garden.

1 cup Italian-style bread crumbs
½ cup finely grated Parmesan cheese, plus more for topping
2 teaspoons dried oregano
2 teaspoons dried parsley
3 large eggs, lightly beaten
4 or 5 splashes hot-pepper sauce
½ cup all-purpose flour
6 zucchini (each 6 to 7 inches long)
salt and freshly ground black pepper, to taste
vegetable oil, for frying
1 to 2 cups pasta sauce, heated (optional)

■ In a pie plate or shallow dish, combine the bread crumbs, ½ cup of Parmesan cheese, oregano, and parsley. Mix lightly.

■ In a bowl, combine the eggs and hot-pepper sauce and whisk until frothy. Set aside near the bread crumb mixture.

■ Spread the flour on a dinner plate and place it near the other dishes.

■ Rinse and dry the zucchini. Slice each one into ¼-inch-thick slices, cutting slightly on the diagonal. Put the slices into a large bowl, sprinkle with salt and pepper, to taste, and toss lightly.

■ Warm a large cast iron or nonstick skillet over medium-low heat and add just enough oil to coat the bottom. Working quickly in batches, dredge each zucchini slice in the flour, dunk it in egg, and then dredge it in the crumbs. Lay each slice in the skillet in a single layer until it is almost full. Cook for 3 minutes on each side, or until golden brown all over. Serve immediately or transfer to a baking sheet and hold in a 300°F oven until ready to serve. Pass the pasta sauce, if using, and Parmesan cheese at the table.

Makes 6 servings.

ZUCCHINI FRESHNESS

Look for firm zucchinis with a heavy body; dull (nonglossy), hard skin; and rich color. Avoid those with cracks, dark or soft spots, or a shriveled body.

Lasagna With Two Sauces
recipe on page 172

main dishes

beef and pork

poultry

fish and shellfish

casseroles and pastas

meatless

Sausage Meat Loaf

This remake of a classic is so much better than good!

1 cup tomato sauce

1 cup tomato-based chili sauce

¼ cup packed light-brown sugar

1 tablespoon apple cider vinegar

½ teaspoon smoked or regular paprika

2 tablespoons olive oil

½ cup finely chopped onion

½ cup finely chopped green bell pepper

½ cup finely chopped carrot

2 cloves garlic, minced

1 large egg

¼ cup milk

2 tablespoons barbecue sauce

2 teaspoons Dijon-style mustard

1½ teaspoons Worcestershire sauce

⅛ teaspoon hot sauce

1½ pounds lean ground beef

½ pound hot or mild Italian sausage
   meat removed from casings

1 teaspoon salt

¼ teaspoon freshly ground black pepper

1 teaspoon dried thyme

¾ cup fine dry bread crumbs,
   plain or Italian-style

■ Preheat the oven to 350°F. Lightly oil a 9x5-inch loaf pan.

■ Combine the tomato sauce, chili sauce, brown sugar, vinegar, and paprika in a small saucepan over medium heat and cook until hot, whisking. Remove from the heat and set aside.

■ Heat the oil in a skillet over medium heat; add the onion, bell pepper, carrot, and garlic; and cook for 7 to 8 minutes, or until soft, stirring occasionally. Remove from the heat and set aside.

■ In a bowl, combine the egg, milk, barbecue sauce, mustard, Worcestershire sauce, and hot sauce. Whisk well and set aside.

■ In a large bowl, combine the meats, salt, black pepper, and thyme. Mix gently by hand, breaking up the large clumps. Add the egg mixture and the cooked vegetables and stir to blend thoroughly. Add the bread crumbs and mix until evenly combined.

■ Spread a layer of the reserved sauce on the bottom of the loaf pan. Transfer the meat mixture to the pan, making a mound in the middle. Make a shallow furrow down the center and spoon half of the remaining sauce over the loaf. Bake for 60 to 75 minutes, or until the juices run clear and a thermometer inserted into the center registers 160°F. Transfer to a cooling rack for at least 10 minutes before serving. Heat the remaining sauce and pass it at the table.

Makes 10 servings.

To me, life without veal stock, pork fat, sausage, organ meat, demi-glace, or even stinky cheese is a life not worth living.

–Anthony Bourdain, American chef and writer (b. 1956)

Southwestern Chipotle Meat Loaf

Here's a loaf with a Southwest accent.

3 tablespoons olive or vegetable oil
1 medium onion, chopped
1 green or red bell pepper, chopped
2 cloves garlic, minced
5 slices white sandwich bread,
    coarsely chopped
⅓ cup milk
1 pound ground chuck
1 pound ground pork or mild Italian
    sausage meat removed from casings
⅓ cup fine dry bread crumbs or fine
    cracker crumbs

1 tablespoon chili powder
1½ teaspoons smoked paprika
1½ teaspoons ground cumin
1½ teaspoons salt
2 large eggs
2 tablespoons buffalo wing sauce or
    ½ teaspoon hot sauce
1 tablespoon Worcestershire sauce
½ cup tomato-based chili sauce
1½ tablespoons puréed canned
    chipotle in adobo (see box)

> ### Canned Chipotles
>
> *Canned chipotles in adobo sauce can be found in the ethnic foods aisle of most supermarkets. To make chipotle purée, empty the contents of the can into the blender and process until smooth. Transfer to a small jar, cover, and refrigerate. It will last for at least a month. Use in a variety of Southwestern dishes, from chili sauce to rice, but use it sparingly— it's hot!*

■ Preheat the oven to 375°F. Line a 13x9-inch baking pan or shallow casserole with parchment paper or greased foil.

■ Heat the oil in a skillet over medium heat, add the onion and pepper, and cook for 8 minutes, stirring often. Add the garlic and cook for 1 minute more. Remove from the heat and set aside.

■ Finely chop the bread by hand or in a food processor. Transfer to a large bowl. Drizzle the milk over the crumbs and toss lightly with a fork to combine. Add the sautéed vegetables, meats, and dry bread crumbs and stir to combine, breaking up all of the large clumps by hand.

■ In a small bowl, mix the chili powder, paprika, cumin, and salt. Sprinkle over the meat mixture.

■ In another small bowl, whisk the eggs, buffalo wing sauce, and Worcestershire sauce. Add it to the meat mixture. Using your hands, combine the ingredients until evenly mixed. Shape into a large loaf and transfer to the baking pan.

■ Mix the chili sauce and chipotle purée in a small bowl. Spoon half of the sauce over the top and sides of the loaf. Bake for 30 minutes. Remove from the oven and spread the remaining sauce on the loaf. Bake for 30 to 40 minutes more, or until a thermometer inserted into the center registers 160°F. Cool for 15 minutes before serving.

Makes 6 to 8 servings.

ONION ADVICE

After peeling onions,
rub salt on your
wet hands to get rid
of the onion smell.

Cottage Pie

A classic!

2 tablespoons vegetable oil
1 large onion, chopped
1 large carrot, cut in a small dice
1 rib of celery, finely chopped
1½ pounds ground beef
2 cloves garlic, minced
2 tablespoons all-purpose flour
1 cup beef broth
1 cup diced canned tomatoes with their juice or
   canned crushed tomatoes
2 tablespoons ketchup
1 teaspoon Worcestershire sauce
¼ teaspoon dried thyme
¼ teaspoon dried rosemary
salt and freshly ground black pepper, to taste
6 cups peeled and coarsely chopped russet potatoes
4 tablespoons (½ stick) unsalted butter, in ¼-inch pieces
⅓ cup sour cream
¼ to ½ cup warm milk
1½ cups shredded cheddar cheese

■ Preheat the oven to 350°F. Oil a large, shallow casserole.

■ Heat the oil in a large skillet over medium heat; add the onion, carrot, and celery; and cook, stirring, for 5 minutes, or until soft. Add the meat and garlic, breaking it up with a wooden spoon, and cook for 4 minutes, or until thoroughly browned. Add the flour and stir to blend. Add the beef broth and tomatoes and bring to a simmer. Add the ketchup, Worcestershire sauce, thyme, and rosemary and cook for 3 to 4 minutes, or until the mixture is saucy and heated through. Add salt and pepper, to taste. Remove from the heat and spread in the prepared casserole.

■ Put the potatoes into a large pot, cover with lightly salted water, and bring to a boil. Reduce the heat and cook for 10 to 12 minutes, or until the potatoes are tender. Drain and transfer to a large bowl.

■ Add the butter and sour cream to the potatoes, pause briefly to let them warm, then mash the potatoes, adding only enough milk to make them soft but textured. Add salt and pepper, to taste.

■ Spoon the potatoes over the meat filling. Sprinkle with the cheese. Bake for 25 to 30 minutes, or until lightly browned. Transfer to a cooling rack for 10 minutes before serving.

Makes 6 to 8 servings.

Who'll dare deny the truth, there is poetry in pie.

–*Henry Wadsworth Longfellow, American poet (1807–82)*

Variations

Shepherd's Pie

Many people are familiar with this dish, a cousin to Cottage Pie.

■ Substitute ground lamb for ground beef.

Two-Root Pie

■ Replace 2 cups of chopped potatoes with 2 cups of peeled rutabaga cut in a ½-inch dice.

■ Cook the rutabaga first (it takes longer), as you would cook the potatoes. When the rutabaga is tender, add the potatoes to the boiling water. Cook until the potatoes are tender, then proceed as directed, mashing them together.

Slow Cooker Barbecue Brisket

You could travel to Texas for outstanding barbecue beef.
Or you could just make this at home.

3 tablespoons vegetable oil
2 large onions, halved and thinly sliced
3 cloves garlic, minced
2 teaspoons smoked paprika
1 teaspoon chili powder
1 bottle (12 ounces) beer
1½ cups tomato-based chili sauce
¾ cup packed light-brown sugar
1 tablespoon Worcestershire sauce
1 teaspoon salt
1 teaspoon onion salt
1 teaspoon dried thyme
½ teaspoon freshly ground black pepper
1 beef brisket (3½ to 4 pounds), trimmed of fat

■ Heat the oil in a large, nonreactive skillet over medium heat, add the onions, and cook for 10 minutes, or until soft. Add the garlic, paprika, and chili powder and cook for 30 seconds, stirring. Add the remaining ingredients, except for the brisket, and cook until heated through. Remove the skillet from the heat.

■ Pour half of the sauce into a large slow cooker. Add the brisket and cover with the remaining sauce. Cover and cook on low for 8 hours.

■ Transfer the brisket to a large casserole and ladle all of the remaining sauce over it. Cool to room temperature. Cover with plastic wrap and refrigerate overnight.

■ Preheat the oven to 350°F. Transfer the meat to a cutting board. Cut the meat across the grain into ⅓-inch-thick slices.

■ Pour the sauce into a large saucepan and bring to a simmer. Return the sauce to the casserole and add the sliced meat. Bake for 30 minutes, uncovered. Transfer the meat slices to a platter and spoon the sauce over the meat.

Makes 8 to 10 servings.

Vegetables are interesting but lack a sense of purpose when unaccompanied by a good cut of meat.

—Fran Lebowitz,
American writer
(b. 1951)

SHALLOTS

Shallots are milder than onions and are often used in French cooking. The small bulbs grow in sections called cloves, similar to garlic. If a recipe calls for a shallot, it means one clove, not the whole bulb.

Bacon Cheddar Burgers

Before drive-in restaurants and fast food, this *was a burger— and it still is!*

1½ pounds ground chuck
2 tablespoons (¼ stick) unsalted butter
2 cloves garlic, minced
1 shallot, minced
½ teaspoon chili powder
½ teaspoon smoked or regular paprika
5 pieces thinly sliced bacon, cut into ½-inch pieces
1 cup shredded sharp or extra-sharp cheddar cheese,
    plus extra to top the burgers, if desired
2 teaspoons Dijon-style mustard
salt and freshly ground black pepper, to taste

■ Put the ground chuck into a large bowl and break up any chunks by hand.

■ Melt the butter in a skillet over low heat, add the garlic and shallot, and cook for 2 minutes, stirring. Add the chili powder and paprika, and cook for 1 minute more, stirring. Add the mixture to the meat, scraping the skillet well.

■ Return the skillet to the heat, add the bacon, and cook until crisp, turning often. Transfer to a plate lined with paper towels. Cool, then crumble or chop coarsely. Add the bacon, shredded cheddar, and mustard to the meat and mix thoroughly by hand. (Do not overwork the meat, or you'll toughen it.)

■ Shape the meat into six ¾-inch-thick patties. Salt and pepper each patty, to taste.

■ Preheat a grill or skillet over medium-high heat. Cook each patty for 3 minutes per side, or to your liking. Top with additional cheese, if desired, in the final 1 to 2 minutes of cooking.

Makes 6 servings.

Two-Bean Slow Cooker Chili

This dish is as easy as 1, 2, 3—the number of steps to completion.

2 tablespoons vegetable oil
1 large onion, finely chopped
1½ pounds ground chuck
3 cloves garlic, minced
2 tablespoons chili powder
1½ teaspoons ground cumin
1 teaspoon smoked paprika
2 cups beef stock
1 large green bell pepper, finely chopped
1 cup tomato sauce
1 can (28 ounces) diced tomatoes (preferably with chiles)
    with their juice
1 can (15 to 16 ounces) black beans, drained and rinsed
1 can (15 to 16 ounces) pinto or kidney beans,
    drained and rinsed
1 can (5 ounces) chopped green chiles
1½ tablespoons light-brown sugar
1 tablespoon Worcestershire sauce
¾ teaspoon salt
1 to 3 tablespoons tomato paste

■ Heat the oil in a large skillet over medium heat, add the onion, and cook for 5 minutes, or until soft. Add the ground chuck and cook to brown thoroughly, breaking up the meat with a wooden spoon. Add the garlic, chili powder, cumin, and smoked paprika and cook for 30 seconds, stirring. Add the beef stock and stir, scraping any bits off the bottom of the skillet.

■ Transfer the beef to a slow cooker and add the remaining ingredients, except the tomato paste. Cook on low for 8 hours or on high for 4 to 5 hours, tasting occasionally to adjust the seasonings, if desired.

■ For liquid with more body, add 1 tablespoon of tomato paste at a time during the last hour, until the liquid reaches the desired thickness.

Makes 6 or more servings.

Corn Chip Chili Bowls

These are perfect for game day, but why wait?

● *Spread ½ to ¾ cup of corn chips in ovenproof bowls. Add a large ladle of hot chili and a thick layer of shredded cheddar, Monterey Jack, or pepper jack cheese. Place under the broiler just long enough to melt the cheese. Garnish with sour cream, if desired.*

If that's too much trouble, do what tailgaters do:

● *Open individual corn chip bags, add some chili and cheese, and dig in!*

Meatball Stroganoff

Also known as "beef stroganoff in the round." Serve over noodles or rice.

3 tablespoons unsalted butter
1 large onion, finely chopped
2 cloves garlic, finely chopped
3 cups thinly sliced mushroom caps
2 tablespoons all-purpose flour
1¾ cups beef stock
¼ cup dry white wine (optional; if omitted, use ¼ cup more beef stock)
¼ teaspoon salt, plus more, to taste
freshly ground black pepper, to taste
2 teaspoons Worcestershire sauce
1 cup sour cream
2 teaspoons chopped fresh dill or ½ teaspoon dried dill
16 to 24 small, cooked meatballs, homemade (page 24)
    or store-bought

■ Melt the butter in a large pot over medium heat, add the onion, and cook for 5 to 6 minutes, or until soft. Add the garlic and mushrooms and cook for 5 to 6 minutes, or until most of the liquid cooks off. Sprinkle with flour, stir, and cook for 1 minute more. Add the beef stock and wine, if using, bring to a simmer, and cook for 3 to 4 minutes, or until the liquid is slightly thick. Add the salt, pepper, to taste, Worcestershire sauce, sour cream, and dill and stir until evenly blended. Add the meatballs and simmer (do not boil) for 5 to 7 minutes, or until the meatballs are heated through. Salt, to taste.

Makes 4 to 6 servings.

If you really want to make a friend, go to someone's house and eat with him . . . . The people who give you their food give you their heart.

–Cesar Chavez, American labor leader (1927–93)

Pot Roast Italian-Style

Aromatic vegetables, red wine, tomatoes, and herbs turn this cut of beef into a tender, succulent roast.

3 tablespoons olive oil
1 beef chuck roast (3 to 4 pounds)
salt, to taste, plus ½ teaspoon
freshly ground black pepper, to taste
1 medium onion, finely chopped
1 rib celery, finely chopped
½ green bell pepper, finely chopped
2 cups thinly sliced mushroom caps
2 cloves garlic, minced
1 cup red wine

2 cups canned crushed tomatoes
1 cup beef broth
3 sprigs fresh thyme or 1 teaspoon
　dried thyme
1 sprig of fresh rosemary or
　1 teaspoon dried rosemary
1 cup coarsely chopped carrots
7 or 8 medium red potatoes, halved
2 to 3 teaspoons brown sugar
　(optional)

■ Preheat the oven to 275°F.

■ Heat the oil in a large pot over medium heat. Pat the roast dry with paper towels, then salt and pepper liberally. Cook to brown for 4 minutes per surface. Transfer to a platter.

■ Add the onion, celery, bell pepper, mushrooms, and garlic to the pot and cook for 5 to 6 minutes, or until soft, stirring often. Add the wine and bring to a simmer for 3 to 4 minutes, scraping any bits off the bottom of the pot with a wooden spoon. Add the tomatoes, beef broth, herbs, salt, and black pepper, to taste. Return the mixture to a simmer. Return the meat to the pot and baste it with the sauce. Scatter the carrots and potatoes over the meat.

■ Cover and bake for 3 to 4 hours, or until the meat is tender. (The heavier the roast, the longer the time required.) Every hour, stir and taste the sauce: If it is too acidic, add 2 to 3 teaspoons brown sugar. Add salt, to taste. At the same time, baste the meat. When the meat is done, remove from the oven and set aside, uncovered, for 30 minutes. Skim the excess fat from the top of the sauce before serving.

Makes 6 to 8 servings.

Fresh vs. Dried

Most herbs keep their flavor when properly dried, and often the taste is concentrated. When cooking, you may be able to exchange fresh for dried, or vice versa. As a general rule:

• For dried, use one-third of the fresh amount.

• For fresh, use three times the dried amount.

For example, 1 tablespoon of a fresh herb, minced and packed, equals about 1 teaspoon of dried.

Steak and Romaine Salad

Got leftover steak? Warming brings out its flavor.

1 to 2 heads romaine lettuce, torn into pieces
1 large cucumber, peeled, halved, seeded, and thickly sliced
2 medium tomatoes, cored and cut into wedges
flesh of 1 to 2 ripe avocados, cut into chunks
Chunky Blue Cheese Dressing (page 82)
12 to 16 ounces leftover steak
¾ to 1 cup beef stock
1½ cups croutons
freshly ground black pepper, to taste

■ Arrange a thick layer of lettuce on each of four to six dinner plates. Arrange cucumber slices, tomato wedges, and avocado chunks on each one. Add dressing, to taste.

■ Thinly slice the steak. Place it in a skillet with just enough beef stock to cover. Bring to a gentle simmer and cook for about 2 minutes, or just until heated through.

■ Place the steak slices directly on the salad, top with croutons, and add pepper, to taste.

Makes 4 to 6 servings.

Variation
No leftover steak? Use packaged beef fajita strips thinly sliced instead.

Lettuce is like conversation; it must be fresh and crisp, so sparkling that you scarcely notice the bitter in it.

–Charles Dudley Warner, American editor and writer (1829–1900)

Gingered Beef, Snow Peas, and Carrots

This is so much better than takeout!

3 cloves garlic, minced

¼ cup soy sauce

¼ cup hoisin sauce

3 tablespoons rice vinegar

2 tablespoons packed
  light-brown sugar

2 tablespoons minced fresh ginger

1 tablespoon lime juice

1 teaspoon sesame oil (optional)

1 to 1¼ pounds flank steak

3 tablespoons vegetable oil,
  divided

2 cups snow peas

1½ cups matchstick-cut carrots

2 teaspoons cornstarch

IT'S ALL IN THE SAUCE

Hoisin sauce, also
called Peking sauce,
is usually made from
fermented soybeans,
garlic, vinegar, chiles,
and a sweetener.

■ Combine the first eight ingredients in a large bowl and stir to blend. Remove half of the marinade and reserve it in a separate bowl.

■ Blot the flank steak dry with paper towels, put it on a baking sheet, and place in the freezer to chill for 30 to 45 minutes, or until hard but still sliceable. (Chilling allows for very thin slicing.)

■ Cut the steak in half with the grain. Then slice across the grain into ⅛-inch-thick pieces. Transfer each slice to the large (not reserved) bowl of marinade.

■ Toss the meat and marinade to mix well. Cover with plastic wrap and refrigerate for 1 to 2 hours.

■ Heat 2 tablespoons of vegetable oil in a large skillet or wok over high heat, add the snow peas and carrots, and cook for 2 minutes, or until tender but still crunchy, stirring often. Transfer to a bowl.

■ Add the remaining 1 tablespoon of oil to the skillet, heat briefly, then add half of the meat, laying each slice across the skillet, and cook for 1 minute, without stirring, to sear. Cook for 2 minutes more, or until all signs of pink are gone, stirring often. Transfer the meat to the bowl of snow peas and carrots. Repeat, cooking the remaining meat without any additional oil. Add the first batch of meat and vegetables to the skillet.

■ Combine the cornstarch and the reserved marinade and whisk to blend. Pour into the skillet and cook for 2 to 3 minutes, or until hot and thick, stirring constantly. Serve hot.

Makes 4 to 6 servings.

CHOP OPTIONS

Pork chops, which
come from the pig's
upper back,
include the sirloin
chop, rib chop, loin
chop, boneless rib
end chop, boneless
center loin chop,
and butterfly chop.

Stuffing-Breaded Pork Chops With Pan Gravy

Dry stuffing mix makes a fine pork chop coating.

Chops:
1½ cups dry stuffing mix
1 egg beaten with 2 tablespoons milk
4 pork chops (about ¾-inch thick)
salt and freshly ground black pepper,
　to taste
onion powder, to taste
garlic powder, to taste
3 tablespoons olive oil

Gravy:
2 tablespoons (¼ stick) butter
¼ cup minced onion
4 teaspoons all-purpose flour
1 cup chicken stock
⅓ cup milk or half-and-half
salt and freshly ground black
　pepper, to taste

For chops:
■ Preheat the oven to 400°F. Line a rimmed baking sheet with foil and put it into the oven to heat.

■ Put the stuffing mix into a food processor and pulse repeatedly, until the stuffing is finely ground. Transfer to a large plate.

■ Put the beaten egg mixture into a shallow bowl (large enough to contain a chop) and set aside.

■ Pat the pork chops dry with paper towels. Lightly salt and pepper the chops on both sides and dust lightly with onion powder and garlic powder.

■ Heat a large skillet over medium heat. Add the olive oil to the skillet. (The pan should be hot, but not hot enough to burn the coating on the chops.) Working with one chop at a time, dip both sides into the egg mixture and then into the stuffing crumbs, coating it heavily. Fry the chops for 2½ minutes on each side, turning once. Transfer the chops to the hot baking sheet and bake for 10 to 15 minutes, or until the internal temperature is 145°F. Remove from the oven and rest for 3 minutes.

For gravy:
■ Melt the butter in the skillet over medium heat, add the onion, and cook for 2 minutes, stirring. Add the flour and cook for 1 minute, stirring. Add the chicken stock and whisk to blend. Simmer until the gravy thickens. Add the milk, whisk to blend, and simmer for 1 to 2 minutes more, adding salt and pepper, to taste. Serve the chops with the gravy on the side.

Makes 4 servings.

SHOPPING FOR BEETS

Look for small to
medium-size roots,
smooth skin, firm flesh,
rich color, and
healthy green leaves.
Avoid cracks,
shriveled or soft roots,
and wilted leaves.

Red Flannel Hash

*This traditional New England dish gets its name and flavor
from the beets.*

3 medium beets, scrubbed
salt and freshly ground black pepper, to taste
3 medium baking potatoes, peeled and cut in a small dice
3 tablespoons unsalted butter or vegetable oil
1 medium onion, chopped
1½ to 2 cups leftover corned beef, cut in a small dice
½ teaspoon paprika
½ teaspoon dried thyme
¼ cup heavy cream
½ teaspoon Worcestershire sauce, plus more, to taste

■ Put the beets into a large saucepan, cover with lightly salted water,
and bring to a boil. Lower the heat and cook for 20 minutes, or until
tender. Drain and set aside to cool. Slip off the skins and cut the beets
into a small dice. Set aside.

■ Put the potatoes into a saucepan, cover with lightly salted water, and
bring to a boil. Cook for 10 minutes, or until barely tender. Drain and
set aside to cool.

■ Melt the butter in a large skillet over medium heat, add the onion,
and cook for 8 minutes. Add the beets, potatoes, and corned beef and
cook for 5 minutes. Add salt and pepper, to taste. Add the paprika
and thyme and stir. Pour the cream over the mixture and stir to blend.
Add the Worcestershire sauce, taste, and add more, if desired. Cook
for 5 to 7 minutes, without stirring, or until it starts to stick to the
pan. Turn the hash, in pieces, with a spatula. Cook for a few minutes
more, and serve.

Makes 4 to 6 servings.

Roast Pork Tenderloin
With Peach–Pepper Jelly Glaze

The sauce is simply luscious!

Glaze:

2 tablespoons (¼ stick) unsalted
  butter
2 cups peeled and chunked ripe
  peaches or canned peaches,
  drained
2 tablespoons light-brown sugar
1 jar (10 ounces) hot pepper jelly

1 tablespoon ketchup
½ teaspoon soy sauce

Pork Loin:

1½ to 2 pounds pork tenderloin
salt and freshly ground black
  pepper, to taste
2 to 3 tablespoons olive oil
¼ cup warm water

For glaze:

■ Melt the butter in a skillet over medium heat, add the peaches
and brown sugar, and bring to a boil, stirring often. Reduce the heat
and simmer for 2 to 3 minutes, or until the peaches are soft. Add
the hot pepper jelly, ketchup, and soy sauce, stir to blend, and return
to a simmer. Cook for 1 to 2 minutes, or until heated through.
Remove from the heat and set aside.

For pork loin:

■ Preheat the oven to 425°F.

■ Rinse the pork tenderloin and pat dry with paper towels. Salt
and pepper, to taste. Heat the oil in a large skillet or large, shallow,
stovetop-to-oven casserole over medium heat. Add the meat and cook
to brown the surface, turning every 60 seconds.

■ Put the skillet into the oven and roast for 10 minutes. Remove
from the oven and pour ¼ cup of warm water into the skillet.
Baste the meat with ½ to ¾ cup of glaze and return it to the oven for
7 to 10 minutes more, or until its internal temperature is 145°F.

■ Transfer to a cutting board and cover with aluminum foil, bunching
it loosely around the meat. Let rest for 3 to 4 minutes. Warm the glaze
over low heat. Slice the meat and serve with the glaze.

Makes 4 servings.

Note: To double the servings, cook two tenderloins and add 3 cups
of peaches to the glaze.

How to Use a Meat Thermometer

*An accurate meat
thermometer can mean
the difference between
a perfectly done roast
and one that's
under- or overcooked.
Old-fashioned
dial-and-needle
thermometers are far
less accurate than
today's digital,
instant-read
thermometers. With
either type, insert the
probe into the thickest
part of the meat. Do
not push it against bone
or clear through to the
pan, or the reading will
be inaccurate.*

Country-Style Root Beer–Glazed Ribs

This glaze is also wonderful as barbecue sauce on chicken, pork chops—even burgers.

**THE ROOT OF
THE MATTER**

Root beer dates from colonial times. The colonists fermented local herbs, barks, roots, and berries with molasses and drank the "beer" while still sweet, before fermentation was completed.

Ribs:

3½ to 4 pounds bone-in,
   country-style pork ribs
salt and freshly ground black pepper,
   to taste
garlic powder, to taste
onion powder, to taste

Glaze:

3 cups root beer (not diet)
¾ cup brewed coffee
½ cup ketchup
1 to 1½ tablespoons tomato paste
2 teaspoons lemon juice
1½ teaspoons yellow mustard
salt and freshly ground black pepper,
   to taste

For ribs:

■ Preheat the oven to 350°F. Line a large, rimmed baking sheet with aluminum foil and place the ribs on it. Salt and pepper, to taste, and dust with the garlic and onion powders. Cover tightly with aluminum foil and bake for 1 hour.

■ Line a second rimmed baking sheet or roasting pan with aluminum foil. Set aside.

For glaze:

■ Pour the root beer and coffee into a large saucepan, bring to a boil, and boil rapidly until the liquid is reduced by two-thirds, or measures about 1¼ cups. (To check, pour the hot liquid into a 2-cup glass measure.) Add the ketchup, 1 tablespoon of tomato paste, lemon juice, and mustard and whisk to blend. Add salt and pepper, to taste, and bring to a simmer. Cook for 5 minutes, stirring occasionally. Remove from the heat. The sauce will thicken as it cools, but to make it thicker or give it more tomato taste, add the remaining ½ tablespoon of tomato paste and whisk to blend.

To assemble:

■ Remove the ribs from the oven (expect a lot of fat in the pan) and transfer them to the other foil-lined pan. Spoon some glaze over each rib. Reduce the oven to 325°F and bake, uncovered, for 50 to 60 minutes more, removing to baste with the remaining glaze after 25 to 30 minutes. Warm any leftover glaze and pass it at the table.

Makes 4 to 6 servings.

Cajun Sausage Stir-Fry

This dish will wake up your taste buds!

3 cups peeled and diced red-skinned potatoes
salt, to taste
2 tablespoons vegetable oil
1 medium onion, chopped
1 green bell pepper, chopped
2 cloves garlic, minced
1 cup frozen corn, thawed
½ pound precooked andouille sausage, in bite-size chunks
Cajun seasoning, to taste (see box)
freshly ground black pepper, to taste
hot sauce (optional)

■ Put the potatoes into a saucepan, cover with lightly salted water, and bring to a boil. Reduce the heat and cook for 5 to 6 minutes, or until barely tender. Drain and spread on a plate to cool.

■ Heat the oil in a large skillet over medium heat, add the onion and bell pepper, and cook for 6 to 7 minutes, or until soft. Add the garlic, corn, and sausage, stir, and cook for 3 to 4 minutes, or until heated through. Add the potatoes, salt, Cajun seasoning, and black pepper, to taste. Cook for 3 to 4 minutes more, or until the potatoes are heated through. Serve, passing the hot sauce at the table, if desired.

Makes 4 servings.

Secrets of Cajun Seasoning

Commercial blends typically combine various peppers, paprika, onion and garlic powders, salt, oregano, thyme, and other seasonings.

If you don't have any prepared mix on hand, experiment by combining some or all of these herbs and spices.

Broccoli and Cheddar Strata

Serve this savory bread pudding as a brunch dish for a crowd.

5 tablespoons unsalted butter, divided (including 2 tablespoons softened)
1 large loaf soft French or Italian bread, crust removed
1 medium onion, chopped
1 clove garlic, minced
2 cups bite-size broccoli florets
1 cup diced smoked sausage
6 large eggs
2½ cups half-and-half or milk
2 teaspoons Dijon-style mustard
1 teaspoon dried basil
¾ teaspoon salt
¼ teaspoon freshly ground black pepper
2 cups shredded sharp cheddar cheese

■ Butter a 13x9-inch casserole or 6 to 8 individual ones lavishly with the 2 tablespoons of softened butter.

■ Cut the bread into 1-inch cubes (about 8 cups) and spread to cover the bottom of the casserole(s).

■ Melt the remaining 3 tablespoons of butter in a large skillet over medium heat, add the onion, and cook for 5 minutes, or until soft. Add the garlic, broccoli, and sausage, and cook for 3 minutes more, or until the broccoli is soft. Remove from the heat and spoon the broccoli mixture over the bread.

■ In a large bowl, whisk the eggs lightly. Add the half-and-half, mustard, basil, salt, and pepper and whisk to blend. Ladle or pour the egg liquid over the bread. Press gently with a large fork or spoon to moisten all of the bread. Sprinkle with cheese, cover with plastic wrap, and refrigerate for at least 2 hours or overnight.

■ Preheat the oven to 350°F. Remove the plastic wrap and bake small casseroles for 25 to 30 minutes or one large casserole for 45 to 55 minutes, or until a knife inserted into the center comes out clean. Transfer to a cooling rack for 10 minutes before serving.

Makes 10 to 12 servings.

A good breakfast is no substitute for a large dinner.
–Chinese proverb

Rice and Sausage–Stuffed Cabbage Rolls

¾ pound (about 3 large links) hot Italian
    sausage meat removed from casings
½ cup finely chopped onion
½ cup finely chopped carrot
2 cloves garlic, minced
1 teaspoon smoked paprika
2¼ cups chicken stock
1 cup long grain rice

¼ teaspoon salt
1 head Savoy cabbage (see box)
1 can (14½ ounces) sauerkraut, drained
    and pressed lightly to remove liquid
2½ to 3 cups tomato sauce
2 cups shredded mozzarella cheese
⅓ cup grated Parmesan cheese

■ Heat a large, preferably nonstick, saucepan over medium heat; add the meat, onion, and carrot; and cook to brown the sausage, breaking it up with a wooden spoon. Spoon off as much of the fat as possible and add the garlic and smoked paprika, stirring briefly. Add the stock and bring to a boil. Add the rice and salt, return to a boil, then reduce the heat to low. Cover and cook for 20 to 23 minutes, or until the rice is done. Remove from the heat and set aside.

■ Put 1½ inches of water into a large pot that has a cover. Bring to a boil. Cut 1 inch deep into the core of the cabbage, remove the core, and put the head into the pot, core side down. Cover tightly and cook for 10 minutes. Transfer the cabbage to a plate and set aside until cool enough to handle.

■ Peel off six to eight of the outer leaves and stack them on a plate. Using a sharp paring knife, cut off the thickest part of the leaf stems, so that the leaves roll up easily.

■ Preheat the oven to 350°F. Grease a large, shallow casserole and spread the sauerkraut evenly in it. Working with one leaf at a time, put a generous portion of the rice mixture into the center. Fold the sides over the filling. Beginning at the stem, roll the leaf to make a neat bundle. Place the bundles close together in the casserole. Spoon the tomato sauce evenly over the cabbage rolls, cover with tented aluminum foil, and bake for 40 minutes. Remove the foil, sprinkle with the cheeses and bake, uncovered, for 10 minutes more.

Makes 6 to 8 servings.

Variation

To make this vegetarian:

■ Omit the sausage. Cook the onion and carrot in 2½ tablespoons of oil for 5 minutes, or until soft. Add the garlic and smoked paprika and cook for 1 minute.

■ Proceed as above, but use vegetable stock, doubling the amount of stock and rice.

About Cabbage

You can use regular green cabbage, but the slightly curly leaves of Savoy cabbage seem to be more tender and easier to peel off and work with. Make the Cabbage Paprikash Soup (page 38) with any leftover cabbage.

Eggplant Parmesan Roll-Ups

Even people who say that they don't like eggplant love this.

2 large eggplants
salt, to taste
2 to 3 tablespoons olive oil
2 cups tomato sauce
2 large eggs
1½ cups Italian-style panko or dry bread crumbs
1 container (15 ounces) ricotta cheese
2 cups shredded mozzarella cheese, divided
¾ cup grated Parmesan cheese, divided
2 tablespoons pesto
1 cup finely diced cooked Italian sausage or meatballs, optional
freshly ground black pepper, to taste

ADD SOME SPICE

To enhance eggplant's mild flavor, add herbs such as basil, oregano, sage, thyme, marjoram, or parsley.

■ From each eggplant, cut six ¼-inch-thick slices, lengthwise, starting in the center, where the vegetable is thickest. (Reserve any unused portions for another use.) Salt both sides of each slice and stand them upright in a colander that has been placed inside a bowl. Set aside for 30 minutes, then blot the slices with paper towels.

■ Preheat the oven to 375°F. Generously oil two large, rimmed baking sheets.

■ Place the eggplant slices on the baking sheets and brush each slice lightly with oil. Bake for 8 minutes, turn over, and bake for 8 minutes more, or until soft. Transfer the baking sheets to racks to cool.

■ Oil a large, shallow casserole. Spread the tomato sauce in it.

■ In a small bowl, beat one of the eggs and set aside. Spread the bread crumbs on a plate.

■ In a large bowl, combine the ricotta cheese and remaining egg and mix. Add 1 cup of mozzarella, ½ cup of Parmesan cheese, the pesto, sausage, if using, and pepper, to taste, and mix to blend. Working with one slice of eggplant at a time, smear a large spoonful of the cheese filling on one side. Beginning at the narrow end, roll the slice into a neat bundle. Brush with beaten egg, roll in the bread crumbs, and place in the prepared casserole, seam side down. Repeat with the remaining ingredients. Do not crowd the roll-ups in the casserole. Sprinkle with the remaining cheeses, drizzle with olive oil, and bake uncovered, for 35 to 40 minutes, or until bubbly. Let rest briefly on a rack before serving.

Makes 6 servings.

Smothered Italian Chicken

The chunky sauce and leftover meat, coarsely chopped, go well with rice or pasta.

3 tablespoons olive oil
4 to 6 pieces boneless, skinless chicken (any combination of
    breasts and thighs), rinsed and patted dry with paper towels
salt, to taste, plus ½ teaspoon
freshly ground black pepper, to taste
1 large onion, halved and thinly sliced
1 large green bell pepper, coarsely chopped
1 large red bell pepper, coarsely chopped
3 cloves garlic, minced
2 cooked Italian sausage links, casings removed, sliced
1 can (28 ounces) diced tomatoes with their juice
1 cup canned chickpeas, drained and rinsed
½ cup dry white wine
1 teaspoon dried oregano
½ teaspoon dried thyme

■ Heat the oil in a large pot over medium heat, add the chicken pieces, sprinkle with salt and black pepper, and cook for 3 minutes on each side, or until browned. Transfer the chicken to a platter. Add the onion and bell peppers to the pot and cook for 5 to 6 minutes, or until soft. Add the garlic and sausage, stir, and cook for 2 minutes more. Add the tomatoes, chickpeas, wine, salt, black pepper, oregano, and thyme, bring to a simmer, and stir, scraping any bits off the bottom of the pot. Return the chicken to the pot, immersing the pieces in the liquid. Cover and simmer for 30 minutes, stirring occasionally. Before removing from the heat, add salt and black pepper, to taste. Let rest, covered, for 20 to 30 minutes before serving, or refrigerate and then reheat before serving the next day.

Makes 4 to 6 servings.

Curried Chicken With Cashews

Add peas or diced potatoes during the last 10 minutes,
if desired.

4 tablespoons vegetable oil, divided
1 medium onion, chopped
1 large carrot, finely chopped
2 pounds boneless, skinless chicken breasts, cut into bite-size pieces
2 tablespoons curry powder, or to taste
1 teaspoon cumin
2 tablespoons all-purpose flour
2 cloves garlic, minced
1 tablespoon minced fresh ginger
1½ cups chicken stock
½ teaspoon salt, plus more, to taste
1 cup coconut milk
¾ cup canned crushed tomatoes
1 can (5 ounces) chopped green chiles
1 cup roasted cashews, coarsely chopped

SPICE OF LIFE

A blend of many
spices, curry powder
traditionally depends
heavily on coriander
for tone, turmeric
for color, and chiles
for heat.

■ Heat 2 tablespoons of the oil in a large pot over medium heat, add the onion and carrot, and cook for 7 to 8 minutes, or until soft. Add the chicken and cook for 5 to 7 minutes, or until the chicken is no longer pink, stirring often. Add the remaining 2 tablespoons of oil, the curry powder, cumin, flour, garlic, and ginger and cook for 1 minute, stirring constantly. Add the chicken stock and salt and stir, scraping any bits off the bottom of the pot. Bring to a simmer, then cover and cook for 10 minutes. Add the coconut milk, tomatoes, and green chiles and stir. Cover and simmer for 10 minutes more, stirring occasionally. Taste and add more salt, if desired. Serve hot, with rice, passing the chopped cashews at the table.

Makes 6 servings.

Note: To reduce the heat of the curry, stir 1 teaspoon of sour cream into the servings of those who desire it or pass sour cream at the table.

Spinach and Cheese–Stuffed Chicken Breasts

Chicken:

2 thick, boneless, skinless chicken breasts

6 tablespoons (¾ stick) unsalted butter, divided

½ onion, finely chopped

1½ cups finely chopped mushrooms

¾ pound fresh baby spinach

1 clove garlic, minced

salt and freshly ground black pepper, to taste

¾ cup ricotta cheese

¼ cup grated Parmesan cheese

1½ teaspoons dried basil

1 cup crumbled feta cheese

1 large egg, lightly beaten

1 cup Italian-style bread crumbs

Lemon–Garlic Butter Sauce:

3 tablespoons butter

2 cloves garlic, chopped

2 tablespoons lemon juice

¼ cup chopped fresh parsley

freshly ground black pepper, to taste

HOW TO POUND CHICKEN BREASTS

Place the chicken breasts between two pieces of waxed paper or plastic wrap.

Using a meat pounder, mallet, or rolling pin, pound the meat gently and evenly, working from the center out, until it is about ¼-inch thick.

For chicken:

■ Preheat the oven to 350°F. Oil a large, shallow casserole and set aside.

■ Halve the chicken breasts and pound the pieces into large, thin cutlets. Cover with plastic wrap and refrigerate.

■ Melt 2 tablespoons of the butter in a large skillet over medium heat, add the onion and mushrooms, stir, and sauté for 5 minutes, or until soft. Add the spinach, garlic, and salt and pepper, to taste, and stir. Cover and cook for 4 to 5 minutes. Uncover and cook for 1 to 2 minutes, or until the excess liquid evaporates.

■ In a small bowl, mix together the ricotta cheese, Parmesan cheese, and basil. Add salt and pepper, to taste, mix, and set aside.

■ Working with one piece of chicken at a time, smear one-quarter of the cheese mixture over the breast, then mound on it one-quarter each of the onion–mushroom mixture and the feta cheese. Fold one side of the chicken over the filling, then roll the chicken into a neat bundle. Brush with the beaten egg and roll in the bread crumbs to coat. Place in the oiled casserole, seam side down, and insert a toothpick through the chicken to secure it. Repeat with the remaining chicken.

■ Melt the remaining 4 tablespoons of butter and spoon over the chicken. Bake for 35 to 40 minutes, or until the chicken is firm, juicy, and no longer pink.

For sauce:

■ Melt the butter in a small saucepan over medium-low heat; add the garlic. Cook for 1 to 2 minutes, stirring constantly, until the garlic is very lightly browned. Remove from the heat and stir in the lemon juice, parsley, and pepper, to taste. Serve over the sliced chicken.

Makes 4 servings.

Braised Chicken Thighs

You may end up wanting to add this simple yet sensational dish to your meal plan every week!

2 tablespoons (¼ stick) unsalted butter
salt and freshly ground black pepper, to taste
6 chicken thighs (boneless and skinless, if preferred)
2 slices bacon, diced
1 medium onion, chopped
1 rib celery, chopped
2 cups thinly sliced mushroom caps
2 cloves garlic, minced
1 cup chicken stock
¾ cup dry white wine
1 to 2 tablespoons Dijon-style mustard, or to taste
½ teaspoon dried thyme or several sprigs fresh thyme
⅓ cup heavy or whipping cream (optional)

■ Melt the butter in a large skillet over medium heat. Lightly salt and pepper the chicken, add to the skillet, and cook for 4 to 5 minutes on each side, or until browned, turning once. Transfer the chicken to a platter.

■ Pour off most of the fat in the skillet, then add the bacon. When it has rendered most of its fat, add the onion, celery, and mushrooms, stir, and cook for 5 minutes, or until soft. Add the garlic, stock, white wine, mustard, and thyme. Return the chicken to the skillet and bring to a simmer. Cover and simmer for 25 minutes. Remove from the heat and let rest for 15 minutes.

■ Transfer the chicken to a platter. Return the skillet to the heat and bring the sauce to a boil. Boil the liquid rapidly, until reduced by half. For a creamy sauce, add ⅓ cup of heavy cream to the reduction and stir before removing the skillet from the heat. Serve the sauce over the chicken.

Makes 4 to 6 servings.

BRAISED RIGHT

Braising is a cooking method in which the main ingredient is seared and then simmered in liquid in a covered pot.

Skillet Chicken With Mushroom Gravy

Down-home and delicious, this goes with just about anything.

Chicken:
2 slices bacon, cut into ½-inch pieces
1 whole cut-up chicken, or 6 to 8
   chicken pieces such as boneless,
   skinless thighs, rinsed and patted dry
salt and freshly ground black pepper,
   to taste

Gravy:
3 ribs celery, finely chopped
1 large onion, chopped
4 tablespoons (½ stick) unsalted butter
3 cups sliced mushrooms
¼ cup all-purpose flour
3 cups chicken stock, divided
freshly ground black pepper, to taste
½ teaspoon dried thyme
¼ teaspoon salt

For chicken:
■ Preheat the oven to 350°F.

■ In an ovenproof skillet or Dutch oven large enough to hold all of the chicken and gravy, cook the bacon over medium heat until it has rendered much of its fat but is not yet crisp. Add the chicken pieces, in batches, if necessary, and cook for 3 minutes per side, or until browned. Salt and pepper each side, to taste. Transfer the chicken to a platter.

For gravy:
■ Add the celery and onion to the skillet and cook over medium heat for 5 minutes, or until soft. Add the butter and mushrooms and cook for 3 to 4 minutes more, or until most of the mushroom liquid has cooked off. Add the flour and cook for 1 minute, stirring. Add 2 cups of the stock and bring to a simmer, stirring. Add the remaining 1 cup of stock and stir. Simmer for 2 minutes, add the pepper, thyme, and salt.

To assemble:
■ Return the chicken pieces to the skillet and baste with the gravy. Cover, put the skillet into the oven, and cook for 30 minutes. Uncover; taste; add salt, if desired; and cook for 30 minutes more. Remove from the oven and cool for 20 to 30 minutes before serving, basting occasionally with gravy.

Makes 6 to 8 servings.

Note: If you have more chicken than will fit in your skillet with the rest of the ingredients, brown the chicken in batches, then transfer the pieces to a large casserole. Make the gravy in the skillet, as directed. Pour the gravy over the chicken, cover, and cook the chicken in the casserole.

> **I come from a family where gravy is considered a beverage.**
>
> *–Erma Bombeck, American humorist (1927–96)*

Chicken Tetrazzini

Better than ever is this classic that once appeared often on supper tables.

6½ ounces (about 4 cups) uncooked wide egg noodles

1½ cups fresh or frozen and thawed green peas

3 cups cooked chicken, cut into bite-size pieces

2 tablespoons vegetable oil

2 ribs celery, finely chopped

1 medium onion, finely chopped

3 cups sliced mushroom caps

2 cloves garlic, minced

4 tablespoons (½ stick) unsalted butter, in pieces

⅓ cup all-purpose flour

2 cups chicken stock

2 cups half-and-half or light cream

1 teaspoon salt, plus more, to taste

¾ teaspoon paprika

freshly ground black pepper, to taste

4 ounces cream cheese, in 5 or 6 pieces

⅔ cup finely grated Parmesan cheese

WHAT'S IN A NAME?

Chicken tetrazzini was named for Italian opera singer Luisa Tetrazzini (1871–1940).

■ Generously oil a large, shallow casserole.

■ Prepare the egg noodles according to the package directions, adding the peas during the last 3 minutes of cooking. Drain and transfer the pasta and peas to the casserole. Add the chicken and toss lightly to combine.

■ Preheat the oven to 375°F.

■ Heat the oil in a large sauté pan or Dutch oven over medium heat, add the celery and onion, and cook for 4 minutes, or until soft, stirring. Add the mushrooms and garlic and cook for 3 to 4 minutes more, or until most of the mushroom liquid has cooked off. Add the butter. When it melts, add the flour, stir, and cook for 1 minute. Add the chicken stock and half-and-half and whisk to blend. Add the salt, paprika, and pepper, to taste. Bring to a simmer, whisking constantly, and cook until the sauce thickens. Remove from the heat and add the cream cheese a piece at a time, whisking in each piece until it melts. Pour the sauce over the pasta and toss lightly. Add half of the Parmesan cheese and toss again. Taste and add salt or pepper, if desired. Sprinkle the remaining Parmesan cheese on top. Bake for 30 minutes, or until bubbly.

Makes 8 to 10 servings.

Note: Whole grain pasta, especially whole wheat thin spaghetti, works well in chicken tetrazzini. To replace the egg noodles, substitute about ¾ pound of spaghetti, breaking the strands in half before cooking.

Spiced Chicken Tenders

Move over, fried chicken: These tenders have all of your charm and great taste, without the fuss or mess.

1 cup all-purpose flour
1 tablespoon onion powder
2 teaspoons paprika or smoked paprika
½ teaspoon cayenne pepper
3 large eggs
½ teaspoon hot pepper sauce
2 cups panko bread crumbs
¼ cup (approximately) vegetable oil, for the pan
1¼ to 1½ pounds chicken tenders
salt and freshly ground black pepper, to taste

■ Combine the flour, onion powder, paprika, and cayenne pepper in a bowl and whisk to mix. Transfer the mixture to a plate near the stove.

■ In a separate bowl, combine the eggs, 2 tablespoons of water, and hot pepper sauce and whisk to blend. Place near the flour.

■ Spread the panko crumbs on a large plate in your work area.

■ Preheat the oven to 250°F.

■ Heat the oil in a large skillet over medium heat. (Too much heat will burn the breading.) Working with one tender at a time, lightly salt and pepper each side. Dredge the tender in the flour, shaking off the excess. Dip the tender in the egg, then roll in the panko crumbs to coat.

■ Place the coated tenders in the skillet without crowding. Cook for 5 to 6 minutes, or until golden, turning once. Transfer to a baking sheet and hold in the oven until ready to serve.

Makes 6 servings.

Panko Prep

Panko bread crumbs are Japanese in origin. The bread dough is kneaded and allowed to rise several times, then "baked" using electric current rather than heat. This gives the bread crumbs their coarse texture.

How to Soften Tortillas

Softening tortillas makes them flexible and easier to fill and roll. There are several ways to do this, but here's a simple method.

- *Warm a nonstick skillet over low to medium heat.*

- *Add 1 teaspoon of oil and, using a paper towel, spread the oil on the bottom of the skillet.*

  - *Lay a tortilla in the skillet and heat for 7 to 8 seconds.*

  - *Flip the tortilla over and heat the other side for 7 to 8 seconds.*

- *Quickly put a second tortilla on top of the first, flip the pile, and heat for 7 seconds. (Tongs and a spatula together can make flipping easy.)*

- *Continue adding a tortilla, heating it, and flipping the pile until all are warmed.*

If necessary, about halfway through the process, spread another teaspoon of oil on the skillet. Tortilla warming can be done in batches. Transfer the pile to a plate and cover with a damp paper towel until ready to use.

Chicken and Cheese Enchiladas

A guaranteed crowd-pleaser

Enchilada Sauce (page 147), divided
4 cups well chopped cooked chicken
⅓ cup sour cream
2 tablespoons finely chopped parsley or cilantro
2 tablespoons minced onion
salt and freshly ground black pepper, to taste
8 to 10 corn tortillas
3 cups shredded sharp cheddar or pepper jack cheese

■ Preheat the oven to 350°F. Lightly oil a large, shallow casserole.

■ Ladle ¾ cup of enchilada sauce into the casserole and spread it evenly across the bottom. Set aside.

■ Put the chicken into a large bowl, add ½ cup of enchilada sauce, and stir. Add the sour cream, parsley, onion, and salt and pepper, to taste. Stir and set aside.

■ Soften the tortillas.

■ Working with one tortilla at a time, spread a portion of chicken filling across the center. Sprinkle with 2 tablespoons of cheese and roll up the enchilada. Place in the casserole, seam side down. Repeat with the remaining tortillas.

■ Spoon the remaining sauce over the enchiladas. Sprinkle with the remaining cheese and bake for 25 to 30 minutes, or until bubbly.

Makes 4 to 6 servings.

Enchilada Sauce

Use this sauce on any dish to which you want to give a Tex-Mex accent.

3 tablespoons vegetable oil
3 tablespoons all-purpose flour
2½ tablespoons chili powder
1 teaspoon cumin
½ teaspoon unsweetened cocoa powder
3 cups chicken stock
¼ cup tomato paste
2½ tablespoons light-brown sugar
¼ teaspoon salt

■ Heat the oil in a saucepan over medium-low heat, add the flour, and whisk for 1 minute. Add the chili powder, cumin, and cocoa powder, whisk to blend, and cook for 30 seconds more. Add the chicken stock, stir, and bring to a boil. Reduce to a simmer; add the tomato paste, brown sugar, and salt; and whisk to blend. Simmer for 10 minutes, stirring often, until it thickens slightly.

Makes about 3 cups.

STOCK VS. BROTH

Stock is made by simmering
bones (or shells)
and vegetables in water.

Broth is made by simmering
meat and vegetables in water.

Turkey Sloppy Joes

Nobody will ever ask, "Where's the beef?"

2 tablespoons olive oil
1¼ pounds ground turkey
1 medium green bell pepper, finely chopped
1 medium onion, finely chopped
2 cloves garlic, minced
1 cup diced tomatoes with their juice
½ cup ketchup or ¼ cup ketchup plus ¼ cup tomato-based chili sauce
¼ cup barbecue sauce
2 tablespoons brown sugar
1 tablespoon yellow mustard
1 teaspoon chili powder
½ teaspoon salt
1 tablespoon apple cider vinegar
Worcestershire sauce, to taste
freshly ground black pepper, to taste

Too few people understand a really good sandwich.

–James Beard, American chef and food writer (1903–85)

■ Heat the oil in a large skillet over medium heat. Add the turkey, breaking it up with a wooden spoon. Add the green pepper, onion, and garlic and cook for 5 minutes, or until the meat is browned. Add the tomatoes, ketchup, barbecue sauce, brown sugar, mustard, chili powder, salt, and 1 cup of water. Bring to a simmer, stirring often. Simmer for 12 to 18 minutes, or until the mixture is thick but still saucy. Near the end of the cooking, add the vinegar plus Worcestershire sauce and black pepper, to taste, and stir to combine. Serve over grilled or toasted rolls or burger buns.

Makes 4 to 5 servings.

Mediterranean-Style Fish and Veggies Cooked in Foil

Serve with rice, to soak up the delicious broth.

2 to 3 cups coarsely chopped baby spinach
2 fish fillets (4 to 6 ounces each), thawed, if frozen
salt and freshly ground black pepper, to taste
1 tablespoon soft butter or olive oil
2 teaspoons chopped fresh basil or 1 tablespoon pesto
1 cup seeded, diced tomato
2 tablespoons minced onion
crumbled feta cheese
chopped olives

■ Preheat the oven to 350°F. Set aside a large, rimmed baking sheet. Tear off two 16-inch-long sheets of aluminum foil and smear oil on the middle, widthwise.

■ Arrange a thick bed of spinach on the oiled areas of each piece of foil. Lay a fish fillet on each spinach bed. Salt and pepper, to taste. Smear each fillet with butter or drizzle with oil. Sprinkle with basil or dab with pesto. Spread diced tomato and onion on each fillet. Fold the foil over the fish and fold the ends to avoid leaks.

■ Place on the baking sheet and bake for 25 to 30 minutes, or until the fillets flake easily. Open the foil packets carefully—steam will be released—and serve. Pass the feta cheese and olives at the table.

Makes 2 servings.

Fish Hash? You'll Be Hooked!

Whenever you have fish leftovers, improvise a hash:

• Combine the flaked fish with pan-fried potatoes, chopped green pepper, onions, and additional seafood seasoning, if desired.

Baked Crab–Stuffed Fish

Double your pleasure with two preparation options.

6 tablespoons (¾ stick) unsalted butter, divided

2 ribs celery, finely chopped

2 scallions, white and light green parts only, finely chopped

3 cups firm white sandwich bread, cut into small cubes

¾ teaspoon seafood seasoning (such as Old Bay)

1 can (5 ounces) crabmeat, drained, with juice reserved

¼ cup mayonnaise

¼ cup finely grated Parmesan cheese

salt and freshly ground black pepper, to taste

4 white-flesh fish fillets, such as cod, haddock, or sole

½ cup panko bread crumbs (optional, for rolling)

1 egg, lightly beaten (optional, for rolling)

READY OR NOT

To determine whether fish is properly cooked, push the point of a knife into the flesh and pull it aside. If the flesh is opaque and separates easily, the fish is done.

■ Preheat the oven to 375°F. Oil a large, shallow casserole.

■ Melt 4 tablespoons of the butter in a large skillet over low heat, add the celery and scallions, and cook for 2 to 3 minutes, or until soft. Add the bread cubes and cook for 2 minutes, stirring, then transfer to a large bowl.

■ Add the seafood seasoning, crabmeat and 1 teaspoon of reserved juice, mayonnaise, Parmesan cheese, and salt and pepper, to taste, to the bowl. Mix to combine.

■ Lightly salt and pepper the fillets.

To bake with stuffing on top:

■ Lay the fillets in the casserole and, working with one fillet a time, place one-quarter of the stuffing on a fillet and spread to cover, pressing down gently. Repeat for the remaining fillets.

■ In a small pan over low heat, melt the remaining 2 tablespoons of butter and drizzle over the fillets. Bake for 20 to 25 minutes, or until the fish flakes easily.

To bake stuffed:

■ Spread the panko crumbs on a plate.

■ Working with one fillet at a time, spread stuffing on the fillet to cover, then roll like a rug. Brush with beaten egg and roll in the crumbs.

■ Place the stuffed, rolled fillet in the casserole, seam side down. Repeat for the remaining fillets.

■ In a small pan over low heat, melt the remaining 2 tablespoons of butter and drizzle over the fillets. Bake for 35 to 40 minutes, or until the fish flakes easily.

Makes 4 servings.

Bourbon and Brown Sugar–Glazed Salmon

Great on the grill, too!

Marinade:

¼ cup bourbon

3 tablespoons packed light-brown sugar

2 tablespoons olive oil

1½ tablespoons soy sauce

1 tablespoon chopped fresh ginger
    or crystallized ginger

1 tablespoon Dijon-style mustard

2 cloves garlic, minced

juice of ½ lime

Salmon:

1½ pounds salmon fillets

freshly ground black pepper, to taste

For marinade:

■ Combine all of the marinade ingredients in a bowl and whisk to blend.

For salmon:

■ Put the salmon into a large plastic freezer bag and add half of the marinade. Reserve the remaining marinade for basting. Seal the bag and turn it several times to coat. Refrigerate for 1 hour, turning the bag occasionally.

■ Preheat the oven to 375°F. Line a large, shallow casserole with aluminum foil. Butter the foil and place the salmon in the casserole, skin side down. Pour the marinade in the bag over the salmon and season with pepper, to taste.

■ Bake for 8 minutes, remove from the oven, and baste with marinade. Bake for 8 minutes more, then baste again. Bake, in total, for 20 to 25 minutes, or until the salmon flakes easily. Spoon any remaining pan juices over the fish when it is served.

Makes 4 servings.

Variation

Glazed Salmon
and Greens
With Bourbon–
Mustard Dressing

■ Add 2 teaspoons of Dijon-style mustard to the reserved marinade and whisk to blend. Baste each baked fillet with 1 to 2 teaspoons of marinade.

■ In a large bowl, make a salad of 1½ cups of thinly sliced green cabbage; 1 cup of grated carrot; 1 cucumber, peeled, seeded, and diced; and 4 to 5 ounces of baby salad greens mix.

■ Drizzle the remaining marinade on the salad and toss to coat. Serve the salad and salmon together, garnished with toasted pumpkin or sunflower seeds and/or thinly sliced crystallized ginger.

Makes 4 servings.

Pan-Fried Fish Fillets on the Grill

Like the popular "blackened" fish recipes that were the rage for so many years, these fillets capture that good grill flavor.

1 tablespoon paprika
1 teaspoon smoked paprika
1 tablespoon garlic powder
1 tablespoon onion powder
2 teaspoons dried thyme
2 teaspoons dried oregano
1 teaspoon salt
½ teaspoon freshly ground black pepper
⅛ teaspoon cayenne pepper
6 tablespoons (¾ stick) unsalted butter
4 fish fillets (6 ounces each), such as catfish or tilapia

■ Combine the paprikas, garlic powder, onion powder, thyme, oregano, salt, pepper, and cayenne pepper in a small bowl. Mix well.

■ Get out a large cast iron skillet or other pan that will tolerate the intense heat of an outdoor grill. Put the skillet on the grill, over high heat, for 3 to 4 minutes.

■ In a separate pan, melt the butter and pour into a shallow casserole or pie plate.

■ Working with one fillet at a time, dip the fish into the butter. Dust one side of the fillet with a generous teaspoon of seasoning and place it in the skillet, seasoned side down. Dust the top of the cooking fillet with seasoning. Repeat, avoiding overcrowding in the skillet. Cook for 2½ to 3 minutes per side, turning once, or until the fish flakes easily. Transfer to dinner plates and drizzle any skillet drippings on the fish.

Makes 4 servings.

Easy Does It

Poaching is a healthy and easy way to cook fish. Place the fish in a shallow pot and add about a cup of vegetable broth or water and some herbs or spices. Cover loosely and simmer gently on the stovetop until the fish is done.

Shrimp Scampi With Artichoke Hearts

This is proof that a classic can get even better.

4 tablespoons olive oil
1 pound large shrimp, peeled and deveined
½ cup finely chopped onion
4 to 6 cloves garlic, minced
¼ teaspoon red pepper flakes
5 tablespoons unsalted butter, in pieces
⅓ cup dry white wine
¼ cup fresh lemon juice
salt and freshly ground black pepper, to taste
½ to ¾ pound angel hair pasta or thin spaghetti
¼ cup chopped fresh Italian parsley
1 to 1¼ cups halved marinated artichoke hearts
finely grated Parmesan cheese

■ Bring a large pot of lightly salted water to a boil for the pasta. Once it boils, turn off the heat and leave it on the stove.

■ Heat the olive oil in a large, nonreactive skillet over medium heat. Add the shrimp and cook on one side for 1 minute. Turn the shrimp and cook for 1 minute more. Add the onion, garlic, and red pepper flakes and cook for 1 minute, stirring. Add the butter, wine, and lemon juice and bring to a simmer. Simmer, partially covered, for 3 minutes. Add salt and pepper, to taste. Remove from the heat.

■ Return the pasta water to a boil and cook the pasta according to the package directions. Drain, reserving 1 cup of the cooking liquid.

■ Add the pasta to the skillet and toss to mix. Add the parsley, artichoke hearts, and ½ cup of pasta water. Toss and add salt and pepper, to taste. Let rest for 5 minutes, covered. (The pasta will soak up some of the liquid.) If necessary, add additional pasta cooking liquid and toss before serving. Pass the Parmesan cheese at the table.

Makes 4 to 6 servings.

CHILL OUT

If using frozen shrimp, defrost in the refrigerator or in cold water. Do not defrost at room temperature or in the microwave— moisture and nutrients will be lost.

Fishermen's Stew

Mussels and clams, having shells, can get messy to eat, but sometimes it's worth it—and this is one of those times.

3 tablespoons olive oil
1 large onion, halved and thinly sliced
1 medium green bell pepper, chopped
2 ribs celery, thinly sliced
2 cups sliced mushroom caps
2 cloves garlic, minced
1 can (28 ounces) crushed tomatoes
2 bottles (8 ounces each) clam juice
1 cup chicken stock
1 cup dry white wine
1 teaspoon salt, plus more, to taste
freshly ground black pepper, to taste
1 teaspoon dried basil
¾ teaspoon fennel seed, preferably crushed
½ teaspoon dried oregano
½ teaspoon sugar, plus more, to taste
1 bay leaf
1 pound cod, haddock, or other firm white fish fillets, cut into large chunks
1 pound shrimp, shelled and deveined
10 to 15 well-scrubbed mussels with beards removed and/or small clams
3 tablespoons chopped fresh Italian parsley, for garnish

■ Heat the olive oil in a large, enameled pot over medium heat. Add the onion, bell pepper, and celery and cook for 6 to 7 minutes, or until soft. Add the mushrooms and garlic, stir, and cook until the mushrooms are soft. Add the remaining ingredients, except the seafood and parsley, and bring to a simmer. Simmer for 10 to 15 minutes, uncovered, tasting to adjust the seasonings.

■ About 15 to 20 minutes before serving, add the seafood. Stir to mix and thoroughly coat. Cover and simmer for 10 to 12 minutes, or until the fish flakes easily and the shellfish have opened. Discard any mussels or clams that have not opened. Remove the bay leaf. Serve in large soup bowls and garnish individual portions with parsley.

Makes 6 or more servings.

Shrimp and Cheddar Cheese Grits

Saucy shrimp dress up the grits, which are fine on their own, too.

Shrimp:

2 slices bacon, cut into 1-inch pieces
1 cup finely chopped onion
½ cup finely chopped green bell pepper
2 or 3 cloves garlic, minced
1 can (15 ounces) diced tomatoes
  with their juice
½ cup chicken stock
salt and freshly ground black pepper,
  to taste
¾ pound shrimp, peeled and deveined
hot sauce, to taste
2 tablespoons chopped fresh parsley

Grits:

2½ cups milk
1½ cups chicken stock
¾ teaspoon salt
1 cup quick-cooking grits
2 tablespoons unsalted butter,
  in several pieces
2 cups shredded sharp or extra sharp
  cheddar cheese
freshly ground black pepper
paprika

For shrimp:

■ Heat a large skillet or Dutch oven over medium heat, add the bacon, and cook until it is crisp. Transfer to a plate lined with paper towels. Add the onion and bell pepper to the bacon drippings in the skillet and cook for 5 minutes, or until soft. Add the garlic and cook for 1 minute more. Add the tomatoes and chicken stock and bring to a boil. Lower the heat and simmer for 5 minutes, to reduce the liquid slightly. Add salt and black pepper, to taste. Add the shrimp, cover, and simmer for 3 to 4 minutes, or until the shrimp are cooked through. Add the hot sauce and parsley and stir.

For grits:

■ Heat the milk, chicken stock, and salt in a large, preferably nonstick, saucepan over medium heat. Gradually add the grits, stirring constantly, and cook for 10 minutes, or until the mixture thickens. Add the butter, stir, and add the cheese 1 cup at a time, stirring between each, until it melts. Cook for 1 to 2 minutes more, or until the grits are thick but still runny. If the grits become too thick, add milk, a teaspoon at a time. Serve hot, with shrimp and sauce on each portion, and pass the black pepper and paprika at the table.

Makes 6 to 8 servings.

Variation

Fried Grits With Eggs and Gravy

Cold, leftover grits firm up like polenta. Here's how to reheat them into a heavenly treat:

■ Transfer leftover grits to a loaf pan, cover with plastic wrap, and refrigerate overnight. Slice the cold grits into slabs. Bread each slice lightly with cornmeal.

■ Melt 1 to 2 tablespoons of butter in a skillet over medium heat. Add the sliced, breaded grits and cook until lightly browned, turning once. Serve with eggs and gravy.

Shrimp Tacos

This combination of lime-flavored slaw and saucy shrimp is perfect on a hot summer day.

Slaw:
¼ cup mayonnaise
2 tablespoons sour cream
1 tablespoon lime juice
2 teaspoons sugar
⅛ teaspoon grated lime zest
3 cups very thinly sliced cabbage
½ cup grated carrot
salt and freshly ground black pepper,
   to taste

Shrimp:
2 tablespoons unsalted butter
1 pound shrimp, peeled and deveined
2 cloves garlic
¾ cup enchilada sauce, homemade
   (page 147) or store-bought
1½ tablespoons tomato paste
salt and freshly ground black pepper,
   to taste
8 large soft corn tortillas or hard
   taco shells
1½ cups guacamole or mashed
   avocado

For slaw:
■ Combine the mayonnaise, sour cream, lime juice, sugar, and zest in a bowl and whisk to blend. Add the cabbage, carrot, and salt and pepper, to taste, and stir. Cover with plastic wrap and refrigerate for at least 1 hour, mixing occasionally.

For shrimp:
■ Melt the butter in a large skillet over medium heat, add the shrimp, and cook for 2 minutes. Add the garlic, turn over the shrimp, and cook for 1 minute more. Add the enchilada sauce and tomato paste and stir to combine. Bring to a simmer and cook for 2 to 3 minutes more, or until the shrimp are firm to the touch and white-pink in color. Add salt and pepper, to taste. Remove from the heat and transfer to a bowl. Cover with plastic wrap and set aside for 15 minutes.

To assemble:
■ Gently warm the soft tortillas in a hot skillet (see page 146). If using hard taco shells, place on a baking sheet and heat for 3 to 4 minutes in a warm (250°F) oven. Spread guacamole or mashed avocado in the tortilla or shell. Add 3 or 4 shrimp, then top with slaw. Fold the tortilla, if using. Repeat for the remaining.

Makes 4 servings.

COUNT CODE

Shrimp are sold by size, and size determines the count, or number of shrimp per pound. For example, "21/25" means that you get 21 to 25 shrimp per pound; "41/50" means 41 to 50 shrimp per pound; "U/15" means under 15 shrimp per pound. The larger the shrimp, the fewer per pound and the higher the price.

Steamed Clams With Garlic and Mushrooms

Have crusty warm garlic bread on hand for sopping up the juice!

3 tablespoons unsalted butter
2 tablespoons olive oil
1 cup finely diced mushrooms
4 cloves garlic, minced
2 shallots, thinly sliced
1 cup dry white wine
1 cup clam juice or water
24 to 48 (about 12 per person) small fresh clams, scrubbed and well rinsed
4 cups cooked linguine (optional)
salt and freshly ground black pepper, to taste
2 to 3 tablespoons chopped fresh Italian parsley, for garnish

■ Heat the butter and olive oil in a large, nonreactive pot over low heat; add the mushrooms, garlic, and shallots; and cook for 3 to 4 minutes, or until soft, stirring occasionally. Add the wine, clam juice, and clams. Cover and simmer for 8 to 9 minutes, or until the clams have opened. Discard any clams that do not open.

■ Divide the linguine, if using, and clams among the serving bowls.

■ Add salt and pepper, to taste, to the broth. Ladle the broth over the clams, garnish with parsley, and serve.

Makes 2 to 4 servings.

Variation
For broth with body:

■ After cooking and removing the clams, return the broth to the heat and bring it to a simmer.

■ In a small bowl, combine 4 teaspoons of all-purpose flour and 4 teaspoons of soft butter.

■ Add the flour–butter mixture to the broth and cook, whisking constantly, for 2 to 3 minutes, or until the sauce thickens slightly. Ladle, as directed, over the clams.

Clams or Mussels

Clams and mussels are different species. Clams are light-colored and short and squat in shape. They live buried in the sand or seabed. Mussels are dark and shaped like elongated teardrops and grow firmly attached to structures like rocks and docks.

Double Cheese Tortellini Casserole

With cheese in the pasta as well as the sauce, even the pickiest eaters will gobble this up!

3 cups frozen small cheese tortellini
3 cups broccoli florets
1 to 1½ cups diced ham or cooked chicken
3 tablespoons unsalted butter
1 clove garlic, minced
2 tablespoons all-purpose flour
1⅓ cups half-and-half or milk
1 cup chicken stock
2 teaspoons Dijon-style mustard
1 teaspoon chopped fresh basil
1½ cups shredded sharp cheddar cheese, divided
salt and freshly ground black pepper, to taste

■ Preheat the oven to 350°F. Butter a medium casserole.

■ Prepare the tortellini according to the package directions. When the tortellini has about 2 minutes of cooking time remaining, add the broccoli.

■ Drain, then transfer the tortellini and broccoli to the casserole. Sprinkle with the diced ham.

■ Melt the butter in a large saucepan over medium heat, add the garlic and flour, and cook for 1 minute, stirring constantly. Add the half-and-half and chicken stock and whisk to blend. Simmer, whisking constantly, for 3 to 4 minutes, until thickened. Add the mustard, basil, and half of the cheese and whisk or stir to blend. Remove from the heat. Add salt and pepper, to taste. Pour the sauce over the tortellini and ham. Mix gently to coat, and sprinkle with the remaining cheese. Bake for 30 minutes, or until bubbly.

Makes 4 to 6 servings.

Navel or Knot?

Legend has it that small, ring-shaped tortellini were first formed in the shape of the navel of Venus, the goddess of love, by a smitten innkeeper near Bologna, Italy. (Some call them a "knot" instead.) They are traditionally stuffed with meat or cheese. Their slightly larger cousin, tortelloni, typically contain vegetable stuffing.

Tuna Noodle Bake

This classic will bring back memories and inspire new ones.

5 ounces (about 3 cups) uncooked wide egg noodles
2 tablespoons plus 1 teaspoon olive oil, divided
3 tablespoons unsalted butter
1 medium onion, finely chopped
2½ tablespoons all-purpose flour
¾ teaspoon seafood seasoning (such as Old Bay)
½ teaspoon paprika
2¼ cups milk
½ teaspoon salt
½ teaspoon ground mustard
¼ cup sour cream or 3 tablespoons cream cheese
1 can (5 to 6 ounces) oil-packed tuna, undrained, flaked
1 medium tomato, seeded and diced
1½ cups shredded sharp cheddar cheese
1 cup fine cracker crumbs

NOODLE THIS

Egg noodles are not actually pasta—although many people refer to them as such. Pasta, which means "paste" in Italian, contains no eggs.

■ Prepare the noodles according to the package directions. Drain, then transfer to a large bowl, drizzle with 1 teaspoon of oil, and toss to avoid clumping.

■ Preheat the oven to 375°F. Butter a medium casserole.

■ Melt the butter in a large saucepan over medium heat, add the onion, and cook for 5 minutes, or until soft. Add the flour, seafood seasoning, and paprika and cook for 1 minute, stirring constantly. Add the milk, salt, and mustard and whisk to blend. Cook for 3 to 5 minutes, or until the sauce thickens, whisking often. Add the sour cream and whisk until blended. Pour the sauce over the noodles.

■ Add the tuna and its oil, tomato, and cheddar cheese and mix to coat. Pour the mixture into the casserole. Sprinkle with the cracker crumbs and drizzle with the remaining olive oil. Bake for 30 minutes, or until bubbly.

Makes 4 to 6 servings.

Super-Creamy Mac and Cheese

So-o-o-o much better than boxed

½ pound elbow noodles
1 teaspoon olive oil
6 tablespoons (¾ stick) unsalted butter, divided
1 medium onion, finely chopped
3 tablespoons all-purpose flour
2 cups milk, divided
1 cup chicken stock
1 tablespoon Dijon-style mustard
1 teaspoon salt
freshly ground black pepper, to taste
3 cups shredded extra sharp cheddar cheese
3 ounces cream cheese, in pieces, softened
¾ to 1 cup fine cracker crumbs or panko bread crumbs

■ Preheat the oven to 350°F. Butter a large, shallow casserole.

■ Prepare the noodles according to the package directions. Drain, transfer to a large bowl, drizzle with oil, and toss to avoid clumping.

■ Melt 3 tablespoons of the butter in a large saucepan over medium heat, add the onion, and cook for 5 minutes, or until soft. Add the flour and cook for 1 minute more, stirring. Add 1 cup of milk and stir. As the sauce thickens, add the remaining 1 cup of milk. Bring to a simmer. Add the chicken stock and heat gently for 3 to 4 minutes, stirring constantly. Add the mustard, salt, and pepper, to taste. Add the cheddar cheese, 1 cup at a time, and stir. Add more as it melts. Add the cream cheese and stir until melted.

■ Pour the sauce over the noodles and stir to coat. Transfer the mixture to the casserole. Sprinkle with cracker crumbs to cover evenly.

■ Melt the remaining 3 tablespoons of butter in a pan over low heat and drizzle over the crumbs. Bake for 30 to 35 minutes, or until bubbly.

Makes 6 servings.

Variations

Bacon Mac and Cheese

■ Add 4 to 5 slices of crisp-cooked, crumbled bacon to the noodles when you add the sauce. Continue as directed.

Pepperoni Pizza Mac and Cheese

■ Add ⅓ cup of chopped pepperoni slices to the noodles when you add the sauce. Instead of cracker crumbs, cover with sliced tomatoes and additional shredded cheese. Bake as directed.

Summer Garden Pasta Sauce

Sensational with any pasta

AT BAY

Bay leaves, the aromatic foliage of the bay laurel *(Laurus nobilis)*, are quite mild; dry leaves are more flavorful.

3 tablespoons olive oil
1 large onion, finely chopped
1 medium green bell pepper, diced
2½ cups diced zucchini or yellow summer squash
3 cloves garlic, minced
4 cups coarsely chopped baby spinach
1 large carrot, grated
1 can (28 ounces) crushed tomatoes
1 can (28 ounces) diced tomatoes with their juice
1 teaspoon salt, plus more, to taste
1 teaspoon dried oregano, or fresh, to taste
1 teaspoon dried basil, or fresh, to taste
½ teaspoon sugar, plus more, to taste
1 bay leaf
2 tablespoons tomato paste, divided
freshly ground black pepper, to taste
2 to 3 tablespoons red wine (optional)
¼ cup chopped fresh Italian parsley

■ Heat the olive oil in a large, nonreactive pot over medium heat, add the onion and bell pepper, and cook for 3 minutes. Add the zucchini and garlic and cook for 3 to 4 minutes more, or until the zucchini starts to soften. Add the spinach and carrot and cook for 2 to 3 minutes more, or until the spinach wilts. Add the crushed and diced tomatoes, salt, oregano, basil, ½ teaspoon of sugar, bay leaf, 1 tablespoon of tomato paste, and black pepper, to taste, and simmer, partially covered, for 30 to 40 minutes, stirring occasionally. Taste, adjusting the herbs, salt, or sugar, if desired. Add 2 to 3 tablespoons of red wine, to taste. Add 1 more tablespoon of tomato paste to thicken, if desired. Add the parsley and remove the bay leaf before serving.

Makes 6 to 7 cups.

Meat and Three-Cheese Manicotti With Summer Garden Pasta Sauce

2 tablespoons plus 1 teaspoon olive oil, divided
¼ cup minced onion
½ pound ground beef
½ teaspoon paprika
1 container (15 ounces) ricotta cheese
1 large egg, lightly beaten
3 cups shredded mozzarella cheese, divided
½ cup finely grated Parmesan cheese
¼ cup pesto or 3 tablespoons chopped fresh basil
salt and freshly ground black pepper, to taste
10 manicotti shells
Summer Garden Pasta Sauce (page 166)

■ Heat 2 tablespoons of olive oil in a large skillet over medium heat; add the onion and ground beef, breaking it up with a wooden spoon; and cook for several minutes, or until the meat is browned. Add the paprika, stir, and remove from the heat. Spoon off as much fat as possible, then transfer the beef to a large bowl. Set aside to cool.

■ To the meat, add the ricotta cheese, egg, 1½ cups of mozzarella cheese, Parmesan cheese, pesto, and salt and pepper, to taste. Mix to combine.

■ Preheat the oven to 350°F. Oil a large, shallow casserole.

■ Cook the manicotti shells according to the package directions. Drain and transfer to a bowl. Drizzle with 1 teaspoon of oil and toss to avoid clumping.

■ Spread a generous layer of Summer Garden Pasta Sauce in the casserole. Stuff the manicotti shells with the meat filling. Cover the shells with sauce. (You may not use all of it.) Sprinkle with the remaining mozzarella cheese. Bake for 30 to 35 minutes, or until bubbly.

Makes 5 to 6 servings.

FUN WITH FILLING

In Italian, manicotti, traditionally tube pasta stuffed with cheese and/or meat, means "muff."

How to Peel Red Potatoes

Place the edge of a small, serrated knife against the cool cooked potato and scrape the edge across the skin; it will peel away easily.

Hash Brown Casserole

A rich and creamy alternative to ordinary mashed potatoes

8 medium red-skinned potatoes, scrubbed
2 cups shredded sharp cheddar cheese, divided
2 strips bacon, chopped
1 medium onion, finely chopped
1½ tablespoons all-purpose flour
1⅓ cups milk
scant 1 teaspoon salt
½ teaspoon dried thyme
freshly ground black pepper, to taste
⅔ cup sour cream
½ cup mayonnaise
paprika, for dusting

■ Put the potatoes into a large saucepan, cover with lightly salted water, and bring to a boil. Reduce the heat to simmer and cook until barely tender. Drain and set aside to cool. Refrigerate for at least 4 hours or overnight.

■ Preheat the oven to 350°F. Butter a medium-large casserole.

■ Peel the chilled potatoes and gently grate on the large holes of a box grater. Transfer to the casserole. Add half of the cheese and toss to mix. Set aside.

■ Fry the bacon in a skillet, preferably nonstick, over medium heat. When it has rendered some of its fat, add the onion and cook for 4 to 5 minutes, or until soft. Add the flour and cook for 1 minute, stirring constantly. Add the milk, salt, thyme, and pepper, to taste, and whisk to blend. Cook, stirring constantly, until the mixture thickens. Add the sour cream and whisk to blend. Heat gently; do not boil. Remove from the heat, add the mayonnaise, and whisk to blend.

■ Pour the sauce over the potatoes and stir gently to combine. Sprinkle with the remaining cheese and dust with paprika. Bake for 30 to 35 minutes, or until golden brown and bubbly.

Makes 8 servings.

Thin Spaghetti Pie

Hearty and delicate all at once—but angel hair pasta is too thin for this dish.

¾ **pound thin spaghetti**
5 **cups pasta sauce, divided**
salt and freshly ground black pepper, to taste
1 **pound ground beef or Italian sausage meat removed from casings**
½ **onion, finely chopped**
1 **cup ricotta cheese**
½ **cup sour cream**
¼ **cup grated Parmesan cheese**
2 **teaspoons dried basil**
1½ **cups shredded mozzarella cheese**
1½ **cups shredded cheddar cheese**

■ Preheat the oven to 350°F. Oil a large, shallow casserole.

■ Prepare the spaghetti according to the package directions, drain, and transfer to the casserole. Cover with 2 cups of sauce, sprinkle with salt and pepper, to taste, and toss to coat. Spread the spaghetti evenly in the casserole.

■ Heat a large skillet over medium heat, add the beef and onion, and cook to brown the meat, breaking it up with a wooden spoon. Remove from the heat and spoon off as much of the fat as possible. Return the skillet to the heat and add the remaining 3 cups of sauce. Cover and simmer for 4 to 5 minutes. Remove from the heat.

■ In a small bowl, combine the ricotta cheese, sour cream, Parmesan cheese, basil, and salt and pepper, to taste, and mix to blend. Drop dollops on the spaghetti and spread with the back of a spoon. Cover with meat sauce and sprinkle with the mozzarella and cheddar cheeses. Bake for 35 to 40 minutes, or until bubbly.

Makes 8 servings.

FLAVOR FACTORS

Traditional Italian sausages usually contain pork and are distinguished as "sweet" or "mild," which are flavored with garlic and fennel seed, or "hot," which contain crushed chiles. Specialty markets may offer more options.

DIY Hot Stuff

You can turn homegrown hot red peppers into flakes:

Wash and dry the best specimens, then remove the stems. Slow-roast them in a 160°F oven for 8 to 10 hours, or until crisp. Cool completely, and crush in a food processor. Wear rubber gloves, open a window when roasting, and process outside, if possible, to avoid sneezing.

Spaghetti With Crunchy Bread Crumbs and Garlic

The secret ingredient is bread crumbs sautéed in olive oil and garlic.

½ loaf Italian bread
½ cup olive oil
5 cloves garlic, finely chopped
⅛ to ¼ teaspoon red pepper flakes (optional)
½ to ¾ pound spaghetti (thin or regular)
2 to 3 tablespoons finely chopped fresh Italian parsley
1 teaspoon dried oregano
freshly grated Parmesan cheese
chopped black or green olives

■ Heat a large pot of salted water to a boil for the pasta.

■ Cut the loaf in half lengthwise, spread it open, and pull off ¼- to ½-inch pieces of the soft inside to make 1½ to 2 cups of bread crumbs. Set aside.

■ Warm the olive oil in a large skillet over medium heat and add the garlic; pepper flakes, if using; and bread crumbs. Sauté the crumbs for 4 to 6 minutes, or until golden, stirring constantly. Remove the skillet from the heat and transfer half of the crumbs to a small bowl.

■ Cook the pasta according to the package directions. Drain, reserving 1 cup of the cooking water.

■ Add the pasta, parsley, and oregano to the crumbs remaining in the skillet. Return the skillet to medium heat and cook for 2 to 3 minutes, tossing the ingredients with two forks to coat. If the spaghetti is dry, add 1 tablespoon of the reserved cooking water to moisten, plus more, if desired. Add the reserved crumbs, mix to combine, and serve, passing the Parmesan cheese and chopped olives at the table.

Makes 4 or 5 servings.

Thin Spaghetti With Garlic, Bacon, and Swiss Chard

1½ pounds Swiss chard
3 slices bacon
½ pound thin spaghetti
1 teaspoon olive oil
1 medium onion, halved and thinly sliced
2 or 3 cloves garlic, minced
¾ cup chicken stock
balsamic vinegar, to taste
salt and freshly ground black pepper, to taste
freshly grated Parmesan cheese, for garnish

▪ Cut out and discard the stems of the Swiss chard. Coarsely chop the leaves and rinse well. Transfer to a colander.

▪ Cook the bacon in a large skillet over medium heat until crisp. Drain on paper towels and, when it's cool enough to handle, crumble.

▪ Prepare the spaghetti according to the package directions, drain, drizzle with olive oil, and toss to avoid clumping.

▪ Add the onion to the bacon drippings in the skillet and cook for 6 to 7 minutes, or until soft. Add the garlic and Swiss chard and cook for 3 to 4 minutes, or until soft. Add the chicken stock, cover, and simmer for 8 to 10 minutes, or until the chard wilts, stirring occasionally. Add the spaghetti and toss to mix. Add balsamic vinegar and salt and pepper, to taste. Serve hot, passing the Parmesan cheese and crumbled bacon at the table.

Makes 4 servings.

Grate Detail

True "Parmesan" cheese is "Parmigiano Reggiano," made from the skimmed or partially skimmed milk of cows raised in and fed fodder from specific portions of the Province of Bologna, Italy, and aged for at least 1 year. Parmesan cheeses produced elsewhere follow less stringent rules.

Lasagna With Two Sauces

A classic crowd-pleaser just got twice as nice!

Meat Sauce:
2 tablespoons olive oil
½ cup finely chopped onion
2 cloves garlic, minced
1 pound lean ground beef
1 pound Italian sausage meat
    removed from casings
2 jars (24 ounces each) tomato sauce
1 can (14 ounces) diced tomatoes
    with their juice
salt and freshly ground black
    pepper, to taste

Filling:
1 container (15 ounces) ricotta
    cheese
1 box (10 ounces) frozen spinach,
    thawed and squeezed of
    excess moisture
1 large egg, lightly beaten
2 teaspoons dried basil
¼ cup Parmesan cheese, plus more
    for topping
salt and freshly ground black
    pepper, to taste

White Sauce:
4 tablespoons (½ stick) unsalted
    butter
¼ cup all-purpose flour
2 cups milk
¼ cup Parmesan cheese
salt and freshly ground black
    pepper, to taste

1 box "oven-ready" or "no-cook"
    lasagna noodles
    (see box, page 175)

For meat sauce:
■ Heat the olive oil in a large pot over medium heat, add the onion, and cook for 5 minutes, or until soft, stirring often. Add the garlic, beef, and sausage. Cook the meat until browned, breaking it up with a wooden spoon. Spoon off as much fat as possible. Add the tomato sauce and diced tomatoes and bring to a simmer. Cook for 20 minutes, sampling occasionally and adding salt and pepper, to taste. Set aside.

For filling:
■ Put the ricotta cheese, spinach, egg, basil, ¼ cup of Parmesan cheese, and salt and pepper, to taste, into a mixing bowl. Mix to combine.

For white sauce:
■ Melt the butter in a saucepan over medium heat, add the flour, and cook for 1 minute, whisking constantly. Add the milk in three portions, as the sauce

thickens. Remove the pan from the heat. Add ¼ cup of Parmesan cheese and salt and pepper, to taste, and whisk to blend.

To assemble:
■ Preheat the oven to 375°F. Oil a large (at least 13x9-inch), deep casserole. Spread a generous layer of the meat sauce in it. Cover with a single layer of noodles, followed by more meat sauce. Dot with one-third of the ricotta mixture in dollops. Spread one-third of the white sauce around the dollops. Sprinkle with Parmesan cheese. Smooth with the back of a spoon, then repeat each layer twice: noodles, meat sauce, ricotta, white sauce, and Parmesan cheese. (You may not use all of the meat sauce.) Cover the pan with tented aluminum foil (it should not touch the sauce) and bake for 25 minutes. Remove the foil and bake for 20 to 25 minutes more, or until golden brown and bubbly. Let rest 10 minutes before serving.

Makes 10 to 15 servings.

Tortilla Flat Facts

- *Tortilla, the bread of Mexico, can be made with corn or wheat flour. In Spain, the word refers to a thin omelet that is stuffed with potatoes, onions, and meat.*

- *A tortilla wrapped around a filling of rice, beans, and/or meat (plus, often, vegetables, salsa, and cheese or sour cream) is a burrito.*

- *A tortilla that is crisp-fried (or not), folded, and filled with meats, vegetables, and cheeses is called a taco.*

- *A large tortilla spread with a vegetable or meat filling and lots of cheese, then folded in half and grilled or cooked until the cheese melts, is a quesadilla.*

Tex-Mex Lasagna

With corn tortillas in place of noodles, this dish looks like lasagna.

2 tablespoons vegetable oil
1 medium onion, finely chopped
1 pound lean ground beef
1 packet (1 ounce) taco seasoning mix
1 can (28 ounces) diced tomatoes with their juice
¾ cup tomato sauce
2 slices bacon, cut into 1-inch pieces
1 can (15 to 16 ounces) black beans, drained and rinsed
salt and freshly ground black pepper, to taste
1 container (15 ounces) ricotta cheese
3½ cups shredded sharp cheddar, Monterey Jack, or pepper jack cheese, divided
8 to 10 corn tortillas (5 to 6 inches in diameter)

■ Preheat the oven to 350°F. Oil a 13x9-inch casserole.

■ Heat the oil in a large skillet over medium heat, add the onion, and cook for 3 to 4 minutes, stirring often. Add the ground beef and cook until browned, breaking up the meat with a wooden spoon. Add the taco seasoning, diced tomatoes, and tomato sauce and bring to a simmer. Cook for 2 to 3 minutes and remove from the heat.

■ Heat a separate skillet over medium heat, add the bacon, and cook until it is crispy and has rendered most of its fat. Add the black beans and ⅓ cup of water. Reduce the heat to low and, using a potato masher, mash the beans, leaving some chunks. Add more water as needed. Add salt and pepper, to taste.

■ In a bowl, combine the ricotta cheese with 2 cups of shredded cheese. Add salt and pepper, to taste.

■ Lay several tortillas in the bottom of the casserole, trimming as needed to make a single layer. Spread one-third of the meat mixture over the tortillas, then one-third of the ricotta mixture over the meat mixture. Cover with a single layer of tortillas and repeat the layers of meat mixture and ricotta mixture. Spread the mashed beans over the ricotta mixture. Add one more layer of tortillas, meat mixture, and ricotta. Sprinkle with the remaining 1½ cups of shredded cheese. Cover loosely with aluminum foil and bake for 25 minutes. Uncover and bake for 20 to 25 minutes more, or until bubbly. Transfer to a cooling rack for 20 to 30 minutes before serving.

Makes 8 servings.

It's hard to imagine civilization without onions.

–Julia Child, American culinary expert (1912–2004)

Using Your Noodle

• Lasagna noodles that go into a dish dry (not boiled) absorb a good deal of the moisture in tomato sauce and thus are well suited to a thin sauce.

• If you use traditional "boiled" lasagna noodles, blot them well with paper towels after boiling. Also, add 1 to 2 tablespoons of tomato paste to your tomato sauce to thicken it, if desired, before removing the sauce from the heat.

Creamy Fettuccine With Vegetables

Heavy cream joins forces with the cream of the crops.

2 tablespoons (¼ stick) unsalted butter
2 cloves garlic, minced
¾ cup chicken stock
1 pound asparagus (top two-thirds of the spears only),
    cut into 1-inch pieces
1 small zucchini or yellow summer squash, diced
½ cup diced green, yellow, or red bell pepper
½ cup finely diced carrot
¼ teaspoon salt
¾ cup heavy cream
½ pound fettuccine
1 cup freshly grated Parmesan cheese, divided
2 tablespoons chopped fresh Italian parsley
freshly ground black pepper, to taste

> It is strange what a taste you suddenly have for things you never liked before. The squash has always been to me a dish of contempt; but I eat it now as if it were my best friend.
>
> *–Charles Dudley Warner, American editor and writer (1829–1900)*

■ Heat a large pot of salted water to a boil for the pasta. When it boils, turn off the heat.

■ Melt the butter in a large, nonreactive skillet or Dutch oven over low heat, add the garlic, and cook for 1 minute. Add the chicken stock, asparagus, zucchini, bell pepper, carrot, and salt and bring to a simmer. Cover and cook for 3 to 4 minutes, or until the vegetables are still a little crunchy. Add the cream, stir, cover, and remove from the heat.

■ Return the pot of water to a boil. Prepare the fettuccine according to the package directions, drain, and set aside.

■ Return the skillet to the heat, bring the vegetables to a simmer, add the fettucine, and heat gently for 3 to 4 minutes, occasionally tossing to avoid clumping. Remove from the heat and sprinkle with ½ cup of Parmesan cheese. Add the parsley and black pepper, to taste. Toss and serve, passing the remaining Parmesan cheese at the table.

Makes 4 to 6 servings.

Pasta Frittata

A frittata is typically a skillet-size baked omelet often made with potatoes. We think that you, too, will prefer pasta.

3 tablespoons olive oil
½ medium onion, thinly sliced
½ green bell pepper, chopped
2 cups cooked pasta (such as spaghetti, rotini, or elbows)
2 cloves garlic, minced
½ cup halved cherry or grape tomatoes
salt, to taste, plus ½ teaspoon
1½ cups diced cooked meatballs or Italian sausage
8 large eggs
1 teaspoon dried basil
freshly ground black pepper, to taste
½ cup grated Parmesan cheese, divided

■ Preheat the oven to 350°F.

■ Heat the oil in an ovenproof skillet over medium heat, add the onion and bell pepper, and cook for 7 to 8 minutes. Add the pasta, garlic, tomatoes, and salt, to taste. Cook for 2 minutes, or until heated through, stirring occasionally. Add the meatballs and cook for 2 minutes more.

■ In a large bowl, whisk the eggs, basil, salt, and pepper, to taste. Add ¼ cup of Parmesan cheese and whisk to combine. Pour the egg mixture over the ingredients in the skillet; do not stir.

■ Bake for 15 to 20 minutes, or until a butter knife inserted into the center comes out clean. Remove from the oven and sprinkle with the remaining ¼ cup of Parmesan cheese. Let rest until the cheese melts, then slice and serve.

Makes 8 to 10 servings.

IS IT FRESH?

To test an egg for freshness, put it gently into a bowl of cold water. If it sinks to the bottom, then it is suitable for use. If it floats, it is too old.

Welsh Rarebit

Legend has it that Welsh peasants were not allowed to eat rabbits caught on the estates of nobility, so they ate warmed cheese as a substitute. Over time, this dish became known as rarebit.

2 tablespoons unsalted butter
2 large egg yolks
¾ cup beer, light cream, or milk
1 tablespoon Dijon-style mustard
½ teaspoon Worcestershire sauce
cayenne pepper, to taste
4 cups shredded extra sharp cheddar cheese
toasted English muffins, warm biscuits, or toast
½ small onion, finely chopped
2 tablespoons chopped fresh Italian parsley

■ Melt the butter in the top of a double boiler set over, not in, simmering water.

■ In a small bowl, combine the egg yolks, beer, mustard, Worcestershire sauce, and cayenne pepper and whisk to blend.

■ Pour the egg mixture into the double boiler. Cook, stirring occasionally, until the liquid is very hot. Add the shredded cheese, 1 cup at a time, adding more as it melts. Cook for 6 to 8 minutes more, or until the rarebit is hot and has a creamy, full-bodied consistency, stirring constantly.

■ Serve over English muffins, biscuits, or toast and pass the onion and parsley at the table.

Makes 4 servings.

> **She who can mix a successful Welsh rarebit is the heroine of the drawing room. The finest evening luncheon is declared to be a Welsh rarebit and a glass of ale.**
>
> –Emily S. Harrison, The Southern Cultivator and Industrial Journal, *1895*

Curried Cashew and Red Lentil Patties With Curried Mayo Sauce

Nuts add a chewy texture, and the curried mayo sauce is the perfect topper.

Patties:
1 cup finely diced carrots
½ cup red lentils
3 tablespoons vegetable or olive oil, divided
1 cup finely chopped onion
1 clove garlic, minced
2 teaspoons curry powder
¾ cup roasted cashews

1 egg yolk
½ cup fine, dry bread crumbs
¼ teaspoon salt, plus more, to taste
freshly ground black pepper, to taste
Sauce:
⅓ cup mayonnaise
½ teaspoon curry powder, plus more, to taste
lemon juice, to taste

NUT TALK

Cashews have a double shell that contains urushiol, the toxin found in poison ivy. For this reason, these nuts are never sold in the shell, or truly raw. Cashews sold as "raw" have been steamed or otherwise processed to remove the urushiol in any shell oil that might have been left on the nut after the shell was removed.

For patties:

■ Combine the carrots and lentils in a saucepan, cover with 2½ cups of lightly salted water, and bring to a boil. Reduce the heat and cook for 15 minutes, uncovered, or until the lentils start to fall apart. Drain through a fine sieve, pressing out excess moisture with the back of a spoon. Spread in a large bowl and set aside to cool.

■ Heat 2 tablespoons of oil in a skillet over medium heat, add the onion, and cook for 8 minutes, or until soft. Add the garlic and curry powder and cook for 1 minute more. Remove from the heat.

■ Coarsely chop the cashews in a food processor. Add the lentils, onion mixture, and egg yolk, and pulse the mixture to combine, leaving a bit of texture.

■ Transfer to a bowl and add the bread crumbs, salt, and pepper, to taste. Shape the mixture into six to eight patties of a ¾- to 1-inch thickness. Place them on a plate lined with plastic wrap. Refrigerate for 1 to 2 hours.

■ Heat 1 tablespoon of oil in a nonstick skillet over medium heat, add the patties, and cook for 3 minutes per side, or until browned.

For sauce:

■ Combine the mayonnaise, curry powder, and lemon juice in a small bowl and mix to blend. Adjust the curry to taste. Serve the patties with or without buns, with the sauce.

Makes 6 to 8 servings.

Southwestern Pumpkin Burgers

Here's a meatless burger that even meat eaters will love.

3 tablespoons vegetable oil, divided
½ cup finely chopped onion
½ cup frozen corn kernels, thawed
¼ cup finely chopped green bell pepper
1 clove garlic, minced
1 teaspoon cumin
1 teaspoon chili powder
½ teaspoon smoked paprika
¾ cup fine-curd cottage cheese
½ cup canned pumpkin
1 egg yolk
2 tablespoons chopped fresh Italian parsley
scant ½ teaspoon salt
freshly ground black pepper, to taste
1¼ cups panko bread crumbs
1 cup shredded pepper jack or sharp cheddar cheese
ranch dressing (optional)

■ Heat 2 tablespoons of the oil in a skillet over medium heat; add the onion, corn, and bell pepper; and cook for 5 minutes, or until soft. Add the garlic, cumin, chili powder, and smoked paprika and cook for 30 seconds more, stirring constantly. Remove from the heat.

■ In a large bowl, combine the cottage cheese, pumpkin, and egg yolk and mix with a wooden spoon. Add the onion–corn–pepper mixture, parsley, salt, and black pepper, to taste. Stir and add the bread crumbs and cheese. Stir until combined. Cover and refrigerate for at least 2 hours, or overnight.

■ Heat 1 tablespoon of oil in a nonstick skillet over medium heat. Shape the pumpkin mixture into six ¾-inch-thick patties. Place them in the skillet and cook, in batches, if necessary, for 3 minutes on each side, or until lightly browned, turning once. Serve with or without buns, passing the ranch dressing at the table, if desired.

Makes 6 servings.

Canned Goods

When buying canned pumpkin, read the label carefully:

• "Pumpkin" or "100% pumpkin" indicates the puréed vegetable.

• "Pumpkin pie mix" indicates the puréed vegetable with spices added.

Do not use the pie mix when pumpkin is required.

Egg Rolls

1½ tablespoons soy sauce

1 tablespoon oyster sauce

2 teaspoons cornstarch

1½ tablespoons vegetable oil

2 teaspoons sesame oil

2 cloves garlic, minced

1 cup chopped shiitake
   mushroom caps

6 scallions, chopped

4 cups very thinly sliced green
   cabbage

2 cups coarsely grated carrot

¼ teaspoon freshly ground black
   pepper

3 to 4 cups oil, for frying

10 egg roll wrappers

duck or plum sauce

■ Combine the soy sauce, oyster sauce, and cornstarch in a small bowl and whisk to blend.

■ Heat the vegetable and sesame oils in a large skillet over high heat, add the garlic, and cook for 30 seconds, stirring constantly. Add the mushrooms and scallions and cook for 1 minute more. Add the cabbage and carrots and cook for 2 minutes more, or until the cabbage is slightly wilted. Add the soy sauce mixture and cook for 1 minute more, or until the liquid thickens slightly and coats the vegetables. Add the pepper and stir. Transfer to a plate to cool.

■ Pour oil to a depth of 1 inch in a deep skillet or Dutch oven. Heat on medium to 340° to 350°F.

■ Working with one wrapper at a time, spread ¼ to ⅓ cup of the vegetable filling in the center, leaving a 1½-inch border on each side. Fold the corner nearest you over the filling. Fold the two sides over the center. Moisten the edge of the remaining corner with a wet fingertip, tightly roll toward the moistened edge, and press to seal. Repeat with the remaining wrappers and filling.

■ When the oil reaches the desired temperature, lower four or five egg rolls in batches into the oil. Fry one side for 4 to 5 minutes, or until golden. Using long-handle tongs, turn over and fry on the other side for 4 to 5 minutes. (If the egg rolls brown too quickly, turn down the heat.)

■ Transfer to a paper towel–lined plate and set aside to cool slightly. Serve with duck or plum sauce.

Makes 5 servings.

Variations

For nonvegetarian:

Pork and Veggie Egg Rolls

■ In a large skillet over medium heat, cook ½ pound of ground pork for 3 to 4 minutes, or until browned and no longer pink, breaking it up with a wooden spoon.

■ Push the meat to the side of the pan and proceed as at left, heating the oil and adding the vegetables to the pan. Add soy sauce, to taste.

Shrimp and Veggie Egg Rolls

■ Add 1 cup of chopped, cooked shrimp to the vegetables 1 minute before removing the mixture from the heat. Add soy sauce, to taste.

Egg Fried Rice

A great way to use leftover rice.

2½ tablespoons vegetable oil, divided
½ teaspoon sesame oil
1½ cups fresh or frozen and thawed green peas
4 scallions, chopped
1 medium carrot, grated
2 cloves garlic, minced
3 to 4 cups cooked long-grain rice that has been refrigerated
3 large eggs
soy sauce, to taste

■ Heat 2 tablespoons of vegetable oil and the sesame oil in a large, preferably nonstick, skillet or wok over medium heat, add the peas, scallions, carrot, and garlic and cook for 2 minutes, stirring often. Add the rice and cook for 3 to 4 minutes, or until heated through, stirring often.

■ In a small bowl, lightly beat the eggs.

■ Move the rice to the perimeter of the skillet and add the remaining ½ tablespoon of oil in the center. Pour the eggs into the center and stir constantly, or until they are soft-cooked. Break up the eggs and stir into the rice, while cooking for 1 to 2 minutes more, or until all ingredients are heated through. Add soy sauce, to taste, and stir.

Makes 4 to 6 servings.

Variation

For nonvegetarian Egg Fried Rice:

■ Prepare the rice with chicken or beef stock.

■ Add 1 to 2 cups thinly sliced, cooked chicken or beef, or coarsely chopped shrimp, during the last few minutes of cooking.

THE LONG AND SHORT OF RICE

When cooked, long-grain rice tends to be fluffier, drier, and less sticky than short-grain types, which makes it a good choice to use as a side dish. You can find several kinds of long-grain rice, including American, basmati, and jasmine.

Triple-Play Grilled Cheese

The combination is a home run.

2 slices fresh sourdough or good sandwich bread (about ½-inch thick)
4 to 5 teaspoons cream cheese, softened and divided
Dijon-style mustard, to taste
⅓ cup loosely packed shredded extra sharp cheddar cheese
2 to 3 very thin slices of ripe tomato (optional)
⅓ cup loosely packed shredded Havarti cheese
1 tablespoon butter, softened

■ Smear one slice of bread with half of the cream cheese and mustard, to taste. Cover with the cheddar cheese. Lay on two or three slices of tomato, if using. Cover with Havarti cheese. Smear the other slice of bread with the remaining cream cheese and more mustard, if desired, and place it, cream cheese side down, on the Havarti cheese.

■ Heat a heavy, preferably cast iron, skillet over medium heat. Spread the butter on the dry side of each of the bread slices.

■ Place the sandwich in the skillet and cook for 2 to 2½ minutes on each side, or until golden brown all over and the cheese starts to ooze. If desired, after cooking for 1 minute, cover the skillet; this helps to melt the cheese. (Do not cover completely, or moisture will form and the bread will soften.)

Makes 1 serving.

Variations

Tomato and Pesto Grilled Cheese

■ Use pesto in place of, or in addition to, cream cheese in the sandwich and use more or thicker tomato slices.

Turkey and Pickles Grilled Cheese

■ Lay several thin slices of cooked turkey and bread-and-butter pickles between the cheese layers.

Eggplant, Tomato, and Rice Casserole

A simple layered casserole made even more delicious by using fresh summer produce

4 large ripe tomatoes
⅓ cup olive oil
1 large eggplant, peeled and cubed
1 medium onion, finely chopped
salt, to taste, plus ½ teaspoon
2 cloves garlic, minced
1 teaspoon dried basil or 1 tablespoon chopped fresh basil
½ teaspoon dried oregano
freshly ground black pepper, to taste
3 cups cooked rice (preferably cooked in vegetable stock), warm or at room temperature
1 cup shredded sharp cheddar cheese or mozzarella cheese

■ Preheat the oven to 375°F.

■ Core and coarsely chop enough of the tomatoes to make 3 cups. Thinly slice the remaining whole tomatoes.

■ Heat the olive oil in a large, preferably nonstick, skillet over medium heat and add the eggplant, onion, and salt, to taste. Cover and cook for 4 to 6 minutes, or until the eggplant softens, stirring occasionally. Add the garlic and cook for 1 minute more. Add the chopped tomatoes, basil, oregano, a scant ½ teaspoon of salt, and pepper, to taste. Cover and cook until the mixture is saucy, about 5 minutes. Remove from the heat.

■ Oil a medium casserole. Spread half of the eggplant mixture on the bottom. Cover with half of the rice, the remaining eggplant, and the remaining rice. Lay the tomato slices on the rice. Sprinkle with cheese. Bake for 40 minutes, or until heated through.

Makes 6 servings.

Color Fast

• *Eggplant flesh will darken after it is exposed to air; dip slices in lemon juice to slow the process.*

• *Avoid cooking eggplant in aluminum pots or pans, which will cause the food to become discolored.*

Ratatouille Poached Eggs

This old favorite is new again when served with poached eggs.

¼ cup olive oil
1 medium onion, finely chopped
1 medium zucchini, cut in a ¼-inch dice
2 cups peeled, finely diced eggplant
2 cloves garlic, minced
½ teaspoon paprika
2 cups finely diced plum tomatoes
salt and freshly ground black pepper, to taste
balsamic vinegar, to taste
8 teaspoons pesto
4 large eggs
chopped fresh parsley, for garnish
chopped pitted olives, for garnish

■ Heat the oil in a large, nonreactive skillet over medium heat, add the onion, and cook for 3 to 4 minutes, or until soft. Add the zucchini and eggplant and cook for 3 to 4 minutes more, or until soft. Add the garlic and paprika and cook for 1 minute. Add the tomatoes and bring to a simmer. Add salt, pepper, and balsamic vinegar, to taste, and simmer for 7 to 8 minutes.

■ With the back of a large spoon, make four depressions in the ratatouille. Drop 2 teaspoons of pesto into each. One at a time, crack each egg into a small bowl, then slide the egg into a depression. Cover the skillet and cook for 4 to 6 minutes, or until the eggs are done to your liking. Garnish with parsley and olives before serving.

Makes 4 servings.

Potato and Onion Pizza
recipe on page 194

pizzas &
savory pies

Pizza Margherita

This is pizza in its most basic or, as some would say, best form.

Topping:
5 to 7 tablespoons olive oil, divided
1 medium onion, chopped
3 cloves garlic, minced
4 cups diced fresh tomatoes
¼ teaspoon sugar, or to taste

salt and freshly ground black pepper,
to taste
¼ cup loosely packed fresh basil
leaves, cut in thin strips
¾ to 1 pound fresh mozzarella
cheese, sliced ⅛-inch thick

For crust:
- Pizza Dough (page 222) or your favorite, prepared as directed.
- Lightly flour a counter or work surface.
- When the dough has doubled, punch it down and turn it out onto the work surface. Divide in half and knead into two balls. Let rest for 5 minutes.
- Preheat the oven to 425°F. Lightly dust two large baking sheets with cornmeal.

For topping:
- Heat 3 tablespoons of olive oil in a large, nonreactive skillet over medium heat. Add the onion and cook for 7 to 8 minutes, or until soft. Add the garlic and tomatoes and stir well. Cover and cook the tomatoes for 6 to 7 minutes, or until soft and saucy, stirring occasionally. Remove the cover and add the sugar, salt, and pepper, to taste. Remove from the heat and add the basil.

To assemble:
- Working with one ball of dough at a time, roll it into a thin, 12½- to 13-inch circle.
- Transfer to a baking sheet. Pinch the edge of the dough to make it slightly higher than the center. Spread on it half of the tomato sauce, followed by half of the sliced mozzarella. Drizzle with 1 to 2 tablespoons of olive oil, then dust with black pepper. Repeat for the other ball of dough. Let rest for 5 minutes.
- If your oven is large enough, bake the pizzas together, on separate oven racks, for 20 to 23 minutes, or until the crust is golden brown around the edges, switching positions halfway through.
- Transfer to a cooling rack for at least 5 minutes.
- Transfer to a large cutting board, then slice and serve.

Makes 6 or more servings.

> **So long as you have food in your mouth, you have solved all questions for the time being.**
>
> *–Franz Kafka,*
> *Austrian writer*
> *(1883–1924)*

Spinach and Meatball Pizza

Topping:
2½ tablespoons olive oil
1 large onion, halved and thinly sliced
2 cloves garlic, minced
½ pound baby spinach, coarsely
   chopped

1 cup tomato sauce
3 cups sliced, fully cooked meatballs,
   store-bought or homemade
   (page 24)
3 cups shredded mozzarella cheese
½ cup crumbled feta cheese

For crust:
- Pizza Dough (page 222) or your favorite, prepared as directed.
- Lightly flour a counter or work surface.
- When the dough has doubled, punch it down and turn it out onto the work surface. Divide in half and knead into two balls. Let rest for 5 minutes.
- Preheat the oven to 425°F. Lightly dust two large baking sheets with cornmeal.

For topping:
- Heat the olive oil in a large skillet over medium heat. Add the onion and cook for 7 to 8 minutes, or until soft. Add the garlic and spinach, stir, and cook for 2 to 3 minutes, or until the spinach is wilted but not thoroughly cooked. Set aside.

To assemble:
- Working with one ball of dough at a time, roll it into a thin, 12½- to 13-inch circle.
- Transfer to a baking sheet. Pinch the edge of the dough so that it's slightly higher than the center. Spread on it half of the tomato sauce. Distribute half of the spinach mixture, half of the meatballs, half of the mozzarella, and half of the feta cheese on it, in that order. Repeat for the other ball of dough. Let rest for 5 minutes.
- If your oven is large enough, bake the pizzas together, on separate oven racks, for 20 to 23 minutes, or until the crust is golden brown around the edges, switching positions halfway through.
- Transfer to a cooling rack for at least 5 minutes.
- Transfer to a large cutting board, then slice and serve.

Makes 6 or more servings.

Topping Ideas

For a change of pace, try goat cheese or feta instead of mozzarella. Mix meat and fruit, such as ham and pineapple.

Pesto, Tomato, and Zucchini Pizza

A fresh-from-the-garden pizza, whether you grow your own or buy at the farmers' market

ALL SQUARED AWAY

Freeze pesto in ice cube trays. Then, transfer the pesto cubes to resealable plastic bags. Pesto can be kept frozen for up to 6 months.

Topping:

2 tablespoons olive oil

2 small or 1 medium zucchini, sliced ⅛-inch thick (on the diagonal, if small)

salt, to taste

½ cup pesto

2 large, ripe tomatoes, cored, halved, seeded, and sliced about ⅛-inch thick

freshly ground black pepper, to taste

1 cup freshly grated Parmesan cheese, divided

For crust:

- Pizza Dough (page 222) or your favorite, prepared as directed.

- Lightly flour a counter or work surface.

- When the dough has doubled, punch it down and turn it out onto the work surface. Divide in half and knead into two balls. Let rest for 5 minutes.

- Preheat the oven to 425°F. Lightly dust two large baking sheets with cornmeal.

For topping:

- Heat the olive oil in a skillet over medium heat. Add the zucchini and salt, to taste, and cook for 2 minutes, or until slightly soft, stirring often. Set aside.

To assemble:

- Working with one ball of dough at a time, roll it into a thin, 12½- to 13-inch circle.

- Transfer to a baking sheet. Pinch the edge of the dough so that it's slightly higher than the center. Spread half of the pesto in the center. Cover with half of the tomato slices and sprinkle with salt and pepper, to taste. Arrange half of the zucchini slices between the tomatoes, then sprinkle ¼ cup of the Parmesan cheese evenly on top. Repeat for the other ball of dough.

- If your oven is large enough, bake the pizzas together, on separate oven racks, for 20 to 23 minutes, or until the crust is golden brown around the edges, switching positions halfway through.

- Transfer to a cooling rack and sprinkle each pizza with ¼ cup of Parmesan cheese. Cool for at least 5 minutes.

- Transfer to a large cutting board, then slice and serve.

Makes 2 pizzas or 6 or more servings.

Portobello Mushroom and Vidalia Onion Pizza

Meaty portobellos and sweet Vidalias make this one memorable pie.

Topping:

6 or 7 large portobello mushrooms

3 tablespoons olive oil, divided,
   plus more for the pizza

3 tablespoons balsamic vinegar, divided

1 very large Vidalia onion, thinly sliced

2 cloves garlic, thinly sliced

⅔ cup freshly grated Parmesan cheese

handful fresh basil leaves, chopped

2 cups shredded mozzarella cheese

For crust:

■ Pizza Dough (page 222) or your favorite, prepared as directed.

■ Lightly flour a counter or work surface.

■ When the dough has doubled, punch it down and turn it out onto the work surface. Divide in half and knead briefly. Let rest for 5 minutes.

■ Preheat the oven to 425° F. Lightly dust 2 large baking sheets with cornmeal.

For topping:

■ Remove the stems from the mushrooms and brush the surfaces with a paper towel. Reserve the stems for another use. Cut the whole caps into ¼- to ⅓-inch-thick slices. Set aside.

■ Heat 1½ tablespoons of the olive oil in a large skillet over medium heat. Add the sliced mushrooms and sauté for 6 to 7 minutes, stirring often. Add 1½ tablespoons of the vinegar and cook for 30 seconds, stirring, then transfer the mushrooms to a large plate or bowl.

■ Add the remaining oil to the skillet, heat, then add the onion. Cook for 7 to 8 minutes, or until golden, stirring often. Add the garlic and cook for 1 minute. Add the remaining vinegar, cook for 30 seconds more, then remove from the heat.

To assemble:

■ Working with one piece of dough at a time, roll into a thin, 13- to 14-inch oblong.

■ Transfer to a baking sheet. Pinch the edge of the dough so that it's slightly higher than the center. Brush it lightly with olive oil. Cover with half of the mushrooms and onions. Sprinkle with ⅓ cup of Parmesan cheese, half of the basil, then half of the mozzarella. Set aside for 5 minutes. Repeat for the other ball of dough.

■ If your oven is large enough, bake the pizzas together, on separate oven racks, for 20 to 23 minutes, or until the crust is golden around the edges, switching positions halfway through.

■ Transfer to a cooling rack for 5 minutes.

■ Transfer to a cutting board, then slice and serve.

Makes 2 pizzas or 6 or more servings.

An empty belly is the best cook.

–Estonian proverb

Potato and Onion Pizza

Potatoes, sweet onions, two cheeses, and rosemary—a scrumptious combination

Topping:

7 medium red-skinned potatoes, peeled and sliced
 ⅛-inch thick

3 tablespoons unsalted butter

2 large Vidalia or other sweet onions, halved
 and thinly sliced

6 cloves garlic, peeled and thinly sliced

salt and freshly ground black pepper, to taste

½ cup freshly grated Parmesan cheese

1 tablespoon chopped fresh rosemary

½ cup heavy cream

2 to 3 cups shredded fontina cheese

For crust:

■ Pizza Dough (page 222) or your favorite, prepared as directed.

■ Lightly flour a counter or work surface.

■ When the dough has doubled, punch it down and turn it out onto the work surface. Divide in half and knead into two balls. Let rest for 5 minutes.

■ Preheat the oven to 425°F. Lightly dust two baking sheets with cornmeal.

For topping:

■ Lightly oil a large casserole.

■ Place the sliced potatoes in a large saucepan and cover with lightly salted water. Over high heat, bring to a boil, reduce heat, and simmer for 4 minutes, or until the potatoes are almost cooked through but firm, stirring occasionally. Drain, then spread the slices in the prepared casserole to cool.

■ Melt the butter in a skillet over medium heat. Add the onion and cook for 7 to 8 minutes, or until soft, stirring often. Add the garlic and cook for 3 to 4 minutes, or until the onions start to turn golden. Set aside.

To assemble:

■ Working with one ball of dough at a time, roll it into a thin, 12½- to 13-inch circle.

■ Transfer to a baking sheet. Pinch the edge of the dough so that it's slightly higher than the center. Layer on half of the onions, then half of the potatoes, overlapping them slightly. Sprinkle with salt and pepper, to taste. Sprinkle with half of the Parmesan cheese and half of the rosemary. Drizzle with half of the cream. Repeat for the other half of the dough.

■ If your oven is large enough, bake the pizzas together, on separate oven racks, for 20 to 23 minutes, or until the crust is golden brown around the edges. Halfway through baking, remove from the oven and sprinkle with the fontina cheese. Return to the oven, switching racks.

■ Transfer to a cooling rack briefly before serving.

Makes 2 pizzas or 6 or more servings.

Deep-Dish Veggie and Sausage Pizza

Stacked with cheese and veggies and sausage and more cheese, it's a handful.

Pans for Pan Pizza

You can bake deep-dish pizza in a variety of pans:

• *any that measure 12 to 16 inches in diameter*

• *a 9-inch springform pan*

• *a 13- to 14-inch round pan*

• *a 13x9-inch baking pan*

If you are not able to roll your dough large enough to run it up the sides and over the edge of the pan, bank it up the sides as high as you can to contain the filling.

Topping:
3 tablespoons olive oil
1 large green or red bell pepper, sliced
1 large onion, halved and sliced
2 cloves garlic, minced
2 cups thickly sliced mushroom caps
2 cups seeded and diced fresh tomatoes
2 teaspoons dried basil

1 pound Italian sausage, fully cooked and thinly sliced or casings removed and in chunks
salt and freshly ground black pepper, to taste
3 cups shredded mozzarella cheese
2 cups tomato sauce
$\frac{2}{3}$ cup freshly grated Parmesan cheese

For crust:

■ Pizza Dough (page 222) or your favorite, prepared as directed.

■ Lightly butter two 9-inch round cake pans or other pans (see box).

■ When the dough has doubled, punch it down and turn it out onto a floured surface. Divide in half and knead into two balls. Let rest for 5 minutes.

■ Preheat the oven to 425°F. Lightly flour a counter or work surface.

For topping:

■ Heat the olive oil in a large skillet over medium heat. Add the bell pepper and onion and cook for 5 minutes, or until soft. Add the garlic and mushrooms and cook for 5 to 7 minutes, or until most of the liquid in the pan cooks off. Add the tomatoes, basil, sausage, and salt and pepper, to taste, and stir. Remove from the heat.

To assemble:

■ Working with one ball of dough at a time, roll it into a 13-inch circle.

■ Drape the dough in a prepared pan, letting the edge hang slightly over the side. Gently tuck the dough into the bottom of the pan. Spread half of the mozzarella cheese in the center. Cover with half of the tomato sauce, followed by half of the veggie and sausage mixture. Sprinkle with half of the Parmesan cheese. Fold the edge of the dough back over the filling. Repeat for the other half of dough.

■ Bake on the center oven rack for 30 to 35 minutes, or until the crust is deeply browned and the filling is bubbling.

■ Transfer to a cooling rack for 10 to 15 minutes, then slice and serve. Do not leave the pizza in the pan for more than 20 minutes, or the crust will trap moisture and become soft.

Makes 2 pizzas or 6 servings.

Eggplant Parmesan Flatbread

Several layers melt into one on thin crust.

Topping:

olive oil

1 large eggplant

salt, to taste

1 medium onion, halved and thinly sliced

2 cups (or more) tomato sauce

1 cup freshly grated Parmesan cheese

½ pound sliced fresh mozzarella cheese

chopped fresh basil, to taste

black pepper, to taste

For crust:

■ Wheaten Flatbread Dough (page 223).

■ Preheat the oven to 425°F. Lightly oil two large baking sheets and dust them with cornmeal.

■ Remove the dough from the refrigerator and set aside for 15 minutes.

■ Turn the dough out onto a lightly floured surface and knead for 30 seconds. Divide in half and let rest for 5 minutes. Working with one piece of dough at a time, roll to about ⅛-inch thick. Transfer to the prepared baking sheets.

For topping:

■ Cut the eggplant into ¼-inch-thick slices.

■ Pour enough olive oil into one or two large skillets to create a thick film, then add as many eggplant slices as will fit in a single layer. Salt, to taste. Cover with lids or aluminum foil and cook for 3 to 5 minutes. Add more oil, then turn the slices and cook for 3 to 5 minutes more, or until fork-soft but not falling apart.

■ Transfer to a plate. Repeat with the remaining eggplant.

■ Add a little more oil to one of the skillets, add the onion, stir, and cook for 6 minutes, or until soft. Remove from the heat.

To assemble:

■ Spread the dough with or dab on ½ cup of tomato sauce (or more, to taste). Arrange the eggplant slices on top, overlapping them slightly. (You may not use all of the eggplant.) Spread with or dab on more sauce. Cover with half of the onions, half of the cheeses, the basil, and pepper, to taste. Repeat with the other half of dough.

■ Bake one flatbread at a time on the center oven rack for 20 to 22 minutes, or until the crust is golden brown.

■ Transfer to a cooling rack for 5 minutes.

■ Transfer to a cutting board, slice, and serve.

Makes 2 flatbreads or 6 servings.

Barbecue Bacon, Shrimp, and Blue Cheese Flatbread

Because you'll need only half a batch of dough, double the topping ingredients and make two or try another type of flatbread.

DISAPPEARING ACT

To devein a shrimp, use a paring knife to make a thin slice down the middle of the back to expose the shrimp's black vein. Lift it out with the tip of the knife.

Topping:
⅓ cup barbecue sauce
1 large, ripe tomato, halved, seeded, and thinly sliced
freshly ground black pepper, to taste
10 to 12 shelled, deveined, and cooked medium shrimp, at room temperature
¾ cup crumbled blue cheese
¾ cup shredded Havarti, Muenster, mild cheddar, or other mild cheese
4 slices crisp-cooked bacon, crumbled

For crust:
■ Wheaten Flatbread Dough (page 223).

■ Preheat the oven to 425°F. Lightly oil a large baking sheet and dust it with cornmeal.

■ Turn the dough out onto a lightly floured surface and knead for 30 seconds. Divide in half. Let one half rest for 5 minutes and refrigerate the other half, if not using. (It will keep in the refrigerator for up to 3 days.) Roll the dough to a ⅛-inch thickness.

■ Transfer to the prepared baking sheet.

To assemble:
■ Spread the barbecue sauce on the dough, then cover with the tomatoes. Dust with pepper, to taste.

■ Bake on the center oven rack for 12 minutes.

■ Remove the flatbread from the oven and sprinkle with the shrimp, cheeses, and bacon. Return to the oven and bake for 10 to 12 minutes more, or until the crust is golden brown.

■ Transfer to a cooling rack for 5 minutes.

■ Transfer to a cutting board, slice, and serve.

Makes 3 to 4 servings.

Sausage, Broccoli, and Cheese Calzone

Filling:

3 tablespoons olive oil

1 large onion, halved and thinly sliced

¾ to 1 pound cooked hot or mild Italian sausage, cut into bite-size pieces

2 cloves garlic, thinly sliced

1 cup tomato sauce, plus extra to serve on the side

salt and freshly ground black pepper, to taste

2 cups small broccoli florets

½ cup freshly grated Parmesan cheese

2 cups shredded cheese (mozzarella, provolone, or a combination)

For crust:

▪ Pizza Dough (page 222), divided as instructed below, or your favorite, prepared as directed.

▪ Lightly flour a counter or work surface. When the dough has doubled, punch it down and turn it out onto the work surface. Divide in half and knead briefly. Let rest for 5 minutes.

▪ Preheat the oven to 425°F. Dust a large baking sheet with cornmeal. Lightly flour a counter or work surface.

For filling:

▪ Heat the olive oil in a large saucepan over medium heat. Add the onion and cook for 5 to 6 minutes, or until soft, stirring often. Add the sausage and garlic and cook for 2 minutes more. Add the tomato sauce, stir, and cook until heated through. Add salt and pepper, to taste. Remove from the heat, add the broccoli, stir to mix, and set aside.

To assemble:

▪ Working with one ball of dough at a time on the work surface, roll it into a 12x10-inch oblong. Draw an imaginary line lengthwise down the center of the dough. Sprinkle one side with half of the Parmesan cheese, leaving a 1-inch border. Spread half of the sausage–broccoli filling over the cheese. Sprinkle with half of the mozzarella. Using a wet fingertip, lightly moisten the edge of the dough. Lift the uncovered half of the dough over the filling and line up the edges (a second pair of hands helps). Pinch the edges to seal, then roll the seam over to make a ropelike edge.

▪ Place on one side of the baking sheet. With a paring knife, make three or four holes, or steam vents. Repeat with the other ball of dough. Let rest for 5 minutes.

▪ Bake on the center oven rack for 23 to 25 minutes, or until golden.

▪ Transfer to a cooling rack for at least 10 minutes. Serve with extra tomato sauce, warmed, if desired.

Makes 2 calzones or 6 servings.

> **After a good dinner one can forgive anybody, even one's own relations.**
>
> *–Oscar Wilde, Irish writer (1854–1900)*

Kale and Three-Cheese Calzone

Hail, kale! It adds great flavor to this cheesy dish.

Filling:

1 box (10 ounces) frozen chopped kale
(or 1 to 1¼ pounds fresh; see box)

1½ cups shredded mozzarella cheese

1 cup crumbled feta cheese

⅔ cup freshly grated Parmesan
cheese

2 tablespoons chopped fresh basil
or 2 teaspoons dried basil

freshly ground black pepper, to taste

2½ tablespoons olive oil

1 large onion, halved and thinly sliced

½ cup tomato sauce, plus extra to
serve on the side

For crust:

■ Pizza Dough (page 222) or your favorite, prepared as directed.

■ Dust a large baking sheet with cornmeal. Lightly flour a counter or work surface.

■ When the dough has doubled, punch it down, turn it out onto the work surface, and knead briefly. Divide in half and knead into two balls. Let rest for 5 minutes.

■ Preheat the oven to 425°F.

For filling:

■ Cook the kale according to the package directions and drain. When the kale is cool enough to handle, squeeze out most of the excess liquid.

■ Transfer to a large bowl and add the cheeses, basil, and pepper, to taste.

■ Heat the olive oil in a large skillet over medium heat. Add the onion and cook for 9 to 10 minutes, or until soft and golden. Remove from the heat.

To assemble:

■ Working with one ball of dough at a time, roll it into a 12x10-inch oblong. Draw an imaginary line lengthwise down the center and pile half of the kale-and-cheese mixture on one side, leaving a 1-inch border. Spread with half of the onions and dot with ¼ cup of the tomato sauce. Using a wet fingertip, lightly moisten the edge of the dough. Lift the uncovered half of the dough over the filling and line up the edges (a second pair of hands helps). Pinch the edges to seal, then roll the seam over to make a ropelike edge.

■ Place on one side of the baking sheet. With a paring knife, make three or four holes, or steam vents. Repeat with the other ball of dough. Let them rest for 5 minutes.

■ Bake on the center oven rack for 23 to 25 minutes, or until golden.

■ Transfer to a cooling rack for at least 10 minutes. Serve with the remaining tomato sauce, warmed, if desired.

Makes 2 calzones or 6 servings.

How to Prepare Fresh Kale

• Strip the leaves from the stems. Discard the stems.

• Place the leaves in a large bowl of water.

Agitate the leaves to remove any grit or dirt.

• Put about 1 inch of water in a large, nonreactive pot and

add the leaves. Bring to a boil, reduce the heat, salt to taste, and cover. Cook at a low boil for 15 minutes, or until tender,

stirring occasionally.

• Drain in a colander and cool. Squeeze out most of the liquid, then chop and use.

Baked Reuben Calzone

A baked version of the famous sandwich

Filling:

3 tablespoons unsalted butter, divided

½ large onion, thinly sliced

1½ cups shredded Swiss cheese

3 tablespoons Russian or Thousand Island dressing

¼ pound thinly sliced corned beef or turkey breast

1 cup sauerkraut, squeezed to remove excess moisture

For crust:

▪ Pizza Dough (page 222), divided as instructed below, or your favorite, prepared as directed.

▪ Dust a large baking sheet with cornmeal. Lightly flour a counter or work surface.

▪ When the dough has doubled, punch it down and turn it out onto the work surface. Knead briefly, then divide in half. Shape one half into a ball and let rest for 5 minutes. Freeze the other half of the dough (see page 223) for another use or double the filling ingredients and make two.

▪ Preheat the oven to 400°F.

For filling:

▪ Melt 2 tablespoons of the butter in a skillet over medium heat. Add the onion and cook for 10 minutes, or until soft and golden, stirring often. Remove from the heat.

To assemble:

▪ Roll the dough into a 14x8-inch rectangle. Draw an imaginary line widthwise across the center, and cover one half with half of the cheese, leaving a 1-inch border. Spread on the onions and dot with the dressing. Layer on the meat, sauerkraut, and remaining cheese. Using a wet fingertip, lightly moisten the edge of the dough. Lift the uncovered half of the dough over the filling and line up the edges (a second pair of hands helps). Pinch the edges to seal, then roll the seam over to make a ropelike edge.

▪ Place on the prepared baking sheet. With a paring knife, make three or four holes, or steam vents. Let rest for 5 minutes.

▪ Bake on the center oven rack for 23 to 25 minutes, or until golden.

▪ Transfer to a cooling rack. Melt the remaining 1 tablespoon of butter and, using a pastry brush, brush it on the dough. Cool for at least 10 minutes before slicing.

Makes 3 servings.

REUBEN'S FATHER?

Food historians agree that the Reuben sandwich can be traced back to the 1920s. They do not, however, agree on who the sandwich was named for—Reuben Kulakofsky of Omaha, Nebraska, or Arnold Reuben of New York City.

Chicken Parmesan Potpie

Use any combination of cooked vegetables on hand. This recipe can also be baked as individual potpies.

Filling:
4 tablespoons (½ stick)
   unsalted butter
1 medium onion, chopped
2 stalks celery, chopped
⅓ cup all-purpose flour
1¼ cups chicken or turkey stock

1¼ cups milk or half-and-half
½ teaspoon crumbled or
   powdered sage
½ teaspoon dried thyme
2½ cups diced, cooked chicken
2½ cups cooked vegetables (corn,
   green beans, peas, or other),
   alone or in combination

½ cup freshly grated Parmesan
   cheese, divided
salt and freshly ground black
   pepper, to taste
1 egg beaten with 1 tablespoon
   milk, for glaze

For crust:

■ Food Processor Tart Dough (page 225), divided as instructed below, or your favorite, prepared as directed.

■ Turn the dough onto a lightly floured counter or work surface. Pack it together, then divide in half. Knead one-half of it two or three times, then flatten into a ½-inch-thick disk. Wrap in plastic wrap and refrigerate for 1 to 2 hours. Repeat with the other half, then wrap, refrigerate, and use within 2 days (or place in a plastic freezer bag and freeze for up to 2 months).

For filling:

■ Melt the butter in a large saucepan over medium-low heat. Add the onion and celery, stir, cover, and cook for 6 to 7 minutes, or until soft, stirring occasionally. Add the flour, increase the heat to medium, and cook for 1 minute, stirring. Add the stock and whisk to blend. As the sauce starts to thicken, add the milk, sage, and thyme and whisk to blend. Add the chicken and vegetables and continue to cook for 3 to 4 minutes, or until heated through, stirring. Add ⅓ cup of the Parmesan cheese and remove from the heat. Add salt and pepper, to taste.

■ Butter a shallow 2- to 2½-quart baking dish. Transfer the filling to the dish and smooth the top. Sprinkle with the remaining Parmesan cheese. Set aside for 15 minutes.

■ Preheat the oven to 400°F.

■ On a sheet of wax paper, roll the pastry to be slightly larger than the dish. Invert the pastry over the filling and peel off the paper. Tuck the pastry edges into the dish. With a paring knife, make several cuts, or steam vents, in the pastry. Brush the pastry with the egg glaze. (If the baking dish is quite full, place it on an aluminum foil–lined baking sheet to catch spillovers.)

■ Bake on the center oven rack for 40 minutes, or until golden and bubbling.

Makes 6 servings.

There is nothing better on a cold wintry day than a properly made pot pie.

—Craig Claiborne, American food writer
(1920–2000)

Turkey Potpies With Stuffing Crumb Topping

Ideal for Thanksgiving leftovers, but why wait? Roast a breast and you're halfway to pie.

Filling:
¾ cup diced carrots
¾ cup fresh or frozen peas
salt, to taste
3½ tablespoons unsalted butter
1 small onion, finely chopped

3 tablespoons all-purpose flour
1⅓ cups chicken or turkey stock
¾ cup half-and-half or light cream
¾ teaspoon dried thyme
3 cups diced, cooked turkey
freshly ground black pepper, to taste

Topping:
1 cup dry stuffing mix
4 tablespoons (½ stick) unsalted
butter

For crust:

■ Food Processor Tart Dough (page 225) or your favorite, prepared as directed.

■ Turn the dough out onto a lightly floured counter or work surface. Pack it together, then knead two or three times. Divide into six equal pieces and shape into balls. Flatten each ball into a ½-inch-thick disk. Wrap in plastic and refrigerate for 1 to 2 hours.

For filling:

■ Put the carrots and peas into a small saucepan; cover with water; salt, to taste; and bring to a boil. Cook for 5 to 7 minutes, or until tender. Drain and transfer to a large bowl.

■ Melt the butter in a large saucepan over medium heat, add the onion, and cook for 5 minutes, or until soft. Add the flour and cook for 1 minute, stirring. Add the stock and whisk to blend. When the sauce becomes thick, add the half-and-half and thyme and whisk to blend. Simmer for 3 to 4 minutes, or until it has full-bodied consistency, whisking often.

■ Pour into the bowl with the vegetables, add the turkey, and stir. Sprinkle with salt and pepper, to taste.

■ Set aside six 1-cup baking dishes or pie pans.

■ Working with one ball of dough at a time on a floured work surface, roll it into a thin circle just large enough to line a baking dish and lay it in. Repeat with the remaining balls of dough. Refrigerate the pie shells for 20 minutes.

■ Preheat the oven to 375°F.

■ Divide the filling among the pie shells (not to overflowing). Place on the center rack and bake for 25 minutes.

For topping:

■ Put the stuffing mix into a plastic freezer bag and, using a rolling pin, crush it into crumbs.

■ Melt the butter in a saucepan over medium-low heat. Add the crushed crumbs and cook for 30 to 60 seconds, or until the butter is absorbed, stirring. Remove from the heat.

■ Remove the pies from the oven and sprinkle each with crumbs. (If desired, put the pies on a baking sheet to catch spills.) Reduce the heat to 350°F and bake for 15 to 20 minutes more, or until golden and bubbling.

■ Transfer to a cooling rack for 10 minutes before serving.

Makes 6 servings.

Meat Pie

Similar to the French Canadian tourtière but with a few nontraditional touches.

Filling:
2½ tablespoons vegetable oil
1 medium onion, finely chopped
2 stalks celery, finely chopped
2 cloves garlic, minced
1½ to 1¾ pounds ground pork or
    ground pork and ground beef,
    combined, in any proportion

1½ cups beef stock
1 large baking potato, peeled and
    cut into ¼-inch dice
1 cup carrots, finely diced
¾ teaspoon regular or smoked
    paprika
¾ teaspoon dried thyme
½ teaspoon salt plus more, to taste
¼ teaspoon cinnamon

¼ teaspoon ground cloves
¼ teaspoon freshly ground
    black pepper
⅓ cup tomato-based chili sauce
1 teaspoon Worcestershire sauce
1 teaspoon Dijon-style mustard
1 egg beaten with 1 tablespoon milk,
    for glaze

For crust:

■ 2 batches of All-Purpose Pie Dough (page 224), refrigerated, or your favorite, prepared as directed.

■ Dust a sheet of wax paper with flour and roll one batch of dough into a 13- to 13½-inch circle. Invert and center it over a 9½- to 10-inch deep-dish pie pan and peel off the paper. Tuck the dough into the sides. Wrap in plastic and refrigerate.

For filling:

■ Heat the oil in a Dutch oven or large skillet over medium heat. Add the onion and celery, and cook for 5 minutes, or until soft, stirring often. Add the garlic and meat and cook to brown the meat, breaking it up with a wooden spoon. Spoon off as much of the fat as possible. Add the stock, potato, carrots, paprika, thyme, salt, cinnamon, cloves, and pepper, stir, and bring to a simmer. Cover and simmer for 10 minutes. Add the chili sauce, Worcestershire sauce, and mustard and simmer for 10 minutes, uncovered, stirring often. When the mixture becomes thick, remove from the heat. Adjust seasonings to taste. Cool.

■ Preheat the oven to 375°F. Spread the filling in the pie shell.

■ Lightly dust a sheet of wax paper with flour and roll the other batch of dough into a 12-inch circle. Moisten the edge of the shell with a wet finger, then invert and center the dough on the pie. Peel off the paper and press the edges together to seal. With a paring knife, trim the excess dough and then make three cuts, or steam vents, in the pastry. Crimp the edge with a fork. Brush the pastry with the egg glaze.

■ Bake for 45 to 50 minutes, or until golden brown. Transfer to a cooling rack for at least 30 minutes before serving.

Makes 8 to 10 servings.

**Don't let love interfere with your appetite.
It never does with mine.**

–Anthony Trollope, English novelist (1815–82)

Crab Potpie

Individual potpies are suggested here, but this recipe can also be assembled in a single baking dish.

Filling:

1 cup peeled, finely diced, red-skinned potatoes

1 cup diced carrots

salt, to taste

4 tablespoons (½ stick) unsalted butter

1 medium onion, finely chopped

2 stalks celery, finely chopped

¼ cup all-purpose flour

2¼ teaspoons seafood seasoning (such as Old Bay)

1½ cups clam juice

1 cup light cream or half-and-half

12 to 16 ounces crabmeat

freshly ground black pepper, to taste

1 egg beaten with 1 tablespoon milk, for glaze

For crust:

■ All-Purpose Pie Dough (page 224) or your favorite, prepared as directed.

■ Turn the dough out onto a lightly floured counter or work surface. Pack together, then knead once or twice. Divide into six equal pieces and shape into balls. Flatten each ball into a ½-inch-thick disk. Wrap in plastic and refrigerate for 1 to 2 hours.

For filling:

■ Combine the potatoes and carrots in a saucepan over medium heat; add enough water to cover; salt, to taste; and bring to a boil. Cook at a simmer for 5 to 6 minutes, or until barely tender. Drain and transfer to a plate.

■ Melt the butter in a saucepan over medium heat, add the onion and celery, and cook for 5 to 6 minutes, or until soft, stirring often. Add the flour and seafood seasoning and cook for 1 minute, stirring. Add the clam juice and light cream and cook for 5 to 6 minutes, or until the sauce thickens, stirring. Add the crab and reserved vegetables and heat for 2 minutes, stirring. Add salt and pepper, to taste. Remove from the heat.

■ Butter six 1-cup baking dishes. Divide the filling among them (not to overflowing). Place the dishes on a large, aluminum foil–lined baking sheet.

■ Preheat the oven to 400°F.

■ Working with one ball of dough at a time on a lightly floured work surface, roll the pastry into circles ½ inch larger than the baking dish. Drape the pastry over the filling, tucking the edges into the dish. With a paring knife, make one or two cuts, or steam vents, in the pastry. Repeat with the remaining pastry.

■ Brush the pastry with the egg glaze. Bake for 20 minutes. Reduce the heat to 375°F and bake for 20 minutes more, or until the pastry is golden and the filling is bubbling.

■ Transfer to a cooling rack for 10 to 15 minutes before serving.

Makes 6 servings.

Vidalia Onion Pie

Vidalia onions star in this creamy pie. If they aren't available, use any sweet onion.

Filling:

3 tablespoons unsalted butter

3 large Vidalia onions, halved and thinly sliced

salt, to taste, plus ½ teaspoon

3 large eggs, at room temperature

¾ cup sour cream

½ cup half-and-half or light cream

½ teaspoon Dijon-style mustard

¼ teaspoon celery seed

freshly ground black pepper, to taste

1½ cups shredded sharp cheddar, fontina, or smoked Gouda cheese

paprika, for dusting

For crust:

■ All-Purpose Pie Dough (page 224), refrigerated, or your favorite, prepared as directed.

■ Lightly flour a counter or work surface. Roll the pastry into a 13-inch circle and line a 9½-inch deep-dish pie pan with it. Chill, partially prebake (see page 215), and cool the shell.

■ Preheat the oven to 400°F.

For filling:

■ Melt the butter in a large skillet or Dutch oven over medium heat. Add the onions and lightly salt, to taste, and cook for 12 to 15 minutes, or until the onions turn golden, stirring often. Remove from the heat.

■ In a large bowl, whisk the eggs until frothy. Add the salt, sour cream, half-and-half, mustard, celery seed, and pepper. Whisk to blend, then set aside.

■ Spread the onions in the pie shell. Pour or ladle the egg mixture over the onions. Sprinkle with the cheese, then dust with the paprika.

■ Bake on the center oven rack for 15 minutes. Reduce the heat to 350°F and bake for 30 to 35 minutes more, or until puffed, golden brown, and set (a knife inserted into the center and then removed shows no evidence of uncooked egg).

■ Transfer to a cooling rack for 30 to 45 minutes before serving.

Makes 8 to 10 servings.

How Sweet They Are!

Vidalia onions, Georgia's official vegetable, are grown in a 20-county region of the state where the climate is mild and the soil is sandy. Look for them in the market from April through mid-September.

PLUM GOOD

Plum tomatoes
have fewer seed
compartments and
a more concentrated
flavor, so they're
great for sauces.

Roasted Tomato Pie

Filling:
3 large eggs
¾ cup light cream or half-and-half
½ cup heavy cream
1 teaspoon dried basil
½ teaspoon salt
freshly ground black pepper, to taste
1½ cups shredded sharp cheddar cheese
Slow-Roasted Plum Tomatoes (page 110)
regular or smoked paprika, to taste

For crust:
■ All-Purpose Pie Dough (page 224), refrigerated, or your favorite,
prepared as directed.

■ Roll the pastry into a 13-inch circle and line a 9½-inch deep-dish
pie pan with it. Chill, partially prebake (see page 215), and cool
the shell.

■ Preheat the oven to 375°F.

For filling:
■ In a large bowl, whisk the eggs until frothy. Add the light cream,
heavy cream, basil, salt, and pepper, to taste, and whisk to blend.

■ Sprinkle a quarter of the cheese in the pie shell. Cover with a layer
of tomatoes and another quarter of the cheese. Pour or ladle the egg
mixture into the shell to barely cover the cheese. Continue the layers,
ending with cheese. (You may not need all of the tomatoes.) Dust
with paprika.

■ Bake on the center oven rack for 45 minutes, or until puffed, golden
brown, and set (a knife inserted into the center and then removed
shows no evidence of uncooked egg).

■ Transfer to a cooling rack for at least 45 minutes before serving.

Makes 8 to 10 servings.

Mexicali Corn Bread Pie

A Tex-Mex casserole with a corn bread crust

Filling:
2 tablespoons vegetable oil
1 large onion, finely chopped
1 green bell pepper, finely
    chopped
1½ pounds lean ground beef
2 cloves garlic, minced
1 packet (1 ounce) taco
    seasoning mix
1 tablespoon all-purpose flour
2 cans (14½ ounces each)
    Mexican-style diced tomatoes
    with their juice

2 cups frozen corn kernels,
    thawed, or 1 can (15 ounces)
    corn, drained
salt and freshly ground black
    pepper, to taste

Crust:
1 cup yellow cornmeal
½ cup all-purpose flour
1½ tablespoons sugar
2 teaspoons baking powder
¼ teaspoon salt
1 large egg
1 cup milk
¼ cup oil

**Baking Powder
Test**

*To test the freshness
of baking powder, add
1 teaspoon to a cup
of hot water. If the
mixture bubbles a lot,
it's good; if it doesn't,
throw it out.*

■ Preheat the oven to 400°F. Lightly oil a 3- to 3½-quart casserole.

For filling:
■ Heat the vegetable oil in a large skillet over medium heat. Add the onion and green pepper and cook for 5 minutes, stirring occasionally. Add the ground beef and cook to brown thoroughly, breaking it up with a wooden spoon. Spoon off half of the fat. Add the garlic, taco seasoning mix, and flour and cook for 30 seconds, stirring. Add the tomatoes and corn and bring the mixture to a simmer. Cover and simmer for 3 to 4 minutes, or until thick and saucy. Add salt and pepper, to taste. Spread the filling in the prepared casserole.

For crust:
■ Combine the cornmeal, flour, sugar, baking powder, and salt in a bowl.

■ In a separate bowl, combine the egg, milk, and oil and whisk to blend. Add to the cornmeal mixture and mix well. Pour over the filling.

■ Bake for 25 minutes, or until golden brown and bubbling. Serve hot.

Makes 8 servings.

Swiss Chard and Ricotta Pie

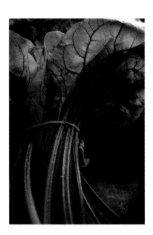

JUST CALL IT CHARD

Swiss chard's dark
green leaves grow on
white, yellow, or red
stalks. In the 19th
century, catalog
publishers dubbed it
"Swiss" to distinguish
it from French spinach.
Today it goes by
many names—leaf beet,
silver beet, and spinach
beet, among others—
yet none of them
reveals its place of
origin: Sicily.

Filling:
¾ pound fresh Swiss chard
4 slices bacon
1 medium onion, finely chopped
2 cloves garlic, minced
salt, to taste, plus ½ teaspoon
½ cup ricotta cheese

½ cup whole milk or half-and-half
3 large eggs
1 teaspoon Dijon-style mustard
freshly ground black pepper, to taste
⅔ cup freshly grated Parmesan
cheese, divided

For crust:
■ All-Purpose Pie Dough (page 224), refrigerated, or your favorite, prepared as directed.

■ Roll the pastry into a 13-inch circle and line a 9½-inch deep-dish pie pan with it. Chill, partially prebake (see page 215), and cool the shell.

■ Preheat the oven to 375°F.

For filling:
■ Cut off and discard the center stems from the Swiss chard. Coarsely chop the leaves and set aside.

■ In a skillet over medium heat, cook the bacon until crisp. Transfer to a paper towel–lined plate.

■ Add the onion to the bacon drippings in the skillet and cook for 5 minutes, or until soft. Add the garlic and chopped Swiss chard, stir, and salt, to taste. When the greens start to wilt, cover and cook for 5 to 6 minutes, or until wilted and tender, stirring occasionally. Remove from the heat.

■ Combine the ricotta cheese, milk, eggs, mustard, salt, pepper, to taste, and ⅓ cup of the Parmesan cheese in a blender and process until smooth.

■ Spread the chard mixture in the pie shell. Crumble the bacon over it. Pour or ladle the egg mixture over the bacon. Sprinkle with the remaining Parmesan cheese.

■ Bake on the center oven rack for about 45 minutes, or until puffed, golden brown, and set (a knife inserted into the center and then removed shows no evidence of uncooked egg).

■ Transfer to a cooling rack. Serve warm.

Makes 8 to 10 servings.

Fresh Corn and Cheddar Spoon Bread

A staple of Southern cuisine, spoon bread is a savory combination of corn bread and soufflé.

2 tablespoons (¼ stick) unsalted
   butter
1 small onion, minced
1½ cups fresh or frozen
   and thawed corn
3 cups milk
¾ cup fine yellow cornmeal

1 teaspoon salt
large dash cayenne pepper
2 teaspoons Dijon-style mustard
2 cups shredded, extra-sharp
   cheddar cheese
2 teaspoons chopped fresh dill
5 large eggs, separated

■ Preheat the oven to 375°F. Butter the bottom only of a 3-quart casserole or gratin dish. Get out a second casserole or baking pan, large enough to hold the first dish. Pour enough hot water into the second pan to come halfway up the sides of the first one. Place this water bath on the center oven rack.

■ Melt the butter in a skillet over medium heat. Add the onion and corn and cook gently for 4 minutes, stirring often. Set aside.

■ In a large saucepan over medium heat, combine the milk and cornmeal and whisk to blend. Using a wooden spoon, stir continuously, as the mixture thickens to a porridgelike consistency. Remove from the heat and add the salt, cayenne pepper, mustard, cheese, and dill, stirring until smooth. Add the cooked corn and onions and stir. Set aside to cool for several minutes, then add the egg yolks, stirring to blend.

■ In a large bowl, beat the egg whites until they hold stiff peaks. Fold one-third of the whites into the cornmeal mixture, until well incorporated. Fold in the remaining whites.

■ Pour the mixture into the prepared casserole and place it in the water bath. Bake for 35 minutes, or until golden and puffed. Serve immediately. (If desired, allow the water bath to cool in the oven. Most of the water will evaporate and it will be easier to remove from the oven later.)

Makes 6 to 8 servings.

> **There is no love sincerer than the love of food.**
>
> –Man and Superman,
> *by George Bernard Shaw,
> Irish-born English writer
> (1856–1950)*

Fresh Tomato Tart

Free-form pastry and summer's best tomatoes make this a work of art.

Filling:
⅓ cup pesto
½ cup finely grated Parmesan cheese, divided
1½ tablespoons fine cornmeal
4 or 5 large, ripe tomatoes, cored, halved, seeded, and sliced ¼-inch thick
salt and freshly ground black pepper, to taste
¼ cup heavy cream
basil leaves, for garnish

For crust:

■ Food Processor Tart Dough (page 225), refrigerated, or your favorite, prepared as directed.

■ Preheat the oven to 400°F. Get out a large, preferably rimless, baking sheet.

■ On a large sheet of floured parchment paper or wax paper, roll the dough into a large rectangle slightly less than ¼-inch thick. If you're using parchment paper, slide the paper and pastry onto the baking sheet and trim the paper so it fits the pan. If you're using wax paper, invert the pastry onto the pan and peel off the paper.

To assemble:

■ Spread the pesto on the pastry, leaving a 1-inch border.

■ In a small bowl, mix ¼ cup of the Parmesan cheese and the cornmeal. Sprinkle over the pesto. Layer on tomato slices (about five slices per row). Salt and pepper, to taste. Fold the edge of the pastry over the perimeter of the tomatoes.

■ Bake on the center oven rack for 20 minutes. Remove from the oven, sprinkle with the remaining Parmesan cheese, and drizzle with cream. Reduce the heat to 375°F and bake for 25 to 30 minutes more, or until the crust is golden and the filling is bubbling.

■ Transfer to a cooling rack for 5 to 10 minutes before serving. Garnish with basil leaves.

Makes 8 servings.

**Appetite,
a universal wolf.**

*—William Shakespeare,
English playwright
(1564–1616)*

SET IT ASIDE

Always allow a quiche to rest for 30 minutes to an hour before cutting or removing from the pan.

Quiche Lorraine

A French classic made with American cheddar and bacon that adds a smoky flavor

Filling:
5 strips bacon
5 large eggs
¾ cup heavy cream
¾ cup whole milk
½ teaspoon salt
freshly ground black or white pepper, to taste
pinch of nutmeg
1½ cups shredded sharp or extra-sharp cheddar cheese

For crust:
■ All-Purpose Pie Dough (page 224), refrigerated, or your favorite, prepared as directed.

■ Lightly flour a counter or work surface. Roll the pastry into a 13-inch circle and line a 9½-inch deep-dish pie pan with it. Pinch the overhanging pastry into an upstanding rim. Chill, partially prebake (see opposite), and cool the shell.

■ Preheat the oven to 400°F.

For filling:
■ In a skillet over medium heat, cook the bacon until crisp. Transfer to a paper towel–lined plate.

■ In a large bowl, whisk the eggs until frothy. Add the cream, milk, salt, pepper, and nutmeg and whisk until evenly blended. Add the cheese and stir.

■ Crumble the bacon into the pie shell. Pour or ladle the egg mixture over the bacon.

■ Bake on the center oven rack for 15 minutes. Reduce the heat to 375°F and bake for 25 to 35 minutes more, or until the quiche is golden brown and the filling is set (a knife inserted into the center and then removed shows no evidence of uncooked egg).

■ Transfer to a cooling rack for at least 1 hour before serving.

Makes 8 to 10 servings.

How to Prebake a Pie Shell

Prebaking ensures against a soggy crust, beans eliminate puffing up, and "plugging" stops leaks.

• *Put the pie shell into the freezer for 15 to 20 minutes to firm.*

• *Preheat the oven to 400°F. Tear off a 16-inch-long sheet of aluminum foil. Press it into the cold pie shell, fitting it like a glove. Fill the shell three-quarters full with dried beans. Fold the edge of the foil over the edge of the pastry to deflect heat from it.*

• *Bake on the center oven rack for 15 minutes. Lower the heat to 350°F. Remove the pie shell from the oven and lift out the foil and beans. (Do not discard the beans; they can be used multiple times.) To prevent the crust from "ballooning" off the bottom of the pan, prick the bottom with a fork six or seven times, twisting it a little. Return the shell to the oven.*

Partially Baked vs. Fully Baked

• *For a partially prebaked pie shell, bake for 10 minutes more, or until light golden brown. Transfer to a cooling rack.*

• *For a fully baked pie shell, bake for 15 to 17 minutes more, or until a rich golden color. Transfer to a cooling rack.*

The Secret to a Leakproof Prebaked Crust

• *Before filling the prebaked crust of a sweet pie, plug the holes with tiny bits of cream cheese.*

• *Before filling the prebaked crust of a savory pie or quiche, cover the holes with shavings of cheese as soon as the shell comes out of the oven; the cheese will melt over the holes.*

What's That Smell?

While cooking broccoli or cauliflower, add a piece of bread to the water to absorb any odor.

Cauliflower Quiche au Gratin

Add crumbled bacon or diced ham, if desired.

Filling:

2½ tablespoons olive oil

1 medium onion, halved and thinly sliced

2 cloves garlic, minced

2½ cups bite-size cauliflower florets

½ cup chicken stock or water

¼ teaspoon paprika

salt, to taste, plus ½ teaspoon

3 large eggs

½ cup heavy cream

½ cup light cream or half-and-half

½ teaspoon Dijon-style mustard

freshly ground black pepper, to taste

1½ cups shredded sharp cheddar cheese

2 tablespoons plain or Italian-style dried bread crumbs

1 tablespoon cold butter

For crust:

■ All-Purpose Pie Dough (page 224), refrigerated, or your favorite, prepared as directed.

■ Roll the pastry into a 13-inch circle and line a 9½-inch deep-dish pie pan with it. Chill, partially prebake (see page 215), and cool the shell.

■ Preheat the oven to 375°F.

For filling:

■ Heat the olive oil in a large skillet over medium heat. Add the onion and cook for 8 minutes, or until soft, stirring often. Add the garlic and cauliflower and cook for 1 minute. Add the stock and paprika, stir, and salt, to taste. Bring to a boil and cook, covered, for 2 to 3 minutes, or until the cauliflower is tender. Uncover and cook until the liquid boils off. Remove from the heat.

■ Whisk the eggs in a large bowl. Add the heavy cream, light cream, mustard, salt, and pepper and whisk to blend.

■ Spread the cauliflower mixture in the pie shell. Sprinkle with half of the shredded cheese. Pour or ladle the egg mixture over the cheese. Sprinkle with the remaining cheese. Sprinkle with the bread crumbs. Slice the butter into five or six slivers and lay them on top.

■ Bake on the center oven rack for 45 minutes, or until puffed, golden brown, and set (a knife inserted into the center and then removed shows no evidence of uncooked egg).

■ Transfer to a cooling rack for at least 30 minutes before slicing.

Makes 8 to 10 servings.

QUICK FIX

When cheese dehydrates in the refrigerator, grate it to use in cooking or as a topping.

'Tis the company that makes the feast.

–*Izaak Walton,*
English writer (1593–1683)

THE DISH ON DILL

Dill is a cooling and
aromatic herb. Its
fresh leaves are used
to flavor fish, eggs,
potatoes, soups,
and stews.

Smoked Salmon, Dill, and Gouda Quiche

Rich enough to turn any meal into an occasion

Filling:
2½ tablespoons unsalted butter
1 large onion, halved and thinly sliced
4 large eggs
1 cup heavy cream
½ cup milk
2 tablespoons chopped fresh dill
1½ teaspoons Dijon-style mustard
¼ teaspoon salt
freshly ground black pepper, to taste
1½ cups shredded Gouda cheese
4 to 6 ounces flaked, smoked salmon

For crust:
■ All-Purpose Pie Dough (page 224), refrigerated, or your favorite, prepared as directed.

■ Roll the pastry into a 13-inch circle and line a 9½-inch deep-dish pie pan with it. Chill, partially prebake (see page 215), and cool the shell.

■ Preheat the oven to 375°F.

For filling:
■ Melt the butter in a skillet over medium heat. Add the onion and cook for 8 to 9 minutes, or until soft and golden. Remove from the heat.

■ Whisk the eggs in a large bowl. Add the cream, milk, dill, mustard, salt, and pepper, to taste, and whisk to blend.

■ Spread the onions in the shell. Sprinkle with half of the cheese. Cover with pieces of smoked salmon. Pour or ladle the egg mixture onto the salmon. Sprinkle with the remaining cheese.

■ Bake on the center oven rack for 40 to 45 minutes, until golden brown and set (a knife inserted into the center and then removed shows no evidence of uncooked egg).

■ Serve warm, cold, or at room temperature.

Makes 8 to 10 servings.

Broccoli Polenta Quiche

This cooks up like spoon bread, a kind of moist corn bread.

Filling:
3 tablespoons unsalted butter
1 medium onion, chopped
2 cups bite-size broccoli florets
salt, to taste, plus ½ teaspoon
1¾ cups milk

⅓ cup fine yellow cornmeal
1½ cups shredded sharp
  cheddar cheese
3 large eggs, lightly beaten
1 teaspoon Dijon-syle mustard
1 teaspoon dried basil

For crust:
■ All-Purpose Pie Dough (page 224), refrigerated, or your favorite, prepared as directed.

■ Roll the pastry into a 13-inch circle and line a 9½-inch deep-dish pie pan with it. Chill, partially prebake (see page 215), and cool the shell.

■ Preheat the oven to 375°F.

For filling:
■ Melt the butter in a large skillet over medium heat. Add the onion and cook for 5 minutes, or until soft, stirring often. Add the broccoli and lightly salt, to taste, cover, and cook for 3 to 4 minutes more, or until the broccoli is almost tender, stirring occasionally. (If necessary, add 1 to 2 tablespoons of water.) Remove from the heat.

■ Combine the milk and cornmeal in a small saucepan over medium heat. Gradually bring to a boil, whisking often, and cook until it has a medium-thick consistency. Remove from the heat and transfer to a large bowl.

■ To the milk and cornmeal, add the cheese, half at a time, and stir, until melted. Let rest for 10 minutes. Add the eggs, mustard, basil, and salt and whisk to blend. Add the broccoli and onion and stir. Pour or spoon the filling into the shell.

■ Bake for 40 to 45 minutes, or until puffed, golden brown, and set (a knife inserted into the center and then removed shows no evidence of uncooked egg).

■ Transfer to a cooling rack for at least 30 minutes before serving.

Makes 8 to 10 servings.

In the Kitchen
Broccoli stalks can be as tender as the florets, if cooked. After washing the broccoli, use a vegetable peeler or paring knife to remove the tough outer layer from the stalks. Cut the stalks into bite-size pieces and drop them into an inch of boiling water for 3 to 5 minutes, or until crisp-tender.

Mexican-Style Quiche

Satisfying anytime—breakfast, lunch, or dinner

Filling:

2 cups diced red-skinned potatoes
   (peeled, if desired)

salt, to taste, plus ½ teaspoon

4 slices bacon

1 medium onion, halved and thinly sliced

1 medium green pepper, halved and
   thinly sliced

1 teaspoon chili powder

½ cup salsa

3 large eggs

1 cup light cream or half-and-half

1 teaspoon dried oregano

1½ cups shredded pepper jack or sharp
   cheddar cheese

All happiness depends on a leisurely breakfast.

–John Gunther, American writer (1901–70)

For crust:

■ All-Purpose Pie Dough (page 224), refrigerated, or your favorite, prepared as directed.

■ Roll the pastry into a 13-inch circle and line a 9½-inch deep-dish pie pan with it. Chill, partially prebake (see page 215), and cool the shell.

For filling:

■ Put the potatoes into a saucepan; add enough water to cover; salt, to taste; and bring to a boil. Reduce the heat and simmer for 6 to 7 minutes, or until the potatoes are barely tender. Drain and transfer to a plate.

■ Preheat the oven to 375°F.

■ In a skillet over medium heat, cook the bacon until crisp. Transfer to a paper towel–lined plate.

■ Add the onion and pepper to the bacon drippings in the skillet and cook over medium heat for 7 to 8 minutes, or until soft. Add the chili powder and cook for 30 seconds, stirring. Add the salsa and potatoes, stir to mix, then remove from the heat.

■ Combine the eggs, light cream, oregano, and salt in a large bowl, whisk to blend, and set aside.

■ Spread the onion mixture in the pie shell. Sprinkle with half of the cheese. Crumble the bacon over the cheese. Pour or ladle the egg mixture over the bacon. Sprinkle with the remaining cheese.

■ Bake on the center oven rack for 45 minutes, or until golden brown and set (a knife inserted into the center and then removed shows no evidence of uncooked egg).

■ Transfer to a cooling rack. Serve warm or at room temperature.

Makes 8 to 10 servings.

Pizza or Calzone Dough

Two methods, one great result.

1¼ cups lukewarm water (105° to 115°F)
½ teaspoon sugar
2¼ teaspoons (1 packet) active dry yeast
3½ cups unbleached all-purpose flour, divided
1½ tablespoons olive oil
1½ teaspoons salt

THE RISING AGENT

To proof, or grow, active dry yeast: Dissolve the dry yeast in lukewarm water (105° to 115°F) to activate it. Bubbles will be evident within a few minutes, indicating that the yeast is viable.

By hand:
■ Pour the water into a large bowl, add the sugar, and sprinkle with the yeast. Set aside for 5 minutes. Add 2 cups of flour, 1 cup at a time, and mix well with a wooden spoon. After the second cup, beat briskly 100 times. Wrap in plastic and set aside for 10 minutes.

■ Add the olive oil, salt, and remaining flour, ⅓ cup at a time, beating well after each addition, until the dough forms a ball. Turn it out onto a floured work surface. Knead with floured hands for 8 to 10 minutes, or until the dough is supple and springy, adding more flour as necessary to keep from sticking. See Finishing Steps.

By food processor:
This is suitable for a processor with a 10- to 12-cup capacity and a metal cutting blade.

■ Reduce the water to 1 cup plus 2 tablespoons and put it into a 2-cup measure. Add the sugar, then sprinkle with the yeast. Set aside for 5 minutes. Add the oil and stir to blend.

■ Put the flour and salt into the processor and pulse to mix. Stir the liquid and, using the feed tube, add it in a 10- to 12-second-long stream, with the machine running. When the mixture forms a dough ball that rides above the blade, process (or knead) for 20 to 30 seconds more.

■ Turn the dough out onto a lightly floured work surface and knead with floured hands for 30 seconds. See Finishing Steps.

Finishing Steps:
■ Lightly oil a large bowl. Place the dough in it, rotating it to coat the surface. Cover the bowl with plastic wrap and set aside to rise in a warm, draft-free spot for 45 to 60 minutes, or until doubled in bulk. Proceed with the recipe as directed.

Makes enough dough for 2 pizzas or calzones.

Wheaten Flatbread Dough

Perfect, if you like thin, crisp crusts! The addition of fat and a period of refrigeration allow you to roll it thinner than "regular" pizza dough, so it bakes up crisper, too.

¾ cup lukewarm water (105° to 115°F)
2¼ teaspoons (1 packet) active dry yeast
1⅔ cups plus 2 teaspoons unbleached all-purpose flour
½ cup whole wheat flour
1 teaspoon salt
½ teaspoon sugar
3 tablespoons cold, unsalted butter, cut into ¼-inch pieces

■ Pour the water into a glass measuring cup, sprinkle with the yeast, stir, then set aside for 5 minutes.

■ Combine the 1⅔ cups of all-purpose flour, wheat flour, salt, and sugar in the bowl of a food processor and pulse to mix. Add the butter and pulse 4 or 5 times more, or until it is cut into fine bits. Using the feed tube, add the liquid in one 6- to 7-second-long stream, with the machine running. Continue processing for about 3 to 4 seconds more. Remove the lid, sprinkle with 1 to 2 teaspoons of flour, then process for 4 to 5 seconds more. The dough should remain balled up and not become sticky or ragged.

■ Transfer the dough to a lightly floured work surface. With floured hands, knead for 30 seconds.

■ Lightly oil a large bowl. Place the dough in it, rotating it to coat the surface. Cover the bowl with plastic wrap and refrigerate for at least 1 hour and up to 24 hours.

Makes enough dough for 2 or 3 flatbreads.

How to Freeze Pizza Dough

After the dough has risen once, shape a portion into a ball. Brush the surface with 1 teaspoon of olive oil, then put the dough into a plastic freezer storage bag. Flatten the dough into a thick disk and place in the freezer.

The night before you plan to use the dough, transfer it to the refrigerator to thaw. You can roll it out while it is still cool, but allow it to sit at room temperature for 10 minutes before filling or shaping.

Bake as usual.

All-Purpose Pie Dough

Use with sweet or savory pies.

7 tablespoons cold unsalted butter, cut into ½-inch cubes
3 tablespoons cold vegetable shortening, in pieces
1½ cups all-purpose flour
½ teaspoon salt
⅓ cup ice-cold water

By hand:

■ Chill the butter and shortening in the refrigerator for 15 minutes.

■ Combine the flour and salt in a large bowl and whisk to blend. Scatter the butter and shortening on top. Using a pastry blender, cut the fat into the flour mixture until it becomes small, split pea–size pieces. Sprinkle with half of the water. Using a large fork, mix the dough briskly. Sprinkle with the remaining water and mix until the dough pulls together. See Finishing Steps.

By food processor:

■ Chill the butter and shortening in the freezer for 15 minutes.

■ Combine the flour, sugar, and salt in the processor, cover, and pulse four or five times, to mix. Scatter the chilled butter and shortening on top. Cover and pulse eight to ten times more in 1-second bursts to break the fat into very small pieces. Using the feed tube, add the water in an 8- to 10-second-long stream, while pulsing. Continue to pulse until the dough forms large, clumpy crumbs. See Finishing Steps.

Finishing Steps:

■ Turn the dough out onto a lightly floured work surface and pack it into a ball. Gently knead once or twice, then flatten into a ½-inch-thick disk. Wrap in plastic and refrigerate for 1 to 2 hours before rolling.

Makes enough pastry for 1 large pie shell or several smaller ones.

Kissing don't last; cookery do.

–George Meredith, English poet (1828–1909)

Food Processor Tart Dough

A tender, flaky crust—guaranteed

1 cup (2 sticks) cold unsalted butter, cut into ½-inch cubes
2 cups all-purpose flour
¾ teaspoon salt
1 large egg beaten with ¼ cup ice-cold water

■ Chill the butter in the freezer for 15 minutes.

■ In a food processor, combine the flour and salt, cover, and pulse four or five times to mix. Scatter the chilled butter on top. Cover and pulse eight to ten times more, in 1-second-long bursts to break the fat into very small pieces. Using the feed tube, add the egg mixture in an 8- to 10-second-long stream, while pulsing. Continue to pulse until the dough forms large, clumpy crumbs.

■ Turn the dough out onto a lightly floured work surface and pack it into a ball. Gently knead once or twice, then flatten into a ½-inch-thick disk. Wrap in plastic and refrigerate for 1 to 2 hours before rolling.

Makes enough pastry for 1 large tart, a 9-inch double-crust pie, or 6 individual pie shells.

**WHAT'S THE
DIFFERENCE?**

Confectioners' sugar (or powdered sugar) is granulated sugar that has been crushed into a fine powder with about 3 percent cornstarch added to prevent clumping.

*Glazed Lemon
Cream Scones
recipe on page 250*

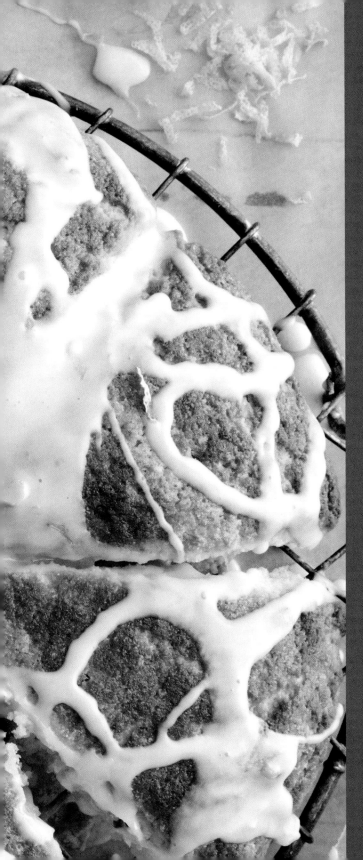

breads

Farmhouse White Loaves

A superior, all-purpose sandwich and toasting loaf like Grandma used to make

2⅓ cups hot milk

2 tablespoons (¼ stick) butter, in several pieces

3 tablespoons sugar

2½ teaspoons salt

¼ cup warm (105° to 115°F) water

2¼ teaspoons (1 packet) active dry yeast

1 egg yolk

6 to 6½ cups unbleached all-purpose flour

■ Pour the milk into a large bowl. Add the butter, sugar, and salt and stir. Set aside to cool.

■ When the milk mixture is almost cooled, pour the water into a small bowl and sprinkle with the yeast. Stir and set aside for 5 minutes.

■ Add the dissolved yeast and egg yolk to the milk mixture. Using a wooden spoon, stir in 4 cups of the flour. Beat well for 100 strokes. Set this "sponge" aside for 5 minutes. Stir in enough of the remaining flour, ⅓ cup at a time, to make a firm dough.

■ Turn the dough out onto a floured work surface and knead for 9 to 10 minutes, or until smooth, supple, and elastic. Dust your hands and work surface with flour, as needed, to keep the dough from sticking.

■ Oil a large bowl, add the dough, and rotate it to coat the entire surface. Cover the bowl with plastic wrap and set in a warm, draft-free spot until doubled in bulk, 1 to 1½ hours.

■ Butter two 8½x4½-inch loaf pans.

■ Punch down the dough and turn it out onto the floured work surface. Knead for 2 minutes. Divide the dough in half, shape into balls, and let rest for 5 minutes. Shape into loaves and place in the pans. Cover the loaves loosely with plastic wrap and set aside in a warm, draft-free spot until almost doubled in bulk.

■ Preheat the oven to 375°F.

■ Uncover the loaves and place them on the lower oven rack, evenly spaced. Bake for 40 to 45 minutes, or until golden.

■ Turn the loaves out of the pans and onto a cooling rack.

Makes 2 loaves.

Good bread is the most fundamentally satisfying of all foods; good bread with fresh butter, the greatest of feasts!

–James Beard, American chef and food writer (1903–85)

TIPS FOR MAKING YEAST BREAD

Prep

Bring ingredients and bowls to room temperature before beginning, unless the recipe specifies otherwise. Cold will throw a chill into dough and slow down the rise.

How to Knead

To knead, flour your hands and work surface and turn the dough out. Push down with your palms, fold the dough over onto itself, give it a quarter-turn, and repeat. Go gently at first, when the dough will be stickier. Expect to knead for 7 to 10 minutes to make the dough smooth, supple, and properly elastic. Continue to dust your hands and work surface with flour, as needed.

How to Know That Dough is Doubled

To check whether dough has doubled, stick a finger about 1 inch into it: If the indentation remains (doesn't spring back), the dough is ready.

How to Get a Good Rise

A glass or ceramic bowl is preferred for rising yeast dough because it is heavy and durable and surrounds the dough with gentle, even warmth. To further ensure best results, before putting the dough into the bowl, fill it with hot water and let stand for 5 minutes. Then, dry the bowl well, oil it, and add the dough, rotating it to coat, as directed.

How to Delay Rising Dough

If you are called away unexpectedly while your dough is rising, don't worry: Just punch it down, cover with plastic wrap, and refrigerate. The dough will continue to rise in the fridge, but the cold will slow it down. When you are ready to resume, punch down the dough again and set it aside at room temperature to double again. This technique works well whether the dough is in the bowl (the first rise) or in the pan (the second rise).

How to Shape a Loaf

To shape a loaf, roll the dough into an approximate rectangle 11 to 12 inches long and almost as wide as your pan. Starting at the short end closest to you, roll the dough up snugly, like a carpet. Pinch the seam, to seal, then pinch the ends and tuck them under. Place the loaf in the prepared pan, seam side down.

How to Prep the Oven

Preheat the oven 10 to 15 minutes before the final rise is finished. To prevent the tops of your loaves from getting too dark, place the oven rack on one of the lower settings.

How to Know When Bread is Done

Many yeast breads are done when, if you turn the loaf out of the pan and immediately tap the bottom, you hear a hollow sound. If the bread is not done, return it to the oven rack, without its pan, and bake for 7 to 10 minutes more. If the bread is rich in dairy products or contains a good amount of oats or other grain flakes, this tap test is less reliable. Total elapsed time is a better indicator.

Cinnamon Raisin Bread

The aroma as this loaf bakes draws people to the kitchen like a magnet!

1 cup old-fashioned rolled oats
2 cups hot milk
3 tablespoons honey
¾ cup warm (105° to 115°F) water
2¼ teaspoons (1 packet) active
    dry yeast

6 to 6½ cups unbleached all-purpose
    flour
¼ cup vegetable oil
2½ teaspoons salt
1 cup raisins

1 cup chopped walnuts or pecans
cinnamon sugar: 2 tablespoons
    sugar mixed with 1 tablespoon
    cinnamon

■ Put the oats into a large bowl, add the milk and honey, and stir. Set aside to cool.

■ Pour the water into a small bowl and sprinkle with the yeast. Stir and set aside for 5 minutes.

■ Add the dissolved yeast and 3½ cups of the flour to the oat mixture. Beat with a wooden spoon for 100 strokes. Cover the bowl with plastic wrap and set this "sponge" aside for 5 minutes. Add the oil and salt to the dough and stir well. Add the raisins and walnuts and stir. Add the remaining flour, ⅓ to ½ cup at a time, stirring after each addition and pausing periodically for 2 to 3 minutes, to allow the dough to rest. The dough will be quite dense.

■ When you have firm dough, turn it out onto a floured work surface. Knead with floured hands for 7 to 10 minutes, or until the dough is supple and elastic. (With all of the raisins and nuts, it won't be particularly smooth.) Dust your hands and work surface with flour, as needed, to keep the dough from sticking.

■ Oil a large bowl, add the dough, and rotate it to coat the entire surface. Cover the bowl with plastic wrap and set aside in a warm, draft-free spot until the dough is doubled in bulk, 1½ to 2 hours.

■ Butter two 8½x4½-inch loaf pans.

■ Punch down the dough and turn it out onto the floured work surface. Knead for 2 minutes. Divide the dough in half, shape into balls, and let rest for 5 to 7 minutes.

■ Working with one ball of dough at a time, roll to about 13 inches long and 8 inches wide at the center. Lightly mist or brush the surface with water. Sprinkle evenly with half of the cinnamon sugar. Starting at the end closest to you, roll up the dough snugly, like a carpet. Pinch the seam to seal and place it in one of the pans, seam side down. Repeat with the other ball of dough. Cover each loosely with plastic wrap and let rise in a warm, draft-free spot until doubled in bulk.

■ Preheat the oven to 400°F.

■ Uncover and place the loaves on the lower oven rack, evenly spaced. Immediately lower the heat to 375°F. Bake for 45 to 50 minutes, or until the tops are golden.

■ Turn the loaves out of the pans and onto a cooling rack. Cool before slicing.

Makes 2 loaves.

Anadama Bread

Slices of this molasses and cornmeal loaf, which is thought to date from Colonial times, are yummy when toasted.

1 cup cold water	3 tablespoons molasses
⅓ cup fine yellow cornmeal	2 tablespoons light-brown sugar
1½ teaspoons salt	½ cup warm (105° to 115°F) water
2 tablespoons unsalted butter, cut into several pieces	2¼ teaspoons (1 packet) active dry yeast
	3½ to 3¾ cups unbleached all-purpose flour

■ Combine the cold water, cornmeal, and salt in a small saucepan and bring to a low boil, while stirring. When it thickens slightly and becomes like a thin porridge, remove from the heat and transfer to a large bowl.

■ Add the butter, stirring until it melts. Add the molasses and brown sugar, stir, and set aside to cool.

■ Pour the warm water into a small bowl and sprinkle with the yeast. Stir and set aside for 5 minutes.

■ Add the dissolved yeast to the cornmeal mixture. Add 1½ cups of the flour and beat well with a wooden spoon for 100 strokes. Set this "sponge" aside for 5 minutes. Stir in enough of the remaining flour, about ⅓ cup at a time, to make a firm dough. It will be sticky.

■ Turn the dough out onto a floured work surface. Using floured hands, knead it, gently at first, for 8 to 10 minutes, until it is smooth, supple, and elastic. Sprinkle with flour, as needed, to keep the dough from sticking.

■ Oil a large bowl, add the dough, and rotate it to coat the entire surface. Cover the bowl with plastic wrap and place in a warm, draft-free spot until the dough is doubled in bulk, 1 to 1½ hours.

■ Butter a 9x5-inch loaf pan.

■ Punch down the dough and turn it out onto a floured work surface. Knead for 2 minutes, then let rest for 5 minutes. Shape the dough into a loaf and place in the prepared pan. Cover the loaf loosely with plastic wrap. Set aside in a warm, draft-free spot until doubled in bulk, about 45 minutes.

■ Preheat the oven to 400°F.

■ Uncover the loaf and place on a lower oven rack. Immediately lower the heat to 375°F and bake for 45 to 50 minutes, or until the top is golden.

■ Transfer to a cooling rack for 1 to 2 minutes. Turn the loaf out onto the rack to cool completely.

Makes 1 loaf.

CHEW ON THIS

For a chewy bread crust, keep a small pan of water in the oven while baking.

Whole Wheat and Oatmeal Sandwich Bread

Delicious when toasted, as French toast, and for grilled cheese

¾ cup old-fashioned rolled oats, plus some for
    dusting the pans
1 cup hot milk
1 cup hot water
¼ cup honey
3 tablespoons unsalted butter, in ¼-inch pieces
¼ cup warm (105° to 115°F) water

2¼ teaspoons (1 packet) active dry yeast
⅓ cup buttermilk or plain yogurt,
    at room temperature
2 cups whole wheat flour
1 egg yolk
2½ teaspoons salt
4 to 4½ cups unbleached all-purpose flour

■ Put the oats into a large bowl and add the milk, hot water, honey, and butter. Stir, then set aside to cool.

■ Pour the warm water into a small bowl and sprinkle with the yeast. Stir and set aside for 5 minutes.

■ Add the dissolved yeast, buttermilk, whole wheat flour, egg yolk, salt, and 1 cup of unbleached flour to the milk mixture. Beat with a wooden spoon for 100 strokes. Set this "sponge" aside for 5 minutes. Add the remaining unbleached flour, ⅓ to ½ cup at a time, stirring after each addition, until you have a firm dough.

■ Turn the dough out onto a floured work surface and knead for 9 to 10 minutes, or until smooth, supple, and elastic. Dust your hands and the surface with flour, as needed, to keep the dough from sticking.

■ Oil a large bowl, add the dough, and rotate it to coat the entire surface. Cover the bowl with plastic wrap and set in a warm, draft-free spot until doubled in bulk, 1 to 1½ hours.

■ Butter two 8½x4½-inch loaf pans and dust them with oats.

■ Punch down the dough and turn it out onto the floured work surface. Knead for 2 minutes. Divide the dough in half, shape into balls, and let rest for 5 minutes. Shape into loaves and place in the prepared pans. Cover loosely with plastic wrap and set aside to rise in a warm, draft-free spot until doubled in bulk.

■ Preheat the oven to 400°F.

■ Uncover and place the loaves on the lower oven rack, evenly spaced. Immediately lower the heat to 375°F. Bake for 45 minutes, or until the tops are golden.

■ Turn the loaves out of the pans and onto a cooling rack.

Makes 2 large loaves.

Ciabatta

The name of this popular rustic bread means "slipper" in Italian, and the resemblance will be apparent once you make it. Prepare the starter early in the day and you will have oven-fresh ciabatta for dinner.

Starter:
1½ cups warm (105° to 115°F) water
2¼ teaspoons (1 packet) active dry yeast, divided
¼ teaspoon sugar
2 cups unbleached all-purpose flour

Dough:
¾ cup warm (105° to 115°F) milk
2 tablespoons olive oil
2 teaspoons salt
3¼ to 3¾ cups unbleached all-purpose flour

For starter:
■ Pour the water into a large bowl and sprinkle with ¼ teaspoon of the yeast and the sugar. Stir and set aside for 5 minutes. Add the 2 cups of flour and beat with a wooden spoon for 100 strokes. Cover the bowl with plastic wrap and set aside in a warm, draft-free spot for 4 to 5 hours to develop a yeasty aroma.

For dough:
■ Pour the milk into a small bowl and sprinkle with the remaining 2 teaspoons of yeast. Stir and set aside for 10 minutes.

■ To the starter, add the dissolved yeast, olive oil, salt, and 1 cup of the flour and stir. Add the remaining flour, ⅓ to ½ cup at a time, stirring between each addition. As the dough becomes firmer and starts to pull away from the sides of the bowl, use a paddling motion to knead the dough in the bowl, dusting with flour as you go. Continue paddling for 2 to 3 minutes, then cover the bowl with plastic wrap and let the dough rest for 10 minutes. It will be slack and sticky.

■ Turn the dough out onto a floured work surface and knead gently with floured hands for 2 to 3 minutes, sprinkling the surface with flour, as needed, to keep the dough from sticking. The dough will feel smooth, supple, and elastic, although more slack than a typical yeast dough.

■ Oil a large bowl, add the dough, and rotate it to coat the entire surface. Cover the bowl with plastic wrap and set aside in a warm, draft-free spot until doubled in bulk, 1 to 1½ hours.

■ Dust a large baking sheet with cornmeal.

■ Punch down the dough and turn it out onto the floured work surface. Knead for 1 minute. Divide the dough in half, shape into balls, and let rest for 5 minutes. Flatten and stretch each ball of dough into a narrow oval. Dust with flour and let rest for 5 to 7 minutes. Continue shaping each portion into a 14x6-inch rectangle—the "slipper" shape. Dust lightly with flour and place the loaves on the prepared baking sheet. Cover loosely with plastic wrap and let rise in a warm, draft-free spot for 30 minutes.

■ Preheat the oven to 425°F.

■ Uncover the loaves and bake on the center oven rack for 25 to 30 minutes, or until golden.

■ Transfer to a cooling rack. Serve warm.

Makes 2 loaves.

Potato and Herb Focaccia

The potato water and potato add velvety softness to this classic Italian bread.

1 large baking potato, peeled
  and cubed
2 teaspoons plus a pinch of salt
1 teaspoon sugar

2¼ teaspoons (1 packet) active
  dry yeast
4½ to 5 cups unbleached
  all-purpose flour
2 tablespoons plus ⅓ cup olive oil

2 cloves garlic, thinly sliced
1½ tablespoons chopped fresh
  rosemary
coarse salt (optional)

■ Put 3½ cups of water and the potato cubes into a large saucepan, add a big pinch of salt, and bring to a boil. Reduce the heat and cook at a low boil for 10 minutes, or until soft. Drain, reserving 2 cups of the cooking water and ¼ cup of the potatoes. (Reserve any remaining water and potato for soup.)

■ Transfer the potato water and ¼ cup of potatoes to a large bowl and break up the potatoes with a fork or masher. Add the sugar, stir, and cool. Sprinkle the yeast over the cooled potato water, stir, and set aside for 5 minutes. Add the remaining salt, 3 cups of the flour, and 2 tablespoons of the olive oil. Beat well with a wooden spoon for 100 strokes. Set aside for 10 minutes. Add the remaining flour, about ⅓ cup at a time, beating well after each addition.

■ When you have firm dough, turn it out onto a floured work surface. Using floured hands, knead for 9 to 10 minutes, or until smooth, supple, and elastic. Dust the work surface with flour, as needed, to keep the dough from sticking.

■ Oil a large bowl, add the dough, and rotate it to coat the entire surface. Cover the bowl with plastic wrap and let rise in a warm, draft-free spot until the dough is doubled in bulk, about 1 hour. Punch down the dough and knead it for 2 to 3 minutes on a floured work surface. Set aside to rest for 5 minutes.

■ Butter a 13x9-inch baking pan and dust with cornmeal.

■ Place the dough in the center of the pan, cover loosely with plastic wrap, and let rest for 10 minutes. Uncover the dough, put a little oil on your fingers, and press the dough out, spreading it evenly in the pan. Re-cover with the plastic wrap and set aside to rise in a warm spot until almost doubled in bulk, 30 to 45 minutes.

■ Preheat the oven to 400°F.

■ Combine the remaining olive oil with the garlic and rosemary in a glass measuring cup.

■ Uncover the dough and, using a finger, make 12 deep, evenly spaced dimples in it. (The dimples will catch the oil.) Spoon the oil-and-herb mixture over the dough. Sprinkle sparingly with coarse salt, if using.

■ Bake on the center oven rack for 25 to 30 minutes, or until golden.

■ Using a spatula, slide the bread out of the pan and onto a cooling rack. Serve warm or at room temperature.

Makes 1 large loaf.

Wheaten Burger Buns

For the perfect burgers (on pages 122 and 180), bake the perfect buns!

⅓ cup warm (105° to 115°F) water
2¼ teaspoons (1 packet) active dry yeast
1 cup milk, warmed to 98°F
1 large egg, lightly beaten
1 tablespoon sugar
1½ teaspoons salt
½ cup whole wheat flour

2 tablespoons (¼ stick)
   unsalted butter, melted
3¼ to 3¾ cups unbleached
   all-purpose flour
1 egg beaten with 1 tablespoon milk,
   for egg wash
sesame seeds or poppy seeds (optional)

■ Pour the water into a large bowl and sprinkle with the yeast. Stir and set aside for 5 minutes. Add the milk, egg, sugar, salt, and melted butter to the dissolved yeast. Add the whole wheat flour and 1½ cups of the unbleached flour, stirring with a wooden spoon between each addition. Beat with the wooden spoon for 100 strokes. Set this "sponge" aside to rest for 5 minutes. Add enough of the remaining unbleached flour, about ⅓ cup at a time, stirring, to make a firm dough.

■ Turn the dough out onto a floured work surface and knead for 9 to 10 minutes, until smooth, supple, and elastic. Dust the work surface with flour, as needed, to keep the dough from sticking.

■ Oil a large bowl, add the dough, and rotate it to coat the entire surface. Cover the bowl with plastic wrap and let rise in a warm, draft-free spot until doubled in bulk, about 1 hour.

■ Lightly oil and dust a large baking sheet with cornmeal.

■ Punch down the dough and turn it out onto the floured work surface. Knead for 2 minutes. Divide the dough into eight equal pieces. Shape each piece into a ball and place them, evenly spaced, on the baking sheet. Lightly oil a sheet of plastic wrap, lay it over the dough balls, and set aside in a warm spot to rest for 20 minutes.

■ Oil your fingers and gently flatten each ball to deflate it. Re-cover with the plastic wrap and let rest another 20 minutes, until puffy.

■ Preheat the oven to 375°F.

■ Uncover and brush the dough with the egg wash. Sprinkle with sesame seeds, if desired. Bake for 20 minutes, or until golden.

■ Transfer the buns to a cooling rack for at least 15 minutes before slicing.

Makes 8 buns.

All sorrows are less with bread.

–Miguel de Cervantes, Spanish writer (1547–1616)

Parker House Rolls

This is the standard for great American dinner rolls, made famous by Boston's Parker House Hotel.

2 cups hot milk

½ cup (1 stick) unsalted butter, divided

2 tablespoons sugar

¼ cup warm (105° to 115°F) water

2¼ teaspoons (1 packet) active dry yeast

2 teaspoons salt

5 to 5½ cups unbleached all-purpose flour

■ Pour the milk into a large bowl and add 3 tablespoons of the butter, cut into pieces. Add the sugar, stir, and set aside and cool.

■ Pour the water into a small bowl and sprinkle with the yeast. Stir and set aside for 5 minutes.

■ Add the dissolved yeast and salt to the milk mixture and stir. Add 3½ cups of the flour and beat well with a wooden spoon for 100 strokes. Set this "sponge" aside for 5 minutes. Stir in enough of the remaining flour, ⅓ cup at a time, to make a firm dough.

■ Turn the dough out onto a floured work surface and knead for 9 to 10 minutes, until smooth, supple, and elastic. Dust the work surface with flour, as needed, to keep the dough from sticking.

■ Oil a large bowl, add the dough, and rotate it to coat the entire surface. Cover the bowl with plastic wrap and set aside in a warm, draft-free spot until doubled in bulk, 1 to 1½ hours.

■ Butter a 13x9-inch baking pan. (You can use a baking sheet instead, but the higher sides of the pan help to prevent the rolls from getting too brown around the edges.)

■ Punch down the dough and turn it out onto the floured work surface. Knead for 2 minutes, then let rest for 5 minutes.

■ Melt the remaining 5 tablespoons of butter and set aside.

■ Lightly flour the work surface and roll the dough to about ½-inch thick. If it springs back, let it rest for 5 minutes more. Press a 2½- to 3-inch biscuit cutter into the dough in close cuts. Leave the cut rolls in place, gather the scraps, knead them into a ball, and set aside, covered.

■ Brush each roll with melted butter. Working with one at a time, make a deep indentation across the roll's diameter with the handle of a wooden spoon or chopstick. Fold the roll in half, so that the buttered halves meet. Place on the sheet, with the fold down. Repeat for the remaining rolls. Reroll, cut, butter, and fold the scraps, then place all of the rolls close together on the baking sheet.

■ Brush each row of the rolls with butter. Cover the pan loosely with plastic wrap and set aside in a warm, draft-free spot until nearly doubled in bulk, 30 to 40 minutes.

■ Preheat the oven to 375°F.

■ Uncover and bake for 20 to 22 minutes, or until browned. Immediately brush with more melted butter. Serve hot, from a cloth-lined basket.

Makes about 30 rolls.

Soft Pretzels

1¼ cups warm (105° to 115°F) water
2¼ teaspoons (1 packet) active
   dry yeast
1 tablespoon light-brown sugar

1½ teaspoons salt
3¼ to 3½ cups unbleached
   all-purpose flour
¼ cup hot water

1 teaspoon sugar
coarse salt (optional)
3 to 4 tablespoons unsalted
   butter, melted

■ Pour the warm water into a large bowl and sprinkle with the yeast. Stir and set aside for 5 minutes. Add the brown sugar, salt, and 2 cups of the flour and beat with a wooden spoon for 100 strokes. Set this "sponge" aside for 5 minutes. Stir in enough of the remaining flour, about ⅓ cup at a time, to make a firm dough.

■ Turn the dough out onto a floured work surface and knead for 6 to 7 minutes, until smooth, supple, and elastic.

■ Oil a large bowl, add the dough, and rotate it to coat the entire surface. Cover the bowl with plastic wrap and set aside in a warm, draft-free spot until the dough is doubled in bulk, about 45 to 60 minutes.

■ Preheat the oven to 425°F.

■ Lightly coat two large baking sheets with shortening or oil, but not butter.

■ Punch down the dough and turn it out onto a lightly floured work surface. Knead for 2 minutes. Divide the dough in half and put one half in the bowl and cover it. Divide the remaining half into three equal pieces. Shape into balls and let rest for 2 to 3 minutes. Working with one piece at a time, roll the dough to make a rope 30 inches long. Shape the rope into a large horseshoe, with the ends pointed away. Holding the ends, cross them about 4 inches from each end, forming a large circle. Twist the ends together once (as you would twist a wire bread tie), pull them toward you, and drape them over opposite sides of the circle to form the classic pretzel shape. Place the pretzel on the baking sheet. Repeat for the other two dough balls, leaving plenty of space between them on the baking sheet.

■ Combine the hot water and sugar in a small bowl, stir, and lightly brush it on the pretzels. Sprinkle with coarse salt, if desired. Let rest for 10 minutes.

■ Bake on the center oven rack for 12 to 15 minutes, or until golden brown.

■ Briefly knead the remaining dough. Shape three more pretzels and place them on the second baking sheet.

■ Transfer the first batch to a cooling rack and immediately brush with the melted butter several times.

■ Bake the second batch as directed. Serve warm.

Makes 6 pretzels.

Variations

Cinnamon Sugar Pretzels

■ Brush each pretzel with hot water, then sprinkle liberally with cinnamon sugar (3 tablespoons of sugar mixed with ¼ teaspoon of cinnamon).

■ Bake and butter, as directed.

Pizza Pretzels

■ Brush each pretzel with hot water, then spread 1 tablespoon of sun-dried tomato pesto on each one. (Store-bought pesto is fine.)

■ Bake and butter as directed.

■ Sprinkle generously with grated Parmesan cheese while still hot.

Monkey Bread

Kids love to help with this one, and nobody knows which is more fun—making this sweet, pull-apart bread or eating it.

Dough:

1⅓ cups hot milk

4 tablespoons (½ stick) unsalted butter, cut into ¼-inch pieces

¼ cup sugar

¼ cup warm (105° to 115°F) water

2¼ teaspoons (1 packet) active dry yeast

2 large eggs, lightly beaten

2 teaspoons salt

4¾ to 5 cups unbleached all-purpose flour

Glaze:

⅓ cup packed light-brown sugar

7 tablespoons unsalted butter, divided

2 tablespoons heavy cream

¾ cup chopped pecans, divided

¾ cup sugar

For dough:

■ Pour the milk into a large bowl, add the butter and sugar, stir, and set aside to cool.

■ Pour the water into a small bowl and sprinkle with the yeast. Stir and set aside for 5 minutes.

■ Add the dissolved yeast, eggs, and salt to the milk mixture and stir. Add 3 cups of the flour and beat with a wooden spoon for 100 strokes. Set this "sponge" aside for 5 minutes. Stir in enough of the remaining flour, ⅓ cup at a time, to make a firm dough.

■ Turn the dough out onto a lightly floured work surface and knead for 9 to 10 minutes, until smooth, supple, and elastic. Dust the work surface with flour, as needed, to keep the dough from sticking.

■ Oil a large bowl, add the dough, and rotate it to coat the entire surface. Cover

Avoid those who don't like bread and children.

—Swiss Proverb

the bowl with plastic wrap and set it aside in a warm, draft-free spot until doubled in bulk, about 1 to 1½ hours.

◼ Generously butter a large (12-cup) Bundt pan. (Do not use a tube pan with a removable bottom; the glaze will run out into the oven.)

For glaze:

◼ Combine the brown sugar, 2 tablespoons of the butter, and the heavy cream in a small saucepan and bring to a low boil. Pour into the Bundt pan and tilt to distribute the glaze evenly. Sprinkle half of the pecans over the glaze.

To assemble:

◼ Punch down the dough and turn it out onto a lightly floured work surface. Knead for 2 minutes.

◼ Melt the remaining 5 tablespoons of butter and pour into a shallow bowl.

◼ Put the sugar into a separate bowl.

◼ Pinch off pieces of dough and shape them into golf ball–size rounds. Coat them with melted butter and roll them in the sugar. Cover the bottom of the pan with the balls, then add a second layer. Sprinkle with the remaining pecans. Continue making balls with the remaining dough. Cover the pan with plastic wrap and let rise in a draft-free, warm spot until doubled in bulk, 35 to 45 minutes.

◼ Preheat the oven to 375°F. Adjust the oven rack to one setting below center.

◼ Uncover the pan and bake for 45 minutes. (The top may get dark, but it won't affect the whole bread. If desired, cover with foil during the last 10 to 15 minutes.)

◼ Transfer to a cooling rack and run a butter knife down the sides of the pan to loosen the bread. Carefully flip the pan over (watch out for hot glaze), letting the bread slide out onto a cooling rack. Cool for at least 20 minutes before serving.

Makes about 8 servings.

SPONGE EFFECT

When the air is humid, flour will soak up moisture. On these days, you may need to use a little more flour than the amount indicated in your recipe.

Cuban Bread

These long, narrow, French-style loaves form the cold cut–and–condiment, sub-style sandwiches that were once the favorite lunch of Cuban workers in South Florida. Also try it buttered and grilled, staled for French toast, or torn for bread pudding.

1½ cups warm (105° to 115°F) water
2 teaspoons sugar
2¼ teaspoons (1 packet) active dry yeast
½ cup whole wheat flour
3¼ to 3½ cups unbleached all-purpose flour
1½ teaspoons salt
2 tablespoons olive oil

■ Pour the water into a large bowl, add the sugar, and stir. Sprinkle with the yeast, stir, and set aside for 5 minutes. Using a wooden spoon, stir in the whole wheat flour and 2 cups of the unbleached flour. Beat well for 100 strokes. Cover the bowl with plastic wrap and set aside for 10 minutes. Add the salt and olive oil and stir to incorporate. Stir in enough of the remaining flour, ⅓ cup at a time, to make dough that pulls away from the side of the bowl.

■ Turn the dough out onto a lightly floured surface and knead for 9 to 10 minutes, or until smooth and elastic. Dust the work surface with flour, as needed, to keep the dough from sticking.

■ Oil a large bowl, add the dough, and rotate it to coat the entire surface. Cover the bowl with plastic wrap and set in a warm, draft-free spot until doubled in bulk, 50 to 60 minutes.

■ Punch down the dough and turn it out onto the floured work surface. Knead for 1 minute. Divide the dough in half and knead each half into a ball. Cover with plastic wrap and let rest for 5 minutes.

■ Lightly oil a large baking sheet and dust with cornmeal.

■ Working with one ball of dough at a time on a lightly floured surface, roll to a 12-inch-long oblong. Roll up lengthwise snugly, like a carpet. With a wet fingertip, dampen the seam and pinch it together. Pinch the ends and tuck them under.

■ Place the loaves on the prepared baking sheet, evenly spaced. Set aside for 15 minutes. Lightly brush the loaves with water. Using a sharp, serrated knife, make three diagonal slashes about ¾ of an inch deep in each loaf.

■ Place the baking sheet on the center oven rack and set the oven to 400° F. (Do not preheat the oven.)

■ Bake for 35 minutes, or until golden.

■ Transfer the loaves to a cooling rack for at least 15 minutes before slicing.

Makes 2 loaves.

60-Minute Bread

This bread is ideal when time is in short supply but sandwiches or a hearty soup or stew are what's for dinner. Allow about 75 minutes to be on the safe side.

¼ cup warm (105° to 115°F) water

2¼ teaspoons (1 packet) active dry yeast

½ cup buttermilk or plain yogurt

1½ cups milk

2 tablespoons sugar

1 cup whole wheat flour

4¼ cups unbleached all-purpose flour, divided

2 tablespoons vegetable oil or canola oil

2 teaspoons salt

1 teaspoon baking powder

1 teaspoon baking soda

■ Pour the water into a small bowl and sprinkle with the yeast. Stir and set aside for 5 minutes.

■ In a small saucepan, heat the buttermilk and milk until slightly warm to the touch.

■ Pour the milk into a large bowl, add the dissolved yeast and sugar, and stir. Add the whole wheat flour and 1 cup of the unbleached flour and whisk to blend. Set this "sponge" aside in a warm, draft-free spot for 15 minutes. Add the oil and salt to the dough and stir.

■ Lightly oil a large baking sheet and dust with cornmeal.

■ In a separate bowl, combine the baking powder and baking soda with 2 cups of the remaining unbleached flour. Add to the dough and stir to blend. Gradually add and stir in enough of the remaining unbleached flour to make a soft dough.

■ Turn the dough out onto a lightly floured surface and knead for 5 minutes. Dust with flour, as needed, to keep the dough from sticking. (The dough is soft, so do not be too forceful.) Divide the dough in half. Shape each half into a stumpy football and place on the baking sheet, evenly spaced apart, leaving plenty of room between them. Dust lightly with flour (not to cover). Set them aside in a warm, draft-free spot for 15 minutes.

■ Preheat the oven to 425°F. Position the oven rack to one setting below center.

■ Using a sharp serrated knife, make 3 diagonal slashes about ¾ of an inch deep in each loaf.

■ Bake for 30 to 35 minutes, or until the loaves are dark golden brown, turning the baking sheet 180 degrees after about 20 minutes.

■ Transfer to a cooling rack. Cool before slicing.

Makes 2 loaves.

Old-Fashioned Date Nut Bread

4 tablespoons (½ stick) unsalted butter, cut into ¼-inch pieces
1 teaspoon baking soda
1½ cups chopped pitted dates
1 cup boiling water
1 large egg
⅔ cup buttermilk
⅓ cup sugar
⅓ cup packed light-brown sugar
1 teaspoon vanilla extract
2 cups all-purpose flour
1 teaspoon baking powder
½ teaspoon salt
¼ teaspoon cinnamon
½ cup chopped walnuts

■ Combine the butter pieces, baking soda, and dates in a bowl. Add the boiling water, stir, and set aside for 30 minutes.

■ Preheat the oven to 350°F. Butter a 9x5-inch loaf pan and line with parchment paper, if desired.

■ In a separate large bowl, combine the egg, buttermilk, sugar, brown sugar, and vanilla and whisk to blend. Add the date mixture, with its liquid, and stir.

■ Sift the flour, baking powder, salt, and cinnamon into another large bowl. Add the walnuts and mix. Make a well, add the date mixture, and stir with a wooden spoon, until the batter is smooth; do not overmix. (The batter will be thin.) Pour the batter into the prepared pan.

■ Bake on the center oven rack for 50 minutes, or until a tester inserted into the center comes out clean and the top is golden.

■ Transfer to a cooling rack for 10 minutes. Turn the bread out of the pan and cool to room temperature before serving.

Makes 1 loaf.

If thou tastest a crust of bread, thou tastest all the stars and all the heavens.

–Robert Browning,
English poet
(1812–89)

Double-Apple Walnut Bread

1 cup sweetened or unsweetened applesauce
½ cup plus 1 tablespoon sugar
½ cup packed light-brown sugar
2 large eggs
¼ cup vegetable oil
¼ cup plain or vanilla yogurt
1 teaspoon vanilla extract
2 cups all-purpose flour
1 teaspoon baking powder
½ teaspoon baking soda
¾ teaspoon salt
½ teaspoon cinnamon
⅛ teaspoon nutmeg
1 cup peeled, cored, and finely diced apple
½ cup chopped walnuts

■ Preheat the oven to 350°F. Butter a 9x5-inch loaf pan and line with parchment paper, if desired.

■ Combine the applesauce, ½ cup of sugar, brown sugar, eggs, oil, yogurt, and vanilla in a bowl and whisk to blend.

■ Sift the flour, baking powder, baking soda, salt, cinnamon, and nutmeg into a separate large bowl. Make a well, add the applesauce mixture, and stir until combined. Fold in the diced apple and walnuts. Scrape the batter into the prepared pan and smooth the top. Sprinkle with the remaining sugar.

■ Bake on the center oven rack for 50 to 55 minutes, or until a tester inserted into the center of the bread comes out clean.

■ Transfer to a cooling rack for 10 minutes. Turn the bread out of the pan and cool thoroughly before slicing.

Makes 1 loaf.

Handy Cover-Up

If the telephone rings while you are working with sticky dough, slip your hand into a plastic bag and use it as a mitten when you pick up the phone.

French Morning Muffins

Irresistible any time of day!

Love the Lumps

Don't use an electric mixer when combining wet and dry muffin ingredients. Beating the batter will cause gluten to overdevelop, which will produce tough muffins. Mix just enough to wet the dry ingredients; a lumpy batter is the goal.

Batter:
2 cups all-purpose flour
⅔ cup sugar
2½ teaspoons baking powder
½ teaspoon salt
¼ teaspoon nutmeg
1 large egg
1 cup plus 2 tablespoons milk

6 tablespoons (¾ stick) unsalted butter, melted and slightly cooled
1 teaspoon vanilla extract

Topping:
½ cup sugar
½ teaspoon cinnamon
2 tablespoons (¼ stick) unsalted butter, melted

For batter:

■ Preheat the oven to 375°F. Butter 12 muffin cups or line with paper liners.

■ Combine the flour, sugar, baking powder, salt, and nutmeg in a large bowl, whisk to mix, and make a well.

■ In a separate bowl, combine the egg, milk, butter, and vanilla and whisk to blend. Pour into the well and stir with a wooden spoon until evenly blended.

■ Divide the batter evenly between the prepared cups.

■ Bake for 15 minutes, then turn the pan 180 degrees and bake for 5 to 6 minutes more, or until golden and the muffins spring back when touched.

■ Transfer to a cooling rack for 3 to 4 minutes, then remove the muffins from the pan and place on the rack.

For topping:

■ Combine the sugar and cinnamon in a small mixing bowl.

■ Generously brush the top of each muffin with melted butter and dip it into the cinnamon sugar. Serve warm.

Makes 12 muffins.

Variation:

■ Divide two-thirds of the batter evenly among the cups. Put 1 teaspoon of your favorite fruit preserves into the center of each one. Distribute the remaining batter among the cups and bake as directed.

FANTASTIC FILLERS

Keep your pantry
stocked with a variety
of additions for muffins:
raisins, nuts, dried
cranberries, dried
blueberries, canned
pumpkin, applesauce,
and pineapple tidbits.

Ginger Bran Muffins

Outrageously good—wholesome, too.

1½ cups all-purpose flour
¾ cup plain oat bran or wheat bran (not packaged bran cereal)
2½ teaspoons baking powder
¾ teaspoon salt
½ teaspoon ground ginger
⅓ cup chopped crystallized ginger
1 large egg
1 cup sweetened or unsweetened applesauce
½ cup packed light-brown sugar
⅓ cup vegetable oil
¼ cup milk
2 tablespoons molasses

■ Preheat the oven to 375°F. Butter 10 muffin cups (or 12, for slightly smaller muffins) or line with paper liners.

■ Combine the flour, bran, baking powder, salt, and ground ginger in a large bowl and whisk to blend. Add the crystallized ginger, mix, and make a well.

■ In a separate bowl, whisk the egg until frothy. Add the applesauce, brown sugar, oil, milk, and molasses and whisk to blend. Pour into the well and stir with a wooden spoon until evenly blended.

■ Divide the batter evenly among the prepared cups.

■ Bake for 23 to 25 minutes, or until the muffins form domes that spring back when touched.

■ Transfer the pan to a cooling rack for 5 minutes, then remove from the pan and place on the rack until ready to serve.

Makes 10 to 12 muffins.

Variation:
■ Substitute ½ cup of raisins for the crystallized ginger.

Cheddar and Onion Drop Biscuits

Add these to the breadbasket when you're serving soup, chili, or stew.

6 tablespoons (¾ stick) cold unsalted butter, divided
1 large onion, finely chopped
2 cups all-purpose flour
1 tablespoon sugar
1 teaspoon baking powder
¾ teaspoon baking soda
½ teaspoon salt
½ teaspoon dried basil
1 cup shredded sharp cheddar cheese
¾ cup sour cream
⅔ cup milk

■ Preheat the oven to 425°F. Lightly grease a large baking sheet.

■ Melt 2 tablespoons of the butter in a skillet over moderate heat, add the onion, and cook for 9 to 10 minutes, or until light golden. Remove from the heat.

■ Combine the flour, sugar, baking powder, baking soda, salt, and basil in a large bowl and whisk to mix. Cut the remaining 4 tablespoons of butter into ¼-inch pieces, add to the dry ingredients, and, using a pastry blender or your fingers, cut or rub it in to make very small pieces. Add the cheese, mix, and make a well.

■ In a separate bowl, combine the sour cream, milk, and onions and stir. Pour into the well and stir with a wooden spoon until evenly combined; do not overmix. Set aside to rest for 3 to 4 minutes.

■ Scoop out the dough in ¼- to ⅓-cup portions and mound these on the baking sheet, leaving space between each one.

■ Bake for 15 to 17 minutes, or until the biscuits have crusty, dark golden highlights. Serve right away, if possible, or transfer to a cooling rack until serving.

Makes 12 to 14 biscuits.

Variation:
■ Use just half of the cooked onions in the dough. Spoon the remainder over the unbaked biscuits.

You don't have to cook fancy or complicated masterpieces—just good food from fresh ingredients.
—Julia Child, American culinary expert (1912–2004)

Glazed Lemon Cream Scones

Delicate, fragrant, and delicious

EASY DOES IT

For light, fluffy scones, avoid kneading the dough too many times. A gentle touch is best.

Batter:

2 cups all-purpose flour

⅓ cup sugar

1 tablespoon baking powder

½ teaspoon salt

finely grated zest of 1 lemon

3 tablespoons cold unsalted butter, cut into ¼-inch pieces

1 egg yolk

1 cup heavy or whipping cream, plus a spoonful or two for tops

½ teaspoon vanilla extract

Lemon Glaze:

1½ cups confectioners' sugar

1 tablespoon light corn syrup

1 tablespoon milk, plus more as needed

⅛ teaspoon lemon extract

1 teaspoon grated lemon zest, for garnish

For batter:

■ Preheat the oven to 400°F. Get out a large baking sheet.

■ Combine the flour, sugar, baking powder, salt, and lemon zest in a large bowl and whisk to mix. Add the butter and, using a pastry blender or your fingers, cut it into the dry mixture to make very small pieces. Make a well.

■ Combine the yolk, cream, and vanilla in a small bowl and stir to blend. Pour into the well and stir until the dough pulls together. Set aside to rest for 3 to 4 minutes.

■ Lightly flour a work surface.

■ Scrape the dough onto the work surface and dust your hands and the dough with flour. Knead the dough gently 4 or 5 times. It will be soft but manageable. Shape the dough into a ball, then flatten it into a disk about ¾-inch thick and 7 to 7½ inches in diameter. Cut the disk into eight equal pie wedges. Place the wedges on the baking sheet, evenly spaced. Lightly brush the tops with cream.

■ Bake for 15 to 17 minutes, or until golden.

■ Transfer to a cooling rack.

For lemon glaze:

■ Sift the confectioners' sugar into a bowl. Add the corn syrup and 1 tablespoon of milk and stir with a wooden spoon, until smooth. Add the lemon extract and stir to blend. Add additional milk, ½ teaspoon at a time, and whisk until the glaze is runny but still thick.

■ When the scones are barely warm, place them on a sheet of wax paper or plastic wrap and drizzle them generously with the glaze. Garnish with lemon zest.

Makes 8 scones.

Warm Brownie Pie
recipe on page 258

desserts

Caramel Apple Crumb Pie

In bygone days, apple pie this good was grounds for a marriage proposal.

All-Purpose Pie Dough (page 224), refrigerated, or your favorite piecrust

Topping:	Filling:	Caramel Sauce:
¾ cup all-purpose flour	8 cups peeled, cored, and sliced	½ cup heavy or whipping cream
½ cup old-fashioned rolled oats	baking apples	⅓ cup packed light-brown sugar
½ cup packed light-brown sugar	⅓ cup plus 1 tablespoon sugar,	2 tablespoons (¼ stick) unsalted
¼ teaspoon cinnamon	divided	butter, in pieces
⅛ teaspoon salt	1 tablespoon lemon juice	½ teaspoon vanilla extract
6 tablespoons (¾ stick) cold unsalted	2 tablespoons cornstarch	½ cup chopped pecans
butter, cut into ¼-inch pieces	⅛ teaspoon salt	

■ Roll the pastry into a 13-inch circle and line a 9½-inch deep-dish pie plate with it. Pinch the overhanging pastry into an upstanding rim. Refrigerate for 15 minutes.

■ Preheat the oven to 375°F.

For topping:

■ Combine the flour, oats, brown sugar, cinnamon, and salt in a food processor. Pulse several times to mix. Scatter the butter pieces over the mixture. Pulse to a sandlike consistency. Transfer to a bowl and rub well with your fingers until the texture is uniform. Refrigerate the crumbs.

For filling:

■ Combine the apples, ⅓ cup of sugar, and lemon juice in a large bowl. Set aside for 10 minutes.

■ In a small bowl, combine the cornstarch and salt with the remaining sugar and mix to blend. Add the mixture to the fruit and stir. Pour the filling into the chilled piecrust, shaping the apples into a smooth mound.

■ Bake on the center oven rack for 35 minutes. Remove the pie from the oven. Spread the crumbs on top. Tamp lightly, to compact. Bake for 25 to 35 minutes more, or until the juices bubble thickly around the edge.

■ Transfer to a cooling rack for at least 1 hour before serving.

For sauce:

■ Combine the cream, brown sugar, and butter in a small saucepan. Bring to a boil and cook for 2 minutes, whisking constantly. Remove from the heat, add the vanilla and pecans, and stir.

■ Transfer to a small bowl and cool completely. Refrigerate briefly for a thicker sauce. Serve the pie with sauce drizzled on each slice.

Makes 8 servings.

GOOD AND FRUITY

Add ½ teaspoon of lemon juice to your fruit filling to bring out the taste of the fruit and help it keep its color.

To avoid a soggy bottom crust in your fruit pie, get the filling into the piecrust and into the oven quickly. If there is extra juice in the bowl, don't pour it into the piecrust.

Fresh Peach Custard Pie

Sweet summer peaches and tangy custard

All-Purpose Pie Dough (page 224), refrigerated, or your favorite piecrust

Topping:
½ cup all-purpose flour
½ cup sugar
4 tablespoons (½ stick) cold unsalted
    butter, cut into ¼-inch pieces

Filling:
¾ cup sugar
3 tablespoons all-purpose flour

¼ teaspoon nutmeg
1 cup sour cream
⅓ cup heavy or light cream
4 large egg yolks
1 teaspoon vanilla extract
3½ cups peeled, pitted, and sliced
    ripe peaches

■ Roll the pastry into a 13-inch circle and line a 9½-inch deep-dish pie plate with it. Pinch the overhanging pastry into an upstanding rim. Chill, partially prebake (see page 215), and cool the crust.

■ Preheat the oven to 400°F.

For topping:
■ Combine the flour and sugar in a large bowl. Add the butter and cut or rub it into the dry mixture to make fine crumbs. Refrigerate.

For filling:
■ In a large bowl, combine the sugar, flour, and nutmeg and whisk to mix. Add the sour cream, heavy cream, egg yolks, and vanilla and whisk until blended.

■ Layer the peaches in the piecrust. Pour the sour cream mixture over the peaches. Nudge the slices with a fork so that the custard settles around them.

■ Bake on the center oven rack for 15 minutes. Reduce the heat to 350°F and bake for 10 minutes more. Remove the pie from the oven. Spread the crumbs on top. Return the pie to the oven, reduce the heat to 325°F, and bake for 25 to 30 minutes more, or until the center is not soupy. Turn off the oven and, with the oven door open, extend the oven rack and rest the pie on it for 10 minutes.

■ Transfer to a cooling rack to cool completely. Refrigerate, uncovered, for at least 6 to 8 hours before serving.

Makes 8 to 10 servings.

Fall Fruit Skillet Pie

This skillet pie has only a top crust, so there is no pie plate to line or fret over.

All-Purpose Pie Dough (page 224), refrigerated, or your favorite piecrust

Filling:

2 tablespoons (¼ stick) unsalted butter

4 cups peeled, cored, and sliced ripe pears

3 cups peeled, cored, and sliced baking apples

2 teaspoons lemon juice

⅓ cup sugar

2 tablespoons cornstarch

¼ teaspoon cinnamon

milk and sugar, for glaze

■ Prepare the dough as directed.

■ Preheat the oven to 350°F.

For filling:

■ Melt the butter in a 10-inch cast iron or other ovenproof skillet over low heat (see Note below). Add the fruit and lemon juice and cook for 1 minute, stirring. Remove from the heat.

■ In a small bowl, mix the sugar, cornstarch, and cinnamon. Add to the fruit, stir, and smooth the top.

■ On a sheet of floured wax paper, roll the chilled dough into a 12-inch circle. Invert the pastry over the fruit, center it, and peel off the paper. Tuck the edge of the pastry between the fruit and inside of the skillet. Lightly brush the pastry with milk and sprinkle with a few pinches of sugar. Poke 2 or 3 steam vents in the dough.

■ Bake on the center oven rack for 45 minutes, or until the fruit is bubbling around the edges and the crust is golden.

■ Transfer to a cooling rack for at least 10 minutes. Serve with a spoon.

Makes 8 servings.

Note: If you do not have an ovenproof skillet, melt the butter separately and pour it into a 10-inch deep-dish pie plate or round casserole. Add the fruit and lemon juice and stir. Continue as directed.

Freshness First

Try to use fresh fruit whenever possible, but especially when baking with apples. Apples can be mushy and bland after storage. Crisp, fresh apples hold up better.

Warm Brownie Pie

Like your brownies gooey-soft in the center and very chocolate-y?
This pie is for you!

All-Purpose Pie Dough (page 224), refrigerated, or your favorite piecrust

Filling:
½ cup (1 stick) unsalted butter
1⅓ cups chocolate chips, divided
2 large eggs, at room temperature
½ cup packed light-brown sugar
⅓ cup sugar
1½ teaspoons vanilla extract
½ cup all-purpose flour
¼ teaspoon salt
1 cup chopped walnuts, preferably toasted

■ Roll the pastry into a 12-inch circle and line a 9-inch (not deep-dish) pie plate with it. Pinch the overhanging pastry into an upstanding rim or trim to be flush with the side of the pan and crimp the edge with a fork. Refrigerate for 15 minutes.

■ Preheat the oven to 350°F.

For filling:

■ Melt the butter in a saucepan over medium heat. Add 1 cup of the chocolate chips and heat for a few seconds more, then remove from the heat. Tilt the pan to make the butter run over the chips. Set aside for 5 minutes. Whisk to smooth the chips.

■ In a large bowl, combine the eggs, sugars, and vanilla and whisk until evenly blended. Add the melted chocolate and whisk to blend. Add the flour and salt and stir until combined. Add the nuts and the remaining ⅓ cup of chocolate chips. Scrape the filling into the piecrust and smooth the top.

■ Bake on the center oven rack for 30 to 35 minutes, or until a crust develops and the pie rises slightly. (A toothpick inserted into the center will not come out clean.)

■ Transfer to a cooling rack. Serve warm.

Makes 8 to 10 servings.

Cut my pie into four pieces, I don't think I could eat eight.
–Yogi Berra,
baseball player, b. 1925

Creamy Peanut Butter Cup Pie

Peanut butter cup lovers will swoon over this pie.

Nut Crumb Crust (page 262), made with roasted peanuts

Filling:
12 ounces cream cheese (not lowfat
  or whipped), softened
1 cup smooth peanut butter
1¼ cups sugar
3 large eggs plus 1 egg yolk, at room
  temperature
½ cup sour cream

1½ teaspoons vanilla extract
¾ cup finely chopped roasted peanuts

Topping:
½ cup heavy or whipping cream
4 ounces semisweet chocolate,
  chopped
10 full-size peanut butter cups,
  coarsely chopped

The Best Spot

When baking a pie, rotate it 180 degrees midway through the baking time. The back of most ovens is typically hotter than the front. Rotating helps baked goods to cook evenly and balances the surface browning.

■ Prepare the crust as directed, using roasted peanuts. Cool thoroughly.

■ Preheat the oven to 325°F.

For filling:

■ Combine the cream cheese and peanut butter in a large bowl and, using an electric mixer on medium speed, beat for 2 minutes, or until smooth. Add the sugar gradually, beating and scraping the bowl. Add the eggs and yolk, one at a time, and beat after each until evenly mixed. Add the sour cream and vanilla and beat until blended. Add the chopped nuts and stir. Scrape the filling into the piecrust and smooth the top.

■ Bake the pie on the center oven rack for 50 minutes, or until the filling is puffed slightly and wobbly but not runny. The center will be shiny; the edges will have a dull appearance.

■ Transfer to a cooling rack and cool thoroughly. Cover with tented aluminum foil and refrigerate overnight.

For topping:

■ Heat the cream in a small saucepan over low heat until the surface shimmers. Remove from the heat and add the chocolate. Let rest for 5 minutes, then whisk to blend. As the chocolate cools, it will start to thicken. When it has a little body, drizzle half over the filling. Randomly place chopped peanut butter cups on top, then drizzle with the remaining chocolate. Refrigerate, uncovered, until serving. Cover with tented aluminum foil and refrigerate after serving.

Makes 10 to 12 servings.

Best-Ever Coconut Cream Pie

In the tradition of great American diner pies

Nut Crumb Crust (page 262), made with almonds

Filling:
½ cup sugar
3½ tablespoons cornstarch
⅛ teaspoon salt
2 cups whole milk
3 large egg yolks
2 tablespoons (¼ stick) unsalted
    butter, cut into ¼-inch pieces
1 teaspoon vanilla extract
½ teaspoon coconut extract
1 cup sweetened flaked coconut

Topping:
½ cup sweetened flaked coconut
¾ cup cold heavy or whipping cream
3 tablespoons sifted confectioners'
    sugar
½ teaspoon vanilla extract

■ Prepare the crust as directed, using almonds. Cool thoroughly.

For filling:
■ In a heavy saucepan, combine the sugar, cornstarch, and salt and whisk. Add the milk and yolks and whisk to blend. Cook over medium heat for 5 to 7 minutes, or until the mixture starts to boil, whisking continuously. Remove from the heat and add the butter, one piece at a time, whisking after each. Add the vanilla, coconut extract, and coconut and whisk to blend. Pour into the piecrust and smooth the top. Press a piece of plastic wrap directly on top of and touching the filling to prevent a "skin" from forming.

■ Transfer to a cooling rack and cool thoroughly. Refrigerate overnight.

For topping:
■ Place a large bowl and your electric mixer's beaters in the refrigerator or freezer to chill for 5 minutes.

■ In a skillet over medium heat, toast the coconut for 3 to 5 minutes, or until golden, stirring constantly. Immediately transfer to a plate.

■ Pour the cream into the chilled bowl and beat until it holds soft peaks. Add the confectioners' sugar and beat to blend. Add the vanilla and beat until the cream is stiff but not grainy. Spread the whipped cream on the filling and sprinkle with the toasted coconut.

Makes 8 servings.

CLEAN CUT

When cutting a cream or custard pie, wet the knife with hot water to make a clean cut that won't tear the filling.

Make It Right

• *For a flaky, tender piecrust, make sure that all the ingredients and utensils are cold.*

• *For the best tasting crust, use butter, preferably unsalted.*

• *Pay attention to the pie while it's baking. Efficiency in the kitchen is great. However, try not to do too many things at once when you are baking pies.*

Nut Crumb Crust

This is the best crust ever for cream pies, icebox pies, and cheesecakes.

¾ cup coarsely chopped almonds, walnuts, pecans, or roasted peanuts
2½ tablespoons sugar
2 tablespoons all-purpose flour
¼ teaspoon salt
1 cup plus 2 tablespoons graham cracker crumbs
¼ teaspoon vanilla or almond extract
¼ cup (½ stick) unsalted butter, melted

■ Lightly butter a 9½-inch deep-dish pie plate.

■ Combine the nuts, sugar, flour, and salt in a food processor. Pulse until the nuts are finely ground.

■ Transfer the mixture to a large bowl. Add the graham cracker crumbs and whisk to blend.

■ In a small bowl, combine the vanilla and melted butter. Add to the crumbs and mix well. Add 2 teaspoons of water to the crumb mixture, then rub with your fingers until it is uniform and clumpy.

■ Transfer the mixture to the pie plate. Press it evenly across the bottom and most of the way up the sides. Refrigerate for 10 minutes.

■ Preheat the oven to 350°F. Bake on the center oven rack for 8 minutes.

■ Transfer to a cooling rack.

Makes one 9½-inch deep-dish piecrust.

Busy Day Cake

Broiled brown sugar–and-coconut icing "takes the cake" when you're up against the clock.

Cake:
¾ cup milk
3 tablespoons unsalted butter, cut into
    ¼-inch pieces
3 large eggs, at room temperature
1⅓ cups sugar
1½ teaspoons vanilla extract
1½ cups all-purpose flour
2 teaspoons baking powder
½ teaspoon salt

Topping:
1 cup flaked sweetened coconut
¾ cup packed light-brown sugar
½ cup (1 stick) unsalted butter, melted
2 tablespoons heavy cream or
    half-and-half

■ Preheat the oven to 350°F. Butter a 9x9-inch baking pan.

For cake:

■ In a small saucepan over low heat, warm the milk until it's hot to the touch (140° to 150°F). Remove from the heat, add the butter, and set aside to let the butter melt.

■ Combine the eggs and sugar in a large bowl. Using an electric mixer, beat on high speed for 3 minutes, or until light and airy. Add the vanilla and beat to blend.

■ In a separate bowl, combine the flour, baking powder, and salt and stir to mix.

■ Add the flour mixture, about one-third at a time, to the egg mixture, beating on low speed after each addition. Add the milk and melted butter and beat on medium-low speed for about 30 seconds, or until blended. Pour into the prepared pan.

■ Bake on the center oven rack for 30 to 35 minutes, or until the top springs back when touched and a toothpick inserted into the center comes out clean.

■ Transfer to a cooling rack for 20 to 30 minutes.

For topping:
■ Turn on the broiler.

■ Combine the topping ingredients in a bowl and mix well. Spoon the topping evenly over the cake. Position an oven rack so that the cake is 4 to 5 inches from the heat and broil for 3 to 4 minutes, or until lightly browned, being careful not to burn the cake. Cool briefly before serving.

Makes 9 servings.

A party without cake is just a meeting.
–Julia Child, American culinary expert (1912–2004)

Maple Pecan Carrot Cake

It travels beautifully in the pan . . . which always seems to come home empty.

Cake:

4 large eggs, at room temperature
1 cup vegetable oil
½ cup maple syrup
½ cup packed light-brown sugar
½ cup sour cream or plain yogurt
1 tablespoon lemon juice
2 teaspoons grated orange zest
1 teaspoon vanilla extract
½ teaspoon almond extract (optional)

2 cups all-purpose flour
1 tablespoon baking powder
½ teaspoon salt
½ teaspoon cinnamon
½ teaspoon allspice
¼ teaspoon baking soda
1⅔ cups pecan halves or pieces
2 cups grated carrots
1 cup raisins

Frosting:

16 ounces cream cheese (not lowfat or whipped), softened
¼ cup (½ stick) unsalted butter, softened
2 cups confectioners' sugar
1 teaspoon vanilla extract

■ Preheat the oven to 350°F. Butter a 13x9-inch baking pan.

For cake:

■ Combine the eggs, oil, maple syrup, brown sugar, sour cream, lemon juice, orange zest, and extracts in a large bowl. Using an electric mixer, beat on medium-high speed for 1 minute.

■ Sift the flour, baking powder, salt, spices, and baking soda into a separate bowl.

■ Put the pecans into a food processor and pulse until chopped fine. Add to the flour mixture, mix, and make a well.

■ Pour the egg mixture into the well and stir with a wooden spoon until evenly combined. Add the carrots and raisins and stir until mixed. Scrape the batter into the prepared pan.

■ Bake on the center oven rack for 30 to 35 minutes, or until the top springs back when touched and a toothpick inserted into the center comes out clean.

■ Transfer to a cooling rack to cool thoroughly.

For frosting:

■ About an hour before serving the cake, combine the cream cheese and butter in a large bowl. Using an electric mixer, beat on medium speed to blend. Add the confectioners' sugar, 1 cup at a time, beating after each addition. Add the vanilla and beat to blend. Frost the cake.

Makes 12 or more servings.

Cherry Tea Cake

Simply dusted with confectioners' sugar, this cake has little to distract from the cherry flavor.

Fresh vs. Frozen Cherries

Frozen cherries are convenient when fresh ones are not in season. If you let them thaw slightly, you can slice them cleanly and they won't lose their juice or streak the batter when you fold them in.

1½ cups all-purpose flour
1 teaspoon baking powder
½ teaspoon baking soda
¼ teaspoon salt
⅛ teaspoon nutmeg
½ cup (1 stick) unsalted butter, softened
1 cup sugar
2 large eggs, at room temperature
2 teaspoons vanilla extract
⅔ cup sour cream, at room temperature
1 teaspoon grated lemon zest
1½ cups frozen pitted cherries, partially thawed and halved (see box)
3 tablespoons confectioners' sugar, for dusting

■ Preheat the oven to 350°F. Butter a 9- or 10-inch springform pan.

■ Sift the flour, baking powder, baking soda, salt, and nutmeg into a bowl.

■ In a separate large bowl, beat the butter with an electric mixer on medium speed until fluffy. Gradually add the sugar, beating after each addition. Add the eggs, one at a time, beating for 1 minute after each. Add the vanilla and beat to blend. Add half of the dry ingredients to the butter mixture, beating on low speed, until blended. Add the sour cream and lemon zest and beat on low speed until blended. Add the remaining dry ingredients and beat on low until the batter is smooth. Fold in the partially frozen cherries. Spread the batter in the prepared pan and smooth the top.

■ Bake on the center oven rack for 35 to 45 minutes (the smaller pan will take the most time), or until the top is golden and springs back when touched and a toothpick inserted into the center comes out clean.

■ Transfer to a cooling rack for 20 minutes. Run a knife around the edge of the pan to loosen the cake, remove the sides, and cool completely. Just before serving, dust with confectioners' sugar using a sifter or sieve.

Makes 8 to 10 servings.

Pineapple Upside-Down Cake

Pure maple syrup sweetness gives this classic a North Country accent.

Topping:
1 can (20 ounces) pineapple slices, drained
¼ cup (½ stick) unsalted butter
2 tablespoons maple syrup
¾ cup packed light-brown sugar
9 maraschino cherries, stems removed
12 pecan halves (optional)

Cake:
½ cup (1 stick) unsalted butter, softened
⅔ cup sugar
2 large eggs, at room temperature
⅔ cup buttermilk, at room temperature, divided

1 tablespoon molasses
1 teaspoon vanilla extract
1½ cups all-purpose flour
1 teaspoon baking powder
½ teaspoon baking soda
½ teaspoon salt
¼ teaspoon cinnamon

For topping:

■ Line a dinner plate with paper towels, lay the pineapple slices on them, and blot the slices dry on both sides.

■ Lightly butter a 9-inch, preferably nonstick, square baking pan (see Notes).

■ Combine the butter and maple syrup in a small saucepan over medium heat. When the butter is melted, add the brown sugar and stir. Bring to a low boil and cook for 30 seconds, stirring.

■ Pour the butter mixture into the prepared pan and tilt it so that the butter mixture covers the bottom. Lay pineapple slices in three rows and put a cherry in the middle of each slice. Press one pecan half, if using, in each gap between the slices.

For cake:

■ Preheat the oven to 350°F. Put the butter into a large bowl and, using an electric mixer on medium-high speed, cream it while gradually adding the sugar. Add the eggs, one at a time, beating well after each. Add ⅓ cup of the buttermilk, the molasses, and the vanilla, beating after each.

■ Sift the flour, baking powder, baking soda, salt, and cinnamon into a bowl. Add half to the butter mixture and beat on low speed until smooth. Add the remaining ⅓ cup of buttermilk, beat to blend, then add the remaining dry ingredients and beat to combine. Scrape the batter over the pineapples and smooth the top.

■ Bake on the center oven rack for 35 to 40 minutes, or until the cake springs back when touched.

■ Invert a platter or baking sheet over the baking pan. Carefully turn the cake onto it and remove the pan. Reposition any pineapple that remains in the pan. Let rest for at least 10 minutes before serving.

Makes 9 to 12 servings.

Notes: You can also use a 9- to 9½-inch cast iron skillet. Heat the butter–maple syrup–brown sugar mixture right in it. Make a ring of pineapple slices, with one in the center, and proceed as directed.

When turning this cake out of any pan, hot glaze can leak out, so consider wearing long sleeves and oven mitts at this stage.

PRESIDENTIAL PLEASURE

Thomas Jefferson loved
peaches and tested
38 varieties at his Monticello
home. By 1811, his South
Orchard contained
163 peach trees, and
thousands more served as
ornamental fences around
fields. Jefferson and
his guests ate peaches fresh
in season or dried in winter.
The fruit was also made
into peach brandy.

Peach Pecan Shortcakes

*Use only the best fresh summer peaches—no canned or bland
January peaches from who-knows-where.*

Shortcakes:

2 cups all-purpose flour

¼ cup sugar, plus extra for sprinkling

1½ teaspoons baking powder

½ teaspoon baking soda

½ teaspoon salt

⅛ teaspoon nutmeg

6 tablespoons (¾ stick) cold unsalted butter, cut into ¼-inch pieces

⅔ cup chopped pecans

1 large egg, lightly beaten

½ cup milk

⅓ cup sour cream

Sauce:

4 to 5 cups peeled, pitted, and sliced peaches

4 tablespoons sugar, divided

1 teaspoon lemon juice

1 cup heavy cream or whipping cream

■ Preheat the oven to 400°F. Line a large baking sheet with parchment
paper or lightly greased aluminum foil.

For shortcakes:

■ Combine the flour, ¼ cup of sugar, baking powder, baking soda, salt,
and nutmeg in a large bowl and whisk to mix. Add the butter and,
using a pastry blender or your fingers, cut or rub the butter into the
flour mixture until it is roughly the size of split peas. Add the pecans
and stir. Make a well.

■ In a separate bowl, combine the egg, milk, and sour cream and whisk until blended. Remove 2 tablespoons to a small bowl and set aside for the glaze. Pour the remaining egg mixture into the well and stir briskly with a wooden spoon until dough forms. Let rest for 3 minutes.

■ Flour your hands (repeat as needed). Scoop up large spoonfuls of dough and shape into eight equal balls. Place them on the baking sheet, spaced evenly. Brush each ball lightly with glaze. Sprinkle with a big pinch of sugar.

■ Bake on the center oven rack for 18 to 20 minutes, or until golden.

■ Transfer to a cooling rack.

For sauce:

■ In a bowl, combine the sliced peaches with 2 tablespoons of sugar. Add the lemon juice and stir.

■ Put a bowl and your mixer's beaters into the refrigerator or freezer to chill for 5 minutes.

■ Pour the heavy cream into the chilled bowl and beat on medium speed until it starts to thicken and mound. Add the remaining sugar and continue beating until the cream is billowy and holds medium-soft peaks.

■ Split the biscuits in half and put the bottoms on individual dessert plates. Cover the bottoms with peaches and a generous dollop of whipped cream. Add the top of the biscuit and serve.

Makes 8 servings.

Whip It Good!

Your whipped cream, that is. Chilling the bowl and beaters helps to keep the cream cool and stable and thus whip up more quickly.

Do not beat too much or the cream will curdle and separate, leaving lumps of butter floating in a pool of buttermilk.

Creamy New York–Style Cheesecake

The texture of this sour cream cheesecake is like velvet on the tongue.

Crust:
1¼ cups fine graham cracker crumbs
2 tablespoons light-brown sugar
⅛ teaspoon salt
4 tablespoons (½ stick) unsalted butter, melted

Filling:
16 ounces cream cheese (not lowfat or whipped), softened
¾ cup sugar
3 large eggs, at room temperature
1 cup sour cream
1 teaspoon vanilla extract
½ teaspoon lemon extract or 1 teaspoon finely grated lemon zest

Topping (optional):
1 cup sour cream
2 tablespoons sugar

MIX LIKE A MASTER

When blending cheesecake ingredients, don't overdo it. It may be desirable to beat air into the batter of other cakes, but beating air into a cheesecake only increases the possibility that it will rise more than it should and then crack as it settles. Go slowly.

■ Preheat the oven to 350°F. Lightly butter the sides of an 8-inch springform pan.

■ Put a shallow pan of hot water on one of the lower racks of your oven (not on the center rack). The water will create steam that will help to prevent your cake from cracking.

For crust:
■ Combine the graham cracker crumbs, brown sugar, and salt in a bowl. Add the melted butter and mix well. Press the crumbs evenly into the bottom and about 1 inch up the sides of the springform pan.

■ Bake on the center oven rack for 8 minutes.

■ Transfer to a cooling rack.

For filling:
■ Put the cream cheese into a bowl and, using an electric mixer, beat on medium speed while gradually adding the sugar, until smooth and creamy. Add the eggs, one at a time, beating after each until just blended. Add the sour cream and extracts and beat until evenly mixed. Pour the filling into the crust.

■ Put the pan on the center oven rack and immediately lower the heat to 325°F. Bake for 50 to 60 minutes, or until the cake rises slightly on the sides. If you nudge the pan, the cake should wobble and not be runny in the center. Turn off the heat and open the oven door slightly. Leave the cake in the oven for 15 minutes.

■ Transfer to a cooling rack.

For topping:
■ Combine the sour cream and sugar in a small saucepan and stir to blend. Cook on low heat, just until runny; do not boil. While the cake is warm, pour the topping over the center and immediately tilt the pan to spread the topping. Set aside to cool.

■ Topped or not, cover the cake with foil in the pan and refrigerate for at least 12 hours before serving.

Makes 8 servings.

Orange Lemon Pudding Cake

On the bottom, smooth citrus pudding; on top, cake so light that it almost floats off of your spoon

1¼ cups sugar, divided
3 tablespoons all-purpose flour
⅛ teaspoon salt
1 cup whole milk
4 large eggs, separated, at room temperature
½ cup orange juice
¼ cup lemon juice
¼ cup (½ stick) unsalted butter, melted
2 teaspoons grated orange zest or lemon zest (or 1 teaspoon of each)
½ teaspoon vanilla extract
2 tablespoons crystallized ginger, coarsely chopped (optional)

■ Preheat the oven to 350°F. Get out a large, shallow casserole and a baking dish that will fit in it.

■ Bring a kettle of water to boil, then turn off the heat.

■ Combine 1 cup of the sugar, the flour, and salt in a large bowl. Add the milk, egg yolks, orange juice, lemon juice, butter, zest, and vanilla and whisk.

■ Combine the egg whites in a clean, dry bowl and, using an electric mixer, beat until frothy. Add the remaining ¼ of cup sugar gradually, beating on high speed until the whites hold soft peaks. Add one-third of the whites to the batter and beat on low speed until just combined. Add the remaining whites and beat on low speed until combined.

■ Pour the batter into the baking dish. Put the baking dish into the casserole. Pour enough boiled water into the casserole to come one-quarter to one-third of the way up the sides of the baking dish.

■ Bake for 40 minutes, or until the top is golden and the pudding on the bottom is set (to check, probe deep into the cake with a butter knife; if it does not come out dripping, the pudding is set).

■ Transfer the baking dish to a cooling rack. Serve warm or at room temperature or cover with plastic wrap, refrigerate, and serve cold.

Makes 6 servings.

Crystal Clear

Crystallized ginger is fresh ginger that has been slowly cooked in sugar water and rolled in coarse sugar for preservation. It has a sweet, spicy taste and can easily be made at home.

Pumpkin Bread Pudding

Like pumpkin pie, but with a firmer, denser texture.

2 large eggs plus 1 egg yolk
1 cup canned pumpkin (not pumpkin pie filling)
1½ cups light cream or half and half
1 cup packed light-brown sugar, divided
1 teaspoon vanilla extract
½ teaspoon cinnamon
½ teaspoon ground ginger
¼ teaspoon nutmeg
¼ teaspoon salt
5 to 6 slices cinnamon raisin bread, crusts removed,
    cut into cubes to make 4 cups (see Note)
2 tablespoons (¼ stick) cold unsalted butter
whipped cream, for garnish

> **The proof of the pudding is in the eating.**
> *—English proverb*

■ Combine the eggs and yolk in a large bowl and whisk until frothy. Add the pumpkin, light cream, ¾ cup of the brown sugar, vanilla, spices, and salt and whisk to combine. Add the bread cubes to the pumpkin mixture and stir gently, just until the bread is soaked and submerged. Set aside for 15 minutes.

■ Preheat the oven to 350°F. Butter a baking dish. Get out a shallow casserole that is large enough to hold the baking dish.

■ Bring a kettle of water to a boil, then turn off the heat.

■ Transfer the pudding mixture into the baking dish. Sprinkle with the remaining brown sugar. Cut the butter into slivers and scatter them on top. Place the baking dish in the casserole. Pour enough boiled water into the casserole to come one-third of the way up the side of the baking dish.

■ Bake on the center oven rack for 45 to 55 minutes, or until the pudding springs back when touched lightly.

■ Transfer the baking dish to a cooling rack. Top with whipped cream before serving.

Makes 8 servings.

Note: Regular white bread can be substituted for cinnamon raisin bread. Add ¾ cup of dark raisins to the mixture when you soak the white bread cubes.

Butterscotch Pudding

For the kids—or the kid in you!

¾ **cup packed dark-brown sugar**
¼ **cup cornstarch**
⅛ **teaspoon salt**
2¾ **cups light cream, half-and-half, or whole milk**
3 **large egg yolks**
2 **tablespoons (¼ stick) unsalted butter, cut into ¼-inch pieces**
1 **teaspoon vanilla extract**
whipped cream and crumbled vanilla wafers, for garnish

■ Combine the brown sugar, cornstarch, and salt in a saucepan (preferably nonstick) and break up any clumps of brown sugar with your fingers. Add the light cream and egg yolks, stir, and cook over medium heat for 5 minutes or until it boils, whisking frequently. When it starts to boil, lower the heat slightly and cook at a low boil for 1 minute, whisking nonstop. Remove from the heat and add the butter, 1 piece at a time, whisking after each addition, and add the vanilla, whisking again.

■ Immediately divide the pudding among six custard cups, ramekins, or single serving bowls. Press a piece of plastic wrap directly on top of and touching the pudding in each to prevent a "skin" from forming.

■ Transfer each to a cooling rack and cool to room temperature. Refrigerate for at least 4 to 6 hours before serving. Serve each portion with a dollop of whipped cream and crumbled vanilla wafers.

Makes 6 servings.

Variation

Butterscotch Banana Trifle

■ Pour the pudding into one casserole dish and set aside to cool.

■ To serve, scoop alternate layers of pudding, whipped cream, banana slices, and 1 or 2 crumbled vanilla wafers into serving dishes. Top with whipped cream and drizzle with butterscotch sauce or Caramel Sauce (page 254), if desired.

Tapioca Pudding

Lemon zest adds citrus fragrance to this childhood favorite.

2¼ cups whole milk, plus a few spoonfuls
3 large egg yolks
⅓ cup plus 1 tablespoon sugar
¼ cup quick-cooking tapioca
⅛ teaspoon salt
½ teaspoon finely grated lemon zest
¾ teaspoon vanilla extract
cream (optional)

■ In a large, preferably nonstick, saucepan, combine the milk, egg yolks, sugar, tapioca, salt, and lemon zest and whisk to blend. Cook over low heat for 3 to 4 minutes, stirring continuously. Increase the heat to medium and continue to cook, stirring nonstop, for 4 to 5 minutes, or until the mixture reaches a full boil. Remove from the heat, add the vanilla, and stir.

■ Transfer the tapioca to a bowl and press a piece of plastic wrap directly on top of and touching the tapioca to prevent a "skin" from forming.

■ Cool to room temperature, adding a spoonful of milk or cream, if using, and stirring occasionally. Refrigerate for at least 1 to 2 hours. Serve topped with whipped cream, if desired.

Makes 6 servings.

Healthy Substitution

Quick-cooking tapioca is often used for thickening puddings, fruit pies, gravies, stews, soups, and sauces. Tapioca is gluten-free and a healthier thickening alternative to cornstarch and flour. Quick-cooking tapioca is also called instant tapioca, quick tapioca, and instant pearl tapioca.

Creamy Vanilla Bean Custard

The vanilla bean is an extra special touch, but you can use vanilla extract instead.

2⅓ cups light cream
1 large, plump vanilla bean, slit in half lengthwise,
    or ¾ teaspoon pure vanilla extract
6 large egg yolks
½ cup plus 2 tablespoons sugar

■ Preheat the oven to 325°F. Get out a large, shallow casserole and six custard cups or ramekins that fit inside it comfortably.

■ Bring a kettle of water to a boil, then remove from the heat.

■ Pour the cream into a saucepan. Using the edge of a paring knife, scrape the seeds out of the vanilla bean and add to the cream. Heat the cream until hot to the touch (140° to 150°F); do not boil. Whisk briefly to separate the vanilla seeds. Remove from the heat.

■ Combine the yolks and sugar in a large bowl. Using an electric mixer, beat on medium speed for 3 minutes, or until thick and lemon-color. Add the cream, ½ cup at a time, stirring with a wooden spoon after each addition.

■ Strain the mixture through a sieve into another bowl. Divide the custard among the cups and place them in the casserole, evenly spaced. Cover each cup with a small piece of aluminum foil. Pour enough boiled water into the casserole to come one-quarter to one-third of the way up the sides of the cups.

■ Bake on the center oven rack for 40 to 50 minutes. When done, the custards will be firm near the edge and wobbly but not soupy at the center. They should not puff up. (If this happens, remove from the oven immediately. You may end up with curdled custard.)

■ Transfer the cups to a cooling rack, uncover, and cool thoroughly. Return the foil lids and chill for at least 4 to 6 hours before serving.

Makes 6 servings.

You eat, in dreams, the custard of the day.

–Alexander Pope,
English poet (1688–1744)

Chocolate Custard Pots

1½ cups heavy cream
1 cup light cream or half-and-half
5 ounces semisweet chocolate, coarsely chopped
5 large egg yolks
⅓ cup sugar
1 teaspoon vanilla extract
1 teaspoon amaretto or coffee liqueur (optional)

■ Preheat the oven to 325°F. Get out a large, shallow casserole and six custard cups or ramekins that fit inside it comfortably.

■ Bring a kettle of water to a boil, then remove from the heat.

■ Combine the creams in a small saucepan and heat until hot to the touch (140° to 150°F); do not boil. Add the chocolate and remove from the heat. Wait 5 minutes, then whisk until smooth.

■ Whisk the yolks and sugar in a large bowl. Gradually add the cream mixture, ⅓ cup at a time, stirring constantly. Add the vanilla and liqueur, if using, and stir to blend.

■ Divide the custard among the cups and place them in the casserole, evenly spaced. Cover each cup with a small piece of aluminum foil. Pour enough boiled water into the casserole to come one-quarter to one-third of the way up the sides of the cups.

■ Bake on the center oven rack for 45 to 50 minutes, checking after 40 minutes. When done, the custards will be set and no longer runny in the center.

■ Transfer the cups to a cooling rack, uncover, and cool thoroughly. Return the foil lids and chill for at least 4 hours before serving.

Makes 6 servings.

Pot Luck

When full custard cups or ramekins are baked in a casserole partially filled with boiled water, the water protects the custards from overheating and separating.

Cherry Berry Cobbler

Filling:

3 cups halved and pitted cherries

3 cups blueberries

2 cups halved strawberries

½ cup sugar

2 tablespoons cornstarch

1 tablespoon lemon juice

2 teaspoons grated orange zest

Topping:

2 cups all-purpose flour

1½ teaspoons baking powder

¼ cup plus 2 tablespoons sugar, divided

½ teaspoon baking soda

½ teaspoon salt

5 tablespoons cold unsalted butter, cut into ¼-inch pieces

1 large egg, lightly beaten

½ cup milk

½ cup sour cream

½ teaspoon vanilla extract

MUSH FACTOR

Do not wash strawberries until you are ready to use them. Moisture will cause the berries to become mushy.

■ Preheat the oven to 400°F. Butter a large, shallow casserole.

For filling:

■ Combine all of the fruit in a large bowl.

■ Combine the sugar and cornstarch in a small bowl and mix. Add to the fruit and mix well. Add the lemon juice and orange zest, stir, and set aside for 10 minutes.

For topping:

■ Combine the flour, baking powder, ¼ cup of sugar, baking soda, and salt in a large bowl. Add the butter and, using a pastry blender or your fingers, cut or rub the butter into the dry ingredients until it is in pea-size pieces. Make a well.

■ In a separate bowl, whisk the egg, milk, sour cream, and vanilla until smooth. Pour into the well and stir with a wooden spoon until a batter forms.

■ Transfer the fruit to the prepared casserole and spread evenly. Using a large spoon, scatter dollops of the topping over the fruit. Do not smooth it. Sprinkle with the remaining sugar.

■ Bake on the center oven rack for 25 to 30 minutes, or until the fruit is bubbly and the top is golden.

Makes 8 servings.

THINK FRESH

Buy extra bags of
fresh cranberries
and store them
in the freezer, where
they will retain their
color and flavor
for up to a year.

Apple Cranberry Crisp

You'll enjoy the hint of cranberry tartness in this blushing fall fruit crisp.

Filling:

6 cups peeled, cored, and sliced baking apples

2 cups fresh cranberries

⅔ cup sugar

2 tablespoons all-purpose flour

2 teaspoons lemon juice

2 teaspoons grated orange zest

Topping:

1¼ cups all-purpose flour

¾ cup packed light-brown sugar

½ teaspoon cinnamon

¼ teaspoon salt

8 tablespoons (1 stick) cold, unsalted butter, cut into ¼-inch pieces

■ Preheat the oven to 350°F. Butter a 9x9-inch baking pan.

For filling:

■ Combine all of the filling ingredients in a bowl. Set aside for
10 minutes, stirring occasionally.

For topping:

■ Combine the flour, brown sugar, cinnamon, and salt in a food processor
and pulse briefly to mix. Scatter the pieces of butter over the dry mixture.
Pulse several times, or until it has a sandlike consistency.

■ Transfer to a large bowl and rub the mixture between your fingers until it
is uniform and clumpy.

■ Spread the fruit in the prepared pan. Sprinkle with the topping.

■ Bake on the center oven rack for 45 minutes, or until the apples are soft
and the cranberries are bubbly.

■ Transfer to a cooling rack for at least 10 minutes before serving.

Makes 8 servings.

A bold page number indicates a photo of the recipe.

ADDITIONAL PHOTO CREDITS

Melissa DiPalma: pages 26, 32, 63, 86, 246

Media Bakery: pages 11–13, 17, 21–22, 27, 36, 38, 42–44, 50, 52–54, 62, 64, 66–70, 72, 74, 77–78, 82, 89, 93–94, 97, 100–101, 103, 105–108, 122–123, 125, 127–128, 130–133, 136, 138–139, 144–147, 155, 160, 162–163, 166, 168–170, 175, 179–180, 183, 185, 191–192, 198, 201, 208–210, 216, 218–219, 222–223, 225, 248, 256, 261, 266, 269, 272, 275, 278

ThinkStock: pages 18, 25, 29, 47–48, 51, 88, 92, 95–96, 98, 102, 104, 110, 113, 118, 137, 142, 151, 154, 159, 167, 171, 177, 214–215, 217, 231, 241, 245, 257, 260, 262, 268, 279–280

Jeff Vanuga/Courtesy of USDA Natural Resources Conservation Service: 207

1901 05812 2211